Screwing the System and Making It Work

Mark D. Jacobs

SCREWING THE SYSTEM AND MAKING IT WORK

Juvenile Justice in the No-Fault Society

The University of Chicago Press

Chicago and London

The University of Chicago Press, Chicago 60637
The University of Chicago Press, Ltd., London

Library of Congress Cataloging-in-Publication Data

Jacobs, Mark D., 1947–
    Screwing the system and making it work : juvenile justice in the
no-fault society / Mark D. Jacobs.
        p.   cm.
    Includes bibliographical references.
    ISBN 0-226-38980-4 (cloth)
    ISBN 0-226-38981-2 (paperback)
    1. Juvenile probation—United States—Case studies.   2. Juvenile
delinquents—United States—Case studies.   3. Probation officers—
United States—Case studies.   I. Title.
HV9104.J3   1990
364.3′6′0973—dc20   90-30126
                                                                          CIP

∞ The paper used in this publication meets the minimum requirements
of the American National Standard for Information Sciences—
Permanence of Paper for Printed Library Materials, ANSI Z39.48-1984.

Contents

Acknowledgments

his book represents a tiny portion of the late Morris Janowitz's intellectual legacy. He supervised this book's inception as a dissertation; it is my sad honor to acknowledge this as one of the last works to bear his aegis. Morris Janowitz's occasional, seemingly off-handed, theoretically elliptical utterances had the power (upon reflection) to open just the right avenues of inquiry. As so many others have already noted, he was a caring and wise mentor.

Gerald Suttles supervised the dissertation through to its conclusion—no mean feat of involvement and perseverance on his part—and provided absolutely crucial direction for shaping it into a book. The very phrase "no-fault society" is his. Irving Spergel and Wendy Griswold also provided helpful comments as members of my dissertation committee. Barry Schwartz, my first graduate adviser, helped arrange my field placement, and has continued through the years as a valued source of encouragement, friendship, and intellectual guidance.

For their camaraderie, advice, and intellectual sparring I thank Charles Bosk, Jack Faris, and Ruth Horowitz. Many members of the Department of Sociology and Anthropology at George Mason University have provided written comments on drafts of one or more chapters: Kevin Avruch, Tom R. Burns, Mark Colvin, Tom Dietz, Lois Horton, Victoria Rader, Karen Rosenblum, and John Stone. I thank all the members of that department for sustaining such a warmly collegial workplace.

Patricia Masters applied her considerable editorial skills to help prepare an "electronic manuscript." Howard Lasus helped produce the camera-ready graphics.

I regret being unable to acknowledge, except generically, the dozens of probation officers, judges, clerks, and administrators with whom I worked. I appreciate their cooperation and—even more—their friendship.

My wife, Erica, has lent her expertise in writing and literary criticism for more hours than either of us would like to recall. Most of all, I am grateful to her, David, and Lauren, simply for being themselves.

Introduction

I t is difficult enough as individuals to organize our attitudes and behavior toward adolescents. Personal memories of our own adolescence are among our most awkward and least readily recalled; the hopes and fears we project onto adolescents are as subject to unconscious conflicts as those of adolescents themselves. Aggressively asserting independence while still dependent on familial support, embodying the promise of the future while endangering the most precious achievements of the past, adolescents conjure opposing images of potency and vulnerability, redemption and ruin. Liminally suspended between the sheltered innocence of childhood and the serious responsibilities of adulthood, adolescence is the most turbulently ambiguous and ambivalent phase of the life cycle.

How much more difficult then to build effective communal and societal institutions for delinquency prevention and treatment. Institution building is problematic even when common goals are clear and the means for achieving those goals are available; the goals of juvenile justice are unsettled and the means elusive. Juvenile delinquency is as inexorable as the social psychological pitfalls of the adolescent passage, a passage even more precarious at greater remove from the beacon of central societal institutions and values. Yet the quality of our public life depends on the success of our collective efforts at building institutions to ease the adolescent passage, especially for youths of peripheral social status. Who shall be responsible for socializing troubled youth?

Not only the symbolic construction but also the stubborn reality of societal and personal dysfunctions frame this study of juvenile justice in the United States today. A broad range of public problems contributes to the problems of delinquents, which in turn promote public ones. Our collective incapacity to correct these problems—or even address them fully—helps explain why parents, public officials, and private treatment-

1

providers as well as delinquents themselves vie so contentiously with each other to evade their respective responsibilities.

For over a decade, I observed probation officers daring to do their best on behalf of the delinquents in their charge. I worked as a research analyst for a model juvenile court in a prosperous and rapidly developing suburban community. The court workers I observed were exceptionally dedicated and competent individuals. Contrary to their scholarly and popular stereotype as "street-level bureaucrats" callously resigned to the rituals of bureaucratic routine, many probation officers I observed immersed themselves fervently in the drama of their clients' lives, exercising remarkable personal resourcefulness to counteract the evasive practices of others. As one probation officer phrased it, they strove diligently to "screw the system and make it work." Yet all too often their efforts to test bureaucratic limits were frustrated, serving only to reexpose institutional gaps and cross-purposes.

This study employs ethnographic, statistical, and literary methods among others to explore the social and cultural disorganization of juvenile justice. In particular, it asks: How do probation officers manage to discharge their duties, despite the disorganization of their task environment? With what effects? How in the face of chronic disappointment do they manage to sustain their motivation? Finally it asks what the disorganization of juvenile justice reveals about ourselves and our society as a whole. The study combines description of selected "special cases" with observation of casework routine, and statistical cohort analysis with symbolic analysis of verbal and written casework accounts. These various strands of analysis all contribute to a concept of the "no-fault society" which describes the larger context of societal disorganization that the juvenile justice system at once reflects and exacerbates.

The rule of confidentiality cloaking the juvenile court's operations and records inhibits meaningful research by outsiders, whose requests for information must be delimited according to prespecified purposes and designs which are warily screened. My job as a research analyst for a juvenile court accorded me privileged access to a wide variety of data sources—from legal files to management information, from a data base of computerized case-processing information to informal conversation in the lunch room and after hours. My official duties included producing the court's annual statistical report, regular activity reports, program evaluations, planning studies, and case-processing and docket management studies. More importantly, however, my position afforded me the opportunity for prolonged participant-observation at the court. I made a point when meeting court workers for the first time to identify my involvement in academic research, which helped overcome their well-founded reticence toward administrators. As I gradually gained their confidence, their reflexive professional curiosity and concern led them to share their experiences with me in a remarkably open manner.

The methodological problem of overidentification with research subjects has received more scholarly attention than the corresponding benefits of protracted participant-observation. Fieldwork success feeds on itself. It is more rewarding for subjects to reveal information about themselves, the more they perceive the observer already knows; conversely, the more the researcher has developed particularistic knowledge and personal ties, the easier it is to pursue inquiry. Access and understanding do not grow at an even pace, but rather traverse a series of thresholds. Increasingly in the last years of my study, probation officers sought me out to recount their best stories, and I sought them out to probe more deeply their feelings of accomplishment and frustration.

Particularly informative were closed monthly meetings I was invited to attend over a period of four years in which probation officers shared experiences and defined common problems among themselves, and sought to educate judges and administrators about their situation. Another invaluable form of fieldwork experience was the opportunity to witness and tape all sessions (forty-three of them) over a six-year period in which departing probation officers described to their supervisors and/ or successors the cases they were leaving behind, as well as all sessions in which probation officers described their active cases to new supervisors. These sessions were serious occasions, in which probation officers concentrated on passing on the most crucial case-related information on the one hand, while accounting for their own professional performance on the other. Ranging in length from one to five hours, the sessions averaged under two hours each. They covered a complete cross section of the court's caseload, indicating among other things how probation officers conceive delinquents' problems and how they allocate attention and effort among types of cases.

These caseload exchanges also provided a grounded basis for identifying systemic dilemmas. Precisely because probation officers would strive to "clean up" their caseloads to leave them in proper "order" for their successors, these sessions highlighted the significance of casework problems that remained outstanding. Especially troublesome cases invariably involved conflicts with representatives of other public agencies seeking to disclaim responsibility for needed services. To explain this pattern of contentious evasion among related agencies, I selected a dozen or so "special" cases for intensive study from among the thousands I heard described in these sessions or in informal conversation, examining all available documents in case files and interviewing all officials involved—not only probation officers and judges but also lawyers, social workers, and school eligibility officials.

The book opens with the story of Larry, one such "special" case, which epitomizes many of the triumphs and disappointments of probation work. Chapters 3 through 5 of part 1 present other cases in which judges and probation officers encounter chronic institutional gaps and cross-purposes as acute dilemmas of individualized casework. Chapter 2 outlines some of the common characteristics of these cases. Relating delinquency to normal processes of adolescent development, it sketches a theory of delinquency as a failure of controls—formal and informal, social and personal—on a number of different systems-levels. It also describes the community setting of this study.

It is necessary to preserve a minute level of detail in recounting these case histories to identify the full scope of systemic disorganization. Despite the varied and diffuse nature of children's problems, related public agencies invoke the vague and contradictory mandates of federal law in defining their cognate competencies and responsibilities in narrowly specialized ways. The resulting pattern of contentious evasion inevitably produces interagency conflicts. Unlike the cases presented in chapter 3, which admit of informal resolution to these conflicts, the cases presented in chapter 4 do not. Chapter 5 examines why, even when explicitly litigated on issues of principle, these conflicts can be resolved on only an ad hoc basis. It thus explores the substantive irrationality resulting from the uncoordinated exercise of discrete fragmentary rationalities.

Although probation officers devote disproportionate resources to "special cases," they employ similar strategies in response to the day-to-day dilemmas of "normal casework." Thus the description of these special cases motivates the more general discussion of the practice, outcome, and ideology of probation casework advanced in part 2. Chapters 6 through 9 inquire how probation officers manage to discharge their duties despite the disorganization of their task environment. In addition to the methods already described, this part of the study relies on dozens of structured interviews with probation officers and judges, lasting on the average several hours each. After examining the essential continuities between "special" and "normal" cases, chapter 6 relates how probation officers ration their limited resources of time, hope, and energy. Chapter 7 describes how they overcome patterns of official evasion by brokering the exchange of services as personal favors among networks of workers in different agencies. Chapter 8 reports strategies for persuading a skeptical and conflicting set of overseers—judges, parents, and lawyers—to grant necessary consent to their case plans. In view of the limited usefulness of detention and traditional public correctional institutions, chapter 9 analyzes the relations of reciprocal patronage probation officers cultivate with private operators of nontraditional residential institutions.

Chapter 10 uses the statistical technique of survival analysis to measure the effectiveness and equitableness of the court's actions. By contrasting offense and treatment histories for a cohort of 629 children processed by the court, this chapter investigates whether court intervention reduces actuarial recidivism risks at various treatment stages, and how the severity of treatments accorded particular types of offenders compares with the recidivism risks they pose. Findings suggest that both probation supervision and removal-from-home are ineffective, and that court decision-making is vulnerable to such situational factors as parents' determination to "dump" their children on the state.

As the focus switches from case outcomes to the ideology of probation work, statistical methods give way to literary ones. The aggregate futility and chronic frustrations of probation work pose obvious dilemmas of morale and accountability for probation officers. To explore how probation officers sustain their motivation and creditable professional identities—as the description of special cases in part 1 suggests they do—chapter 11 examines the poetics and dramaturgy of casework narratives as cultural objects. Everyday reports—formal or informal, verbal or written—that probation officers make about delinquents' pasts and prospects fit the genre of tragic narratives, casting delinquents (and reflexively, therefore, probation officers as well) as modern tragic heroes. By capturing the mutually ambivalent attitudes of the public, probation officer, and delinquent that govern their complex system of moral transactions, these narratives attribute meaning and motivation essential to social control on a number of different systems-levels. Yet as this chapter argues, the expressive satisfactions these narratives provide to all parties only compound the limitations of instrumental rationality in probation work.

The concluding chapter reflects on the macrosociological significance of these findings by relating problems of juvenile justice to more general societal problems of integration and authority, and thus of social control. This chapter defines the "no-fault society" in terms of erosion in the very bases of individual and institutional accountability, as the combined result of three interrelated conditions: constrictive individualism, confusion of public and private action realms, and laxity in the rule of law. The rhetoric of modern tragedy serves the interpersonal strategies of artifice and special pleading imposed on delinquents and probation officers alike partly because they cannot rely on law to enforce mutual obligations in an openly authoritative manner. This rhetoric at once expresses and promotes the spirit of mutual exculpation and immunity from evaluation characteristic of the no-fault society—a spirit that can be shown to pervade the narrative accounts of cases like Larry's.

This study builds on the seminal ethnographies of juvenile justice by David Matza (1964), Aaron Cicourel (1968), and Robert Emerson (1969). Their varying portrayals of the situated, negotiated, and mystified character of the court's decision process have helped shape my own analysis. Paradoxes Matza poses about causality, will, and justice provide starting points for my own exploration of the court's ideology.

Yet, as always happens to ethnographers, none of these existing theories equipped me to make full sense of my own field observations. Each theory accentuates different determinants of court routine: Matza stresses caseload pressures and the need to satisfy conflicting expectations; Cicourel stresses organizational contingency; Emerson stresses imperatives of interagency exchange. Despite these differing emphases, all describe probation work as a dull, dispassionate set of bureaucratic routines. None of these theories, then, prepared me for my initial overwhelming impression of probation work as high drama, reflexively constructed around genuine involvement in the drama of delinquents' lives—a sense of drama motivating probation officers to persevere in those involvements rather than submitting to bureaucratic impediments. Explaining that sense of drama naturally suggested itself as my basic research problem.

Of course the juvenile court I observed was vastly changed from the time of those earlier studies. Indeed, the very influence of those studies helped precipitate some of those changes. Partly in response to their demystification of juvenile justice, the Supreme Court extended to juveniles many (but not all) of the due process protections already guaranteed to adults, starting with the *Kent* decision in 1966 (Kent v. U.S., 383 U.S.). Affirming the official decline of the rehabilitative ideal, the federal government funded research, training, and demonstration projects to promote vaguely defined alternative policies: the Juvenile Justice and Delinquency Prevention Act of 1974 (P.L. 93–415, 88 Stat. 1109, codified at 42 U.S.C. 5601 et seq.) was the first legislation not only to authorize federal funds, but even to acknowledge any federal responsibility for the delinquency problem. Among other things, federal involvement created additional strain for the juvenile court. Amendments to that act in 1977 (P.L. 95–115, 91 Stat. 1048) explicitly assigned the court responsibility for enforcing the rights and entitlements of children, even as other federal legislation (particularly the Title XX Social Security Amendments of 1974 [P.L. 93–647 S2, 88 Stat. 2337, codified at 42 U.S.C. 1396–97S] and the Education for All Handicapped Act of 1975

[P.L. 94–142, 89 Stat. 774, codified at 20 U.S.C. 1401 et seq.]) expanded those rights in such areas as special education and foster care. The ambiguity of the new policies, compounded by the more punitive ideological turns of the eighties, promoted new forms of mystification. Well before the Reagan administration solicited the commercialization of juvenile corrections, a mislabeled policy of "de-institutionalization" had started funding the increasing removal of children from their own homes to a network of privately operated nontraditional residential institutions.

Contemporary theories of juvenile justice must reckon with these changes. Juvenile courts are more formal and legalistic than Cicourel and Emerson found them. Their staffs are more professional and their responsibilities expanded. The courts' political environments are no longer merely local, but national; confused federal statutes are now important features of those environments. Thus their interorganizational fields are more complex (Anne Mahoney's 1987 case study makes this point nicely). Court decision-makers scan a more varied range of private dispositional alternatives than did their predecessors of twenty years ago.

Yet as significant as these new realities are, they do not account for my unexpected observation of the high drama in probation work. To construct a theory capable of explaining that observation, I found it necessary to expand the conceptual schemes employed by Cicourel and Emerson, along lines suggested by Matza's analysis of delinquency. In explaining court decision-making as a simple by-product of organizational constraint, Cicourel and Emerson adopt utilitarian models of human action, overlooking not only the crucial variability of culture as the very medium of practical interest, but also the autonomy of will inherent in the dialectic of agency and structure. In emphasizing the narrowly situated nature of practical judgment, both theorists also overlook ways in which microlevel interactions reflect their macrosocial and macrocultural contexts.

Thus, I have attempted to fill out their models in several important respects. I have focused on ways in which probation officers exercise agency in struggling against structural constraints—by "screwing the system to make it work." I have traced the subtle interplay between instrumental and expressive rationality in the workaday culture of probation. In indicating the relation between the spirit of modern tragedy and the core themes of Christian theodicy, I have identified a link between narrative strategies of everyday interaction and the deep culture of American society. In demonstrating the symbiotic fit between the rhetoric of modern tragedy and the most general problems of social control in the "no-fault society," I have suggested one way in which micro- and macrolevel processes help shape each other.

In attempting to construct a more adequate conceptual framework for analyzing problems of juvenile justice and of social control more generally, I have benefited from recent developments in social theory—in particular, the surge of interest in the sociology of culture and in the role of human agency in the micro-macro link, and the new-found respectability of "blurred genres" (Geertz 1983, chap. 1). However I have also been able to draw upon more venerable intellectual traditions, particularly some of the most general themes associated with "Chicago sociology": John Dewey's symbolic interactionist concern with the aesthetic and ethical dimensions of practical judgment; Edward Shils's macro-sociological concern with the problematic but constitutive relation between center and periphery; and Erving Goffman's dramaturgical concern with the struggle to maintain a creditable self.

This study is indebted to the traditions of Chicago sociology in other ways as well. The case narratives presented in the book's opening chapters hearken to Clifford Shaw's "natural histories of delinquent careers," though indicating (thanks primarily to Cicourel and Emerson) how much of what we regard as natural is shaped by bureaucratic concerns. In broad outline, the book's argument combines early Chicagoans' emphasis on ecological determinism with later Chicagoans' emphasis on symbolic constructions. The work of Morris Janowitz provides the contour for such a synthesis. In particular, his concepts of institution building, citizenship, and social control inform this analysis of juvenile justice in the no-fault society.

1

Larry: "Screwing the System and Making It Work"

Dear members of the diagnostic team,

The young man I am sending you today is in great need of help. At the age of thirteen years, Larry has spent four of his last five years in a penal institution. The conduct of the authorities in this case has been incredibly inept.

There is perhaps no way that we at this point can reverse the failures of the past. Larry is hurt, confused, and hard to manage. His educational and emotional needs are enormous. Shortly, his hurt will turn to bitterness, his confusion to violence, and we will have a very dangerous adult felon in our community.

Whatever plan you develop for Larry will be restricted by the following parameters: (1) I will not send Larry to the Department of Corrections; (2) I will be hostile to any institutional setting.

In short, I am asking you to do the impossible. I am confident that if over the next five years we can turn Larry into a functioning adult, we all will have done a service of inestimable value for the community.

I dare you to do your best.

To all appearances, Larry had been treated most unjustly by juvenile authorities in the nearby state he had just left. He seemed primarily neglected rather than delinquent, yet those authorities had warehoused him in various residential institutions for the four years since age nine, when his street cop father was caught in the act of robbing a bank, and his overwhelmed mother, keeping just two of her children, abandoned Larry and two others without support.

His offenses in the nearby state had consisted of running away, breaking and entering, vandalism, and a number of auto thefts and unauthorized uses of automobiles; but these offenses all occurred after his family's disintegration, and many of the offenses were associated with attempts to escape the succession of foster homes, group homes, and state institutions in which he was placed. (Of all these placements, only a Jesuit group home offered Larry a sense of belonging and stability. But even from there he ran within a year, taking the Jesuit father's car after he was disciplined for breach of the home's strict rules.) For his various offenses, so easily understandable, Larry had spent one and a half years in the largest juvenile institution operated by that state's Department of Social Services and had twice been committed to the juvenile training school operated by that state's Department of Corrections.

When Larry's probation officer learned of this treatment, it offended his sense of decency. Here was Larry, still only thirteen, with a record of prior institutionalization longer than any the counselor had ever encountered, except for that of a brutal and deliberate murderer. Larry had just moved in with his father, who had been released early from the penitentiary because of a nervous breakdown and had been living in the court's venue. After supervising Larry for five years, the other state's juvenile authorities had released him directly to the custody of his father without arranging for courtesy supervision as provided by an interstate compact; despite Larry's previously diagnosed severe educational deficiencies, he was enrolled in regular public school classes. When the first set of new complaints were brought against Larry for incorrigibility and unauthorized use of his stepmother's car, a probation officer had been working with Larry's older brother, whom he had already sent to a harsh state training school.

Larry's treatment history so outraged this probation officer, as well as the judge and other staff members who became involved in the case, that the court mobilized an extraordinary degree of commitment to help Larry. The probation officer brought Larry's records to a judge who had been on the bench less than a year and was determined to make the system work. After reviewing the case overnight, the judge decided on the course of noncorrectional treatment for Larry. To demonstrate his intense interest in Larry's case, the judge also made the unprecedented gesture of communicating this decision in a handwritten letter to the director of the court's diagnostic team, an interagency coordinating group that explores all possible dispositional alternatives for youth who have frustrated previous treatment efforts or who seem headed for commitment to the state. The judge called together the probation officer and the director of the diagnostic team into his chambers, personally delivering the challenge of doing "the impossible" and pledging himself to secure any special resources they might need in their efforts. The judge followed their progress with weekly meetings in chambers and frequent meetings over lunch.

"To Make a Difference"

It is neither accidental nor arbitrary that Larry's case received such an extraordinary level of attention from the juvenile court; a combination of mutually reinforcing factors qualified it for special treatment. Larry's prior treatment seemingly exemplified a commonly perceived model of juvenile justice at its worst, in which the system had itself compounded Larry's vulnerability. And Larry was personally an especially appealing boy, able to elicit most intensely the court's normative commitment to care for and protect children in need. The staff's sense of injustice intensified this normative commitment, while Larry's personal appeal intensified the sense of injustice. As the probation officer described his attraction to Larry:

> I responded emotionally to this case because I thought we could make a difference. Larry has a very appealing manner about him when you meet him. It's because there's something very redeeming there, and I can't put my finger on it—something very child-like, something that never grew up, something that is four or five years old, just like our children, that makes you say, "what he needs is someone to really care for and love him—and by golly, I'm the one!"

Although determined to "make a difference" and armed with the judge's full support, Larry's probation officer and the head of the diagnostic team found it exceedingly difficult to arrange a suitable disposition within the scope of the judge's instructions. They considered it necessary to find a small homelike residential placement for Larry because of both the father's character and his desire to be rid of Larry. Yet those very reasons made Larry a poor candidate for community placement, since those placements were trying to recruit children whose families were "workable." Some placements were inappropriate because they did not offer specialized-enough services; Larry required special education for severe language and reading problems, emotional disturbance, and borderline mental retardation. Other placements were inappropriate because the services they offered were too specialized; at least one placement, for example, rejected Larry on the grounds that his behavior disorder was not "organic." Of course the determination of these clinical

11

diagnoses is flexible; underlying these various grounds for rejecting Larry was a sense that someone with Larry's extensive history of institutionalization was too "hard-core."

It was difficult even to complete the application materials for these various placements because the other state's juvenile agency withheld its extensive diagnostic and treatment reports about Larry. In response to a letter from Larry's probation officer requesting those reports, the agency sent only scanty information. They had sent a much fuller set of reports to the schools, which Larry's probation officer was able to obtain from school authorities with the consent of Larry and his father. Still, to obtain such routine information as Larry's exact offense history, dates of institutional stay, and reasons for release, the director of the court's diagnostic team had to make a special trip to inspect the other state's court records, after the judge had interceded to gain permission for him to do so. (The authority of a juvenile court to subpoena records does not extend across state lines.)

Despite all these efforts, it was not until three years later that Larry's probation officer or anyone else on the court staff learned the other half of Larry's story, because the other state had segregated its correctional from its social services records. As it turned out, Larry had suffered years of neglect and physical abuse even before his father's arrest. His parents neither fed nor clothed him properly nor saw him to school regularly, and when he did attend school he often exhibited massive bruises from his father's drunken beatings. His mother often failed to return home at night. Larry's records at the other state's court did not state that at the time of his first court contact there, his family was already under active investigation by a protective services worker.

For six weeks, Larry's probation officer devoted half of every day exclusively to Larry's case: making phone calls, consulting with the head of the diagnostic team, meeting with the judge, seeing Larry at the detention home and Larry's father in his office, visiting possible placements, and trying to gain release of Larry's full records. The diagnostic team coordinator also devoted considerable time to this case. After six weeks, all they had to show for their efforts were dozens of rejections from placements. It was not possible to place Larry anywhere within the state.

Inspiration and Triumph

Finally, the probation officer and diagnostic team coordinator hit on the inspired idea of placing Larry at Boys Town in Nebraska, which not only offered the ideal residential setting they were seeking for Larry, but—uniquely among private agencies—was well enough endowed financially so that funding was not an issue. At first, Boys Town too rejected Larry's application, on the familiar grounds that Larry was too disturbed and too educationally deficient. However the probation officer and diagnostic team coordinator refused to accept this rejection. They had a new educational evaluation performed which found Larry not quite as far below normal achievement levels as had previous testing. Larry's probation officer brought his own personal camera to the detention home and took pictures that highlighted the boy's cheerful demeanor even there. The diagnostic team coordinator wrote back to Boys Town, reporting the new educational test results, enclosing the photographs, stressing again the judge's personal interest in Larry, and requesting that the admissions committee interview Larry in person before reaching a final decision. The diagnostic team coordinator tracked down Larry's father, who had since moved to an adjoining county, to procure Larry's air fare to Nebraska for the interview. The court director had to have an exception made to established financial regulations in order to arrange air fare for Larry's probation officer to accompany Larry. Larry was charming as ever in his appearance before the admissions committee at Boys Town; they accepted him.

It was, reports Larry's probation officer, one of the great emotional moments in his career at the court. The probation officer, the diagnostic team coordinator, and the judge went out to lunch together in celebration. "We really did it—we made the system do something it heretofore had never done—we really screwed the system and made it work, for one impossible kid."

Even after Boys Town's decision, the diagnostic team coordinator had to negotiate a maze of bureaucratic review before concluding arrangements for the out-of-state placement. Because of the judge's concern to decriminalize Larry's case and to ensure the delivery of the services Larry needed, the judge was unwilling to transfer correctional supervision of the case to Nebraska to monitor the placement at Boys Town. For its part, Boys Town required compliance with the Interstate Compact on the Placement of Children, administered by the state Departments of Welfare. The diagnostic team coordinator persuaded Larry's father to pay transportation and medical expenses and a token monthly tuition fee to Boys Town. This obviated the need to secure state funding, since Boys Town was willing to assume the remaining costs. Yet even so, the process of securing approval for Larry's placement took a solid week.

From the county's Department of Social Services, the diagnostic team coordinator had to arrange certification that local or in-state placements were either inappropriate or unavailable. The diagnostic team coordinator also obtained from this department names of the state officials whose approval was required for the Interstate Compact. When the diagnostic team coordinator had finally traced through the welfare chain of command, the response came down that approval was dependent on the recommendation of the state's commissioner of corrections. The diagnostic team coordinator had to start all over again, identifying and satisfying every step in an extended chain of command, this time within the state Department of Corrections. Final approval for Larry's placement at Boys Town required not only document production at every level of review, but personal phone calls from the judge to the directors of the state departments of Welfare and of Corrections.

Aftermath and Hindsight

Larry went off to Boys Town with hope and enthusiasm. However the triumphant climax to his case was quickly overtaken by a tragic denouement: just two weeks after his admission to Boys Town, while the regular houseparents of his cottage were away on leave, Larry left campus without permission and acted as an accomplice to armed robbery, abduction, and attempted rape. Larry's probation officer was shocked to hear a probation officer from Nebraska level the very accusation against him that he had earlier addressed to a probation officer in the state where Larry's case originated: "You dumped on us and didn't even bother to notify us." When he heard the news, the diagnostic team coordinator wept.

Larry was committed to a juvenile correctional facility in Nebraska. Despite running away several times, he finally finished serving his sentence and hitchhiked back to his father's house. In short order, he faced new complaints in several jurisdictions for grand larceny, auto theft, and driving while intoxicated and without a license. Larry's probation officer, now seeing the case as hopeless, wanted to recommend that the juvenile court certify Larry to stand trial as an adult in the circuit court. Anticipating resistance to this plan, however, he instead recommended that Larry be sentenced to the adult jail for one year—the longest term the juvenile court could impose. Larry's case went in before a different judge, who rejected even this recommendation since Larry was still only sixteen and instead committed Larry to yet another state training school.

While awaiting transfer to the training school, Larry and a companion escaped from the juvenile detention home by beating a guard senseless with a baseball bat. The two escapees drove a stolen car across three states before wrecking it in a drunken crash; Larry was in a coma for several days but survived. Returning from the scene of the crash, he escaped yet once again at the airport, but was recaptured to face charges of attempted murder.

Although hindsight obviously changes the assessment of this case, subsequent events do not detract from the dedicated and resourceful casework demonstrated by Larry's placement at Boys Town, which at the time represented the last best hope for a most troubled and troubling youth. "I started out thinking the system ruined this kid," reflected Larry's probation officer. "That's not true; this kid was destroyed by age eight. We could not have saved him, if save is the word. There is probably no institutional program that could have helped him. . . . My impression now is that it's always been hopeless, that we were fooling ourselves, that we acted—consciously—not with the facts in front of us, but from our hearts. Still, what the judge did then was noble."

1

Institutional Gaps and Cross-Purposes as Dilemmas
of Individualized Casework

2

What Makes Some Cases Special?

L
arry's case and the others I report in the next chapters, though accorded special attention by court staff, epitomize the challenges,
meanings, triumphs, and disappointments common to more routine
cases. These cases reveal the profound disorganization of the court's task
environment: the failure of such community institutions as family and
school to provide adequate informal controls or help foster the development of adequate personal controls in adolescents, on the one hand,
and the failure of such formal institutions as health, welfare, and correctional agencies to provide adequate habilitation or punishment, on the
other. Caseworkers resort to inspirational strategies of decision making
because the organization's technology is incomplete and even its objectives are uncertain. The very resourcefulness caseworkers must exercise
as individuals to secure needed support from clients and colleagues testifies to the scarcity of resources on the systems level; the very density
of bureaucratic regulation governing interagency, interjurisdictional,
and intergovernmental cooperation indicates as well the absence of
domain consensus and the sparseness of administrative coordination.
These cases test the definition and relevance of the court's institutional
ethos while straining the limits of its organizational competence, with
judges and probation officers encountering institutional gaps and cross-
purposes as dilemmas of individualized casework and justice.

As the formal agency of last resort in maintaining control over
adolescents in the community, the juvenile court confronts most pro-
foundly the dilemma that adolescent behavior is essentially uncontrollable through direct, external means. Social control depends primarily
on the indirect, informal controls created by the integration of individual
personalities in the social and economic institutions that embody central
values and the prevailing technology; as Talcott Parsons puts it, "the
most fundamental mechanisms of social control are to be found in the

normal processes of interaction in an institutionally integrated social system" (1951: 301). Adolescents develop moral judgment, as Jean Piaget describes that process, not from the exercise of adult authority, but rather in the natural course of interacting with their peers:

> the sense of justice, though naturally capable of being reinforced by the precepts and the practical example of the adult, is largely independent of these influences, and requires nothing more for its development than the mutual respect and solidarity which holds among the children themselves. It is often at the expense of the adult and not because of him that the notions of just and unjust find their way into the youthful mind. (1965: 198)

The means of legitimate coercion that the court commands are limited in their extent as well as their effectiveness. Due to the inordinate public expense of confining large numbers of individuals to correctional institutions, and the resulting scarcity of prison capacity relative to the criminal population, even chronic offenders often escape incarceration for their crimes. Conversely, not only are means of legitimate coercion scarce, so is the wisdom to know when to refrain from intervention.

Larry's and these other cases indicate how intricate are problems of working with troubled adolescents. Adolescence is the most marginal status within the age structure—a treacherous passage between youth and adulthood when, for both psychodynamic and psychosocial reasons, personal and social controls are weakest. The rejection of parental ego support in the disengagement from infantile dependencies compounds the intensification of libidinal drives due to biological maturation, creating a psychodynamic situation where, in Anna Freud's phrase, "a relatively strong id confronts a relatively weak ego" (quoted in Blos 1962: 177). The adolescent ego must draw on these expanded drive energies to rework earlier developmental crises; Peter Blos asserts that "the task of psychic restructuring by regression represents the most formidable psychic work of adolescence" (1979: 152). Since this task includes radical revision of the superego, with its origin in oedipal and pre-oedipal object relations, "superego disturbances constitute a uniquely adolescent deviancy" (152).

In psychosocial terms, Erik Erikson describes adolescence as a "moratorium" before the assumption of adult family and work responsibilities, a period of provocative playfulness on the part of youth and of selective permissiveness on the part of society. The maturational task of the adolescent is to develop a sense of inner identity: "The young person, in order to experience wholeness, must feel a progressive continuity between that which he has come to be during the long years of childhood and that which he promises to become in the anticipated future: between that which he conceives himself to be and that which he perceives others to see in him and to expect of him" (1968: 87). Crucial to this process is the adoption of work goals which provide an outlet for sublimating infantile instinctual aims and transforming passivity into activity in a way that matches the corresponding demands and opportunities of social reality.

Discovering an identity depends then in large part on institutional support. School curricula, for example, must be "relevant" in the sense of instilling technological skills that will equip children to participate in productive adult life: "the configurations of culture and the manipulations basic to the prevailing technology must reach meaningfully into school life, supporting in every child a feeling of competence" (Erikson 1968: 126). "Adolescence . . . is least 'stormy' in that segment of youth which is gifted and well trained in pursuit of expanding technological trends, and thus able to identify with new roles of competency and invention" (129–30). In a more attenuated fashion, the process of identity formation "depends on the support which the young individual receives from the collective sense of identity characterizing the social groups significant to him: his class, his nation, his culture" (89). It is in adolescence that the ego-ideal attains its definitive organization, which as Freud noted in "On Narcissism" has a social as well as an individual side, being "also the common ideal of a family, a class, or a nation" (1957: 101).

Larry's case and these others suggest the usefulness of Albert Reiss's conception (1951) that delinquency is a failure of social as well as personal controls. The failure of social controls extends far beyond ineffective rule enforcement by criminal justice agencies, to problems stemming from community disorganization. In Erikson's psychosocial terms, an adolescent's drift into delinquency is the embrace—most likely only temporary—of a negative identity in an attempt to escape from identity confusion. In institutional terms, delinquent drift results largely from the disarticulation between schooling, on the one hand, and the structure of employment opportunities on the other. Lacking are such "linking institutions" as apprenticeship, work-study, or community service programs to ease the transition from school to employment. Lacking too are linking institutions for strengthening the family in its role of preparing children for school. In disorganized communities, both primary groups and secondary institutions are unstable, isolated, and inadequate in resources. Community disorganization helps cause delinquency directly by weakening the "stakes in conformity" that constitute the most effective social controls and indirectly through a more crescive process of contributing to the formation of weakened personal controls.

Institutional incapacity to provide routes to valued goals weakens ego controls, while institutional discontinuities in socialization and discipline weaken superego controls. Thus while delinquents, like all adolescents, occupy the most marginal status within the age structure, they tend also to be marginally situated within the stratification structure, peripheral to the central institutional system.

As individuals, their problems are multiple, diffuse, and ambiguous. Was Larry, for example, predominantly a hurting child or a hardened predatory criminal, and when? Larry was abused, neglected, emotionally disturbed, borderline mentally retarded, deficient in language and reading skills, alcoholic, and violent. These sorts of problems are not just multiple and diffuse, but synergistic. Low intelligence compounds the effects of emotional disturbance, and vice versa. Larry's outbreaks of violent behavior repeatedly frustrated attempts to provide the nurturance he needed. For another boy, a worsening physical disability helped create and perpetuate severe emotional instability, while the emotional instability prevented him from receiving the preferred treatment for his physical deterioration. In yet another case, a violent and self-destructive heroin addict contracted a serious case of hepatitis, with each aspect of her condition rendering inaccessible required emergency treatment for the other. As intractable as these types of problems are singly in their own right, in combination they defy ministration.

Larry's case and these others illustrate the displacement of child welfare functions assumed by court staff. Judges and probation officers find themselves increasingly responsible to procure, for especially hard-to-serve children who are without adequate parental support, basic nurturance, shelter, health, and educational services that more directly qualified agencies are either unwilling or unable to provide. This responsibility is increasing in part because of statutory revisions inspired by federal delinquency and child welfare legislation, expanding the court's formal authority over other agencies to enforce both the "right to treatment" and the civil liberties of children. The interorganizational role of the juvenile court within the network of child welfare agencies has become more central even as the partly conflicting formal rights and liberties of children have been simultaneously expanding. These recent trends are perhaps best exemplified by probation officers' involvement in obtaining educational services for handicapped students; descriptions of several such cases follow. The same trends also surface in other cases described below, in which probation officers seek either to secure foster care for their clients from the Department of Social Services or to arrange such foster care on their own in anticipation of rejection by that depart-

ment; these trends reappear in still other cases, in which probation officers must deal with hospitals, mental hospitals, and other organizations
for treatment.

The effective authority of the court is inadequate to fulfill its expanding formal responsibility for child welfare. Not only are the clients it
treats marginal in the age and stratification systems, but in practice the
court is itself marginal, relegated to the "borderland of criminal justice"
(Allen 1964), mediating between the system of law and coercion on the
one hand and the welfare system on the other, peripheral to both. Delinquency results in large measure from the institutional disarticulation
between schooling and the structure of work opportunities; the juvenile
justice system is disarticulated as well. The network of correctional and
welfare agencies that appears to children and parents as remote, fragmented, and overspecialized affronts its workers with goal confusion,
inadequacy of resources, and lack of administrative coordination. The
agencies loosely linked in this network defend their organizational
boundaries by harboring information, enforcing red tape, establishing
waiting lists, and arguing legal proceedings against each other. These
agency boundaries are semipermeable, through the medium of specialized diagnosis, only to casework strategies of "problemization"—strategies that as Margaret Rosenheim argues, "counter . . . the wisdom of
'normalizing' as much delinquent conduct as we possibly can" (1976: 52).

Community Setting

This study is set in a prosperous and rapidly developing suburban
county. The county's social landscape—a four hundred square mile pas-
tiche of landed estates and trailer parks, one-lane bridges and interstate
highways, colonial landmarks and new towns, horse farms and office
towers—attests to the tumultuous pace of change. During the study period (from 1975 to 1985), population grew from 580,000 to 690,000.
The preceding decades had seen even more dramatic growth: from a
dairy farming community of only 40,000 residents in 1940, the county
had undergone transformation to a bedroom community after the war
(its population reaching 120,000 in 1950), and then to a multinucleated
secondary metropolitan center of a service economy (its population expanding from 270,000 in 1960 to 480,000 by 1970). As recently as 1959,
24 percent of the county's total acreage was devoted to agricultural use;
by 1983, only 7 percent of the acreage remained agricultural—less than
the acreage zoned for commercial and industrial use. From 1973 to
1983, the number of commercial and industrial firms located in the

county increased nearly two and a half fold; a plurality of those firms (over a quarter of them) were "high tech," formally classified as "research and technical manufacturing firms."

By any measure of wealth or status, the county ranks among the highest in the nation. In 1984, 48 percent of all its residents twenty-five years of age or older were college graduates. In 1980, 77 percent of its employed work force was white collar. Median household income in 1983 was more than double the national figure. In 1983, when the nation's unemployment rate neared 10 percent, the county's remained under 3 percent. The county has never undergone the shock of fiscal crisis, consistently maintaining AAA bond ratings. Although residential integration is increasing slowly, the county remains predominantly white: whites comprised 93 percent of the county's population in 1970, and 86 percent in 1980. Despite the relative transience of its population, community controls are strong. The county's social life revolves around civic, church, and voluntary groups, and rates of participation in these groups are high.

Yet as in any metropolitan jurisdiction, there are pockets of community disorganization and poverty, situated according to the familiar ecological pattern in "areas of transition" immediately surrounding zones of commercial and industrial development. Not surprisingly, these areas spawn a disproportionate share of the delinquency complaints received by the juvenile court. As might be presumed from its favorable demographics, the countywide delinquency problem is relatively mild by national standards: in one year during the study period, for example, not a single case of murder was reported in the county. Nonetheless, the juvenile court received between 3,500 and 6,200 complaints of juvenile delinquency annually (in addition to traffic, custody, and certain adult complaints).

The particular juvenile court that I studied differs from most others in one significant aspect of its organizational structure: the chief judge does not administer the probation department. Although according to the state code all court employees serve "at the pleasure of the judge," workers in the court's probation, residential, and administrative divisions are county employees supervised by the court director. Their employment is governed by the terms of the county's civil service system, even though a portion of their salaries is reimbursed by the state. This bifurcation of authority is unusual, according to a study conducted by the National Center for State Courts (Stapleton, Aday, and Ito 1982). Along the other dimensions of organizational structure and procedure determined by this study to differentiate juvenile courts, the court I studied is unexceptional: its jurisdiction includes status offenders; judicial adjudication and disposition can be collapsed into a single stage; a prosecutor does not screen criminal petitions; and intake officers have limited discretion to assign children to informal supervision.

Despite the element of disorganization introduced by conflict and confusion over the division of authority between chief judge and court director, this court is in many ways a national model for excellence, as indicated by any number of prestigious awards. By national standards, probation officers' salaries are high (indeed, probation officers with seven year's experience receive more generous salaries than newly tenured college professors at the local branch of the state university), while their caseloads are low. As a result, there is active competition for probation jobs at the court, yielding a highly qualified staff with relatively little turnover. A majority of probation officers have master's degrees. Like the county government in general, the court's administration has consistently embraced modern management techniques. The court was among the first to automate its case processing and management information. (Characteristically however, the computer system that won national awards for the court has never really worked: its records are at once redundant, incomplete, and inaccurate, often failing to capture such essentials as findings of guilt or innocence, and yielding key workload indicators that are inflated by as much as 30 percent.)

This court deliberately articulated its own development with federal policy goals. When it formally separated from the county's circuit court in 1965, the juvenile court's staff consisted of a single judge and a handful of probation officers and clerks. By 1975, the staff had grown to ninety, including three judges; seven years later, the court numbered five judges among a staff that had more than doubled in size. The court's aggressive and successful application for Law Enforcement Assistance Administration grants during the seventies helped accelerate its growth. During that decade the court received over a million dollars in grants to help plan for new secure and less-secure detention homes, to design and implement a computerized information system, and to start a wide variety of programs: family counseling, work training, community service, drug counseling, emergency foster homes, group homes, volunteer services, and outreach detention, among others.

The community and organizational settings of this study lend it more than parochial interest. The conscious articulation of the court's development with federal policy makes it a testing ground for national trends. The rapidity of growth in both the county and court creates a propitious opportunity to study the effects of social change. In particular the special advantages enjoyed by the county and court provide a hard test of the assumption that societal change produces institutional disarticulation, since the types of social and cultural disorganization found in an exemplary juvenile court in a relatively well-organized community are likely to exist elsewhere as well.

This setting, then, is well suited to the research questions that inspire this study: How do probation officers manage to discharge their duties, despite the disorganization of their task environment? With what effects? How in the face of chronic disappointment do they manage to sustain their motivation? These issues inform the particulars of the "special" cases selected for examination in the remaining chapters of part 1, suggesting some of the generalizations offered throughout the rest of the book about the practice, outcomes, and ideology of probation casework.

3

Daring the Impossible: Michael, Mary, Jerome

S he came from one of the best neighborhoods in the county; the two
boys, of different races, came from among the worst. Mary and
Jerome were physically and personally appealing; Michael was physically grotesque. All were uncontrollable. Each had suffered parental loss
or abandonment and lacked effective family supervision. None would
cooperate with educational or residential programs; each needed foster
care and special education; all were ill served by the public schools and
Department of Social Services. Their probation officers were their dedicated advocates, since the probation officers perceived their helplessness,
while others were repelled by their dangerousness. Each child confronted the probation officer with the urgent need to do something to
resolve a desperate situation for which there was nothing to be done.

Helpless or Dangerous?

Helpless or dangerous? Insane or criminal? Their backgrounds were
all marked by a mixture of misfortune and misbehavior which confounds
such determinations. The director of the community mental health center could not decide whether Michael was sane enough to be legally
competent to stand trial and so referred the case to a state psychiatric
hospital for a thirty-day evaluation. Members of the court's diagnostic
team, reviewing Michael's case at the time of his first offense, disagreed
whether to recommend probation as a punitive measure or merely to
suggest the need for some form of treatment. As a child he had been
abused and neglected. A protective services worker had investigated his
family when Michael was still in elementary school, and Michael was
actually placed in foster care when his mother left with another man,
after his father had undergone protracted hospital treatment for alcoholism and cirrhosis. These considerations alone would have inspired sym-

pathetic understanding for Michael's aggressive and disruptive behavior; beyond these considerations, however, Michael—a slight, short boy with a terrible skin condition—bore the extraordinary handicap of a rare eye disease which rendered him legally blind and doomed gradually to lose the little vision he had.

Yet his offenses were most serious. Complaints brought against Michael in his early adolescence for vandalism and fire-setting were handled informally. The state school for the blind expelled him for repeatedly running away and for emotional outbursts. The Department of Social Services had to remove him from a foster home because he was sexually active with the foster parents' daughter. And by the time he attained his eighteenth birthday, he had come to court at different times for assaulting a teacher, sodomizing a little girl, and raping and sodomizing a boy who had spited him—offenses for which he experienced little remorse.

Similar ambiguity surrounded the nature of Mary's case. At a critical point in the course of her court supervision, Mary was in the regional detention home, experiencing the throes of heroin withdrawal and having contracted a yet undiagnosed case of life-threatening hepatitis. During a forty-five-day spree following her escape from a mental hospital, Mary and her boyfriend—a paroled adult felon, also a heroin addict—had committed over 120 larcenies in at least four adjoining jurisdictions, stealing and fencing tens of thousands of dollars worth of cars and other valuables; the police finally captured the pair in a prolonged high-speed car chase ending with a wreck. The judge in one of the other jurisdictions wanted Mary held in detention for trial; Mary's probation officer, backed by his judges, wanted her released for psychiatric and medical treatment.

During the year before she first came to court, Mary had been in and out of mental hospitals, for runaways, sexual activity, and drug use. This pattern of behavior developed to its full extent several months after Mary's mother had died of a heart attack. Initially, Mary and her rather stiff military father responded to their loss by drawing closer to one another, more on the level of friends and equals than of parent and child; but they soon began to grow increasingly alienated from each other until he admitted her involuntarily to a mental hospital for evaluation, a month after he married another woman.

Mary's probation officer described her as "one of those kids who could charm the pants off anyone. She has a physical magnetism—not sensual, but the appeal of a poor, hopeless little girl." Evaluating the success of her treatment at yet another private psychiatric hospital, to which she was committed for the string of larcenies, the probation officer wrote,

"Mary's progress has been remarkable in the fact that she has been virtually drug-free and has gained a great deal of understanding through therapy for the first time." This probation officer, who had worked with Mary for eighteen months, left the court soon thereafter; the probation officer who took over Mary's case saw it differently, believing that correctional treatment would have been more appropriate than psychiatric treatment. Six months later, as Mary turned eighteen on the run from a community halfway house and under suspicion of still more larcenies, her new probation officer concluded the case termination summary: "Mary struck us as an extremely manipulative girl who took advantage of, rather than used, the rehabilitative services which were arranged for her." Disputing one of the psychiatric diagnoses, this new probation officer (who herself had mental health training) asserted, "She was never schizophrenic . . . she was really a criminal personality." Reflecting on the case two years later, Mary's original probation officer independently endorsed this judgment: "Mary was a sociopath. She was really manipulative. But I couldn't acknowledge that, because that would have made the case unworkable."

Hopelessly and dangerously criminal requiring commitment, or workable with the nurturing supervision never provided by parents? Jerome's case too embodies this ambiguity. The youngest of two children, Jerome lost his mother to leukemia at age three and his father to a mentally incapacitating automobile accident five years later. By Jerome's fourteenth birthday, no one could contain him: not his loving older sister, who was trying to raise him along with three other siblings and three children of her own, while at the same time contending with a physically abusive spouse; not the regular public school, which officiously documented Jerome's every truancy, tardiness, class cut, classroom disruption, and fight; not the teacher of a small alternative school for court-involved children, who found Jerome "constantly and totally disruptive, refusing assigned work, and verbally abusive"; not foster parents licensed by the Department of Social Services, who could not control Jerome's comings and goings; not group-home parents under contract to the court, who were shocked when in a fit of temper Jerome threw a pool ball across a room, and who feared for the safety of their own seven-year-old son whom Jerome picked on frequently; not a group-centered wilderness program, which expelled Jerome after only two weeks for his inability to control himself whenever he was not receiving direct individual attention. Citing Jerome's record of nearly twenty court intakes, Department of Social Services workers, the court's group-home coordinator, and the court's coordinator of special placements all felt that Jerome was too "criminal" for their services.

The only person to whom Jerome seemed responsive was his probation officer, who dedicated herself to his welfare and who saw his behavior in a different light. To her, Jerome was no menacing delinquent, but
a youngster who delighted in gardening and fishing and was afraid of
the dark. "Poor baby—I like that kid—damn. . . . It's clear to him that
no matter what he does, I will like him. I will have to do things if he
doesn't do what he's supposed to do, but I do like him." Jerome would
always behave himself for her, sitting quietly in the lobby outside her
office for hours at a time on days when he was suspended from school.
"Jerome is a kid who loves people very easily. Your first impression of
him is that he's going to run you in circles—he *can*. But if you can hang
in there through the first three or four weeks, he's workable, he really is.
He does take a lot of energy, there's no two ways about it. That kid is
desperate; he has *never* had any parenting. I mean, he's a fourteen-year-
old who's got a hell of a background. And he's bright—you don't think
so at first, but the more you work with him the more you realize he is
bright." As for Jerome's extensive record of court intakes, most alleged
such noncriminal behavior as incorrigibility, violation of probation, or
failure to appear in court. "If you really look at his record," the probation
officer argued, "the only real heavy-duty on there is one that says 'strong-
arm robbery,' and that consists of taking a bike-seat away from another
kid. It's mostly trespass, petty stuff—just being a little piss-ant. He is just
that—a little red piss-ant." She viewed Jerome's expulsion from the wilderness program as unfair: "He didn't hit anybody; he didn't run away;
he didn't threaten to run away; basically, it's just that *they* couldn't give
him the attention he needed. They said very clearly he wasn't appropriate for their program because he needs one-on-one supervision. . . .
They're understaffed right now." Jerome's tendency to get into fights she
regarded as attention-seeking behavior normal for a parentless child
from a large family. "The sad thing is, he's not a bad kid. He's your kid
who's going to end up getting very little out of the system. And that's the
kind of kid I want to be able to help."

Desperate Dilemmas

The greatest "help" Jerome's probation officer could hope to offer was
long-term residential placement, forestalling his commitment to a state
training school. Jerome, who was unable to stay out of trouble in the
community, had already been warned in court that he would be committed for the very next incident. And although Jerome's sister genuinely
cared for him, she had asked to be relieved of his custody because she

simply could not handle him. She had no telephone, consistently missed appointments at both school and the probation office, and even failed to appear at court hearings. Despite the sister's inaccessibility and reticence to discuss her own situation, Jerome's probation officer finally learned, indirectly, a partial explanation for her behavior: she had been seeking refuge from her husband in the local women's shelter. Given Jerome's expulsion from two schools, the foster home, group home, and group-centered wilderness program, it seemed that only a highly structured, individualized residential program would be able to contain him; given his learning disability, sharply limited classroom attention span, and interest in outdoor activity, he seemed to require a placement that emphasized such activity. "This is a kid who needs one-to-one supervision. Anything less than that, he's going to drive the place crazy."

Finding such a placement—finding an appropriate place that would admit and keep Jerome, and that Jerome would agree to enter—seemed like an impossible task. "I look at the resource manual and I think, 'Where the hell does a Jerome fit?'" The two local community-based residential programs for boys were not structured enough for Jerome's needs; a network of privately owned adolescent group homes operated by paid shift-workers which claimed to provide residents with individual attention had just been closed down in scandal. There did seem to be one program that might possibly work for Jerome, which placed emotionally disturbed children one at a time in "community teaching homes." Run by couples specially trained in behavior modification, this program simultaneously trained the children's natural parents in the same technique in preparation for the children's return home. However it seemed unlikely that Jerome's sister would be able to sustain the participation this program required of her; at any rate, there were few openings and a long waiting list of applicants. The mere process of arranging the battery of educational, psychological, and medical evaluations and completing the paperwork required even to apply for this program was forbidding; for several months, though, it seemed like Jerome's—and his probation officer's—last chance.

Jerome's probation officer faced a dilemma. If she kept Jerome on probation, in the unlikely hope of arranging placement, she would almost certainly see him return to court on some violation or petty new offense leading to commitment; by releasing him from probation, she would not have to be party to Jerome's return to court, and he might be less likely to return. "Part of me just wants to turn him loose and see where he goes." But the public schools had agreed to pay Jerome's tuition at a private school offering special education while the court was in the process of arranging placement. If released from probation, Jerome would lose his eligibility for that school, and the regular public school would not accept him back for long.

The probation officer decided to hold on to supervision, and Jerome's case took a serendipitous turn. On the basis of his initial good adjustment to the private special school, Jerome was admitted to a wilderness program affiliated with that school. This wilderness program, reputed to be less selective than most others, managed to overcome Jerome's initial resistance and keep him for at least four months. Thus was Jerome's probation officer able to arrange residential placement, staving off commitment to a state training school.

Michael's case took no such turn. His particular combination of emotional disturbance, learning disability, and visual impairment thwarted repeated rounds of efforts to arrange placement for him; in consequence, he was committed to state training schools on two separate occasions. The initial round of efforts followed a complaint against Michael for assaulting his teacher, the first complaint against him to be heard before a judge. Since the Department of Social Services (DSS) had legal custody over Michael, and the public schools were contracting for his program of special education, these efforts involved collaboration among the court's diagnostic team coordinator, Michael's DSS counselor, and a contract services specialist from the public schools. Initially, because of the inordinate amount of additional paperwork and delay entailed in using Title XX funds for placing children out of state, these collaborators limited their search for possible placements accordingly; when the in-state search proved fruitless, they canvassed placement possibilities nationwide in consultation with a clearinghouse for residential institutions. Over a hundred informal inquiries generated only about a dozen formal referrals, all ending in rejection for similar reasons. Programs for emotionally disturbed youngsters would be unable to accommodate Michael because of his visual impairment; programs for the blind would be unable to contain Michael's emotional outbursts. Michael was too handicapped for most programs; for at least one program, however, he was not handicapped enough, so that the other residents would be relatively more vulnerable to possible attack. Moreover, as an older adolescent Michael was of a most inconvenient age, which made him ineligible for many placements.

After a five-month search proved unsuccessful, the judge reluctantly agreed to abandon this first round of efforts. DSS retained legal custody over Michael while he continued to live with his father, and the public schools enrolled him in another local special education program. One month later, however, the task of securing placement assumed renewed and indeed greater urgency as the only alternative to commitment to a state training school, when Michael returned to court for raping a younger boy. Yet the same insurmountable combination of conditions obtained. The judge could do no more than stay Michael's commitment an extra several weeks to give the last possible placements the fullest opportunity to consider accepting Michael. Despite special provisions to teach Michael braille during his stay at the training school, no one expected him to benefit from commitment, but nothing could be done to avert it.

The final round of efforts to place Michael began five months after his release by the state, when Michael came back before the court yet again, this time for sodomizing a young girl. These efforts were constrained by the judge's stipulation that any placement be locked; however, the search was expanded to include secure psychiatric institutions, since Michael reported enjoying his thirty-day stay at a forensic unit of a state mental hospital for evaluation of his competence to stand trial. But Michael was by then too old for any such juvenile facility, yet not old enough, hardened enough, or "crazy" enough for any such adult facility. In consequence, he was committed a second time to the state Department of Corrections.

Michael and Jerome posed casework challenges framed by the danger of commitment; the challenge of Mary's case was framed, with even greater urgency, by life-threatening disease. Compounding the difficulty of this challenge were the synergy of its legal, medical, and psychological dimensions and the antagonisms or evasions of the various jurisdictions, agencies, or units that were called on to collaborate. Mary was being held in the regional detention home for a series of thefts she had committed with her adult boyfriend in several different jurisdictions after escaping from a psychiatric hospital. When her probation officer visited her in detention, he was struck by how terribly ill she looked—as it turned out, from a combination of heroin withdrawal and infectious hepatitis. He tried with the judge's support to have her moved to a hospital, but the judge in the jurisdiction that formally admitted her to the detention home insisted that she be kept there instead. To circumvent this injunction, the probation officer advised Mary's father to initiate mental commitment proceedings, since by statute such proceedings take precedence over criminal misdemeanor ones. Despite the refusal of the court's intake counselors to grant a mental petition, the probation officer persuaded a judge to issue such a petition during a preliminary hearing on a violation-of-probation charge. On the basis of the mental petition, the probation officer was able to have Mary transferred for temporary observation back to the mental hospital from which she had originally escaped.

However doctors at the mental hospital refused to keep Mary when they discovered her hepatitis. Nor would the county hospital agree to admit her, since they claimed she constituted a security risk. Nor for that matter would the sheriff's department willingly transport her, since her disease was infectious. The probation officer obtained court orders both for Mary's transportation and for her medical treatment; even so, he had to wait six hours in the hospital's emergency room before Mary was finally admitted, to be kept under police guard. The decision to commit Mary to a mental hospital for longer-term treatment commanded no less grudging compliance. The secure state mental institution for juveniles refused to accept Mary because it was "against policy" to admit infectious patients. On behalf of the judge, the court's supervisor of special services finally negotiated an ad hoc compromise with the state director of mental hospitals to place Mary under guard at a medical center on the grounds of a different state mental hospital. Still, Mary's admission to that facility was delayed several hours after her arrival there while the intake staff maintained that they lacked authorization to admit her; the sheriff who had transported her there, bearing the mental commitment order, finally just notified the administrator in charge that he was returning alone. When the hepatitis cleared up, Mary transferred to a private psychiatric hospital where, during the six-month period of her commitment, she seemed to make progress for the first time.

Recalcitrance as Usual

Measured against the competing demands for their attention represented by numerous other cases, the amounts of time probation officers invested in Mary, Jerome, and Michael were inordinate. During the three weeks it took Mary's probation officer to improvise and orchestrate an interorganizational resolution to Mary's crisis, he had little time left over—less than ten hours a week—to do anything for the other forty-odd children under his supervision; the proddings of his own supervisor and of co-workers were necessary to recall him to his other duties. Jerome's probation officer devoted more time to him—hundreds of hours over a two-year period—than to almost any other child in over thirteen years of probation work. Michael's multiple problems consumed the intensive casework services not only of the court but also of the Department of Social Services, the public schools, and different agencies for the handicapped for months at a time, generating hundreds of phone calls, dozens of letters, hours of conferences, and reams of photocopied reports.

Despite the extensiveness of their efforts on behalf of these children, all the various probation officers still encountered significant resistance to their plans from the children themselves. Between them, Jerome and Michael managed to get expelled from an entire range of foster homes, group homes, schools, special schools, and residential placements; Mary ran away from a foster home, a group home, a succession of psychiatric hospitals, and a community halfway house. Upon the expiration of her mental commitment, Mary ruined her probation officer's attempt to place her in a structured community-based residential program by proclaiming her defiance at the preadmission interview. When the interagency team of caseworkers reluctantly abandoned their first round of efforts to find a placement for Michael, the judge approved a package of community-based treatments they had put together instead, including private special education for emotionally disturbed students and a diversified day-program offered by a local mental health center. Disregarding the judicial order, Michael foiled the plans for him by proclaiming during the application interviews his unwillingness to participate in either program. In much the same manner, no sooner had Jerome arrived at the wilderness camp that his probation officer had found through sheer tenacity as the last hope to steer him away from commitment than he declared his intention to leave. The school director persuaded Jerome to stay by pointing out how much time he had recently spent in a juvenile detention home and how likely he was to wind up in an adult jail unless he changed his ways. Nonetheless, Jerome ran away the very next day, after being disciplined for striking a boy who had failed to accede to one of his demands. He enlisted his sister's support for his action by calling her to complain that they had not allowed him to eat at the camp. Several phone calls later, Jerome's probation officer convinced him to return by confronting him with the alternative of commitment.

Weak Trump

Probation officers encounter resistance not only from their clients, but also from the set of organizations whose correctional and welfare services they are called on to broker. The poor quality of state training schools epitomizes the sparseness of remedial resources in the court's institutional environment. Short of treating children as adults by sentencing them to jail, commitment to these schools constitutes the ultimate sanctions available to the court. In holding out the threat of commitment to the state as their final trump card over clients, probation officers play a shallow suit indeed, as Michael's experience illustrates. To limit the backlog of committed youth awaiting transfer to state facilities from local jails and detention homes, the largest training school for boys keeps its residents an average of only four months. Although the length of stay varies slightly according to the boy's behavior inside the institution, it bears almost no relation to his background or offense history; four months is generally sufficient for the training school staff to certify successful completion of the individualized treatment plan prepared by the reception and diagnostic center. So it was with Michael. Training school officials sought to release him on their normal schedule, despite his parole officer's repeated written protestations to those officials about the seriousness of Michael's offense. By refusing to accept responsibility for parole supervision in the community until Michael had completed a second successful home visit, the parole officer was able to get the training school to extend Michael's commitment—but only by a single month. Michael "earned" his release with a report that claimed, "Michael has shown good improvement in understanding human sexuality and normal heterosexual relationships. . . . We spent much time going over his charge of abduction and sodomy . . . and he should avoid such an incident easily in the future." It was only five months later that he sodomized a little girl.

Although the penultimate sanction available to the juvenile court—commitment to a state training school—is hollow, the ultimate sanctions—sentence to the adult jail for up to a year or, worse, transfer to the circuit court for trial and sentence as an adult—are even further to be avoided. And to have a child's case transferred to circuit court, the prosecuting attorney must prove that the defendant is not amenable to any form of treatment as a juvenile. Fortunately for Michael, he was represented on his second sodomy charge by a court-appointed lawyer who was aggressive enough to strike a deal with the prosecuting attorney not to press for transfer. At first, reacting to the repulsive nature of Michael's act and his record of prior commitment, Michael's parole officer thought that this time it was appropriate to treat him as an adult; on second thought, however, he did not object to the deal: "I began to think how Michael, almost blind and small in stature, would do in a prison setting—he'd be victimized so badly he'd probably kill himself."

Resistance from Within

State training schools and adult correctional institutions are outside the court's control, which explains in part why they offer probation officers so little support. But probation officers experience lack of support from their own organization as well. The various residential facilities administered by the court itself are even more likely than state or private institutions to reject truly difficult children—or to expel them, once admitted—because these facilities are not programmed for children with serious emotional disturbances. Recall that Jerome was expelled from a court-operated group home for engaging in the same sort of hostile behavior toward the group houseparents' seven-year-old son as he was wont to practice toward his many own natural siblings. Jerome's probation officer, so desperately seeking possible placements, did not even apply to the court-operated probation house, feeling that Jerome would be beyond their control. Mary was refused admission on several occasions to court-operated group homes; at the time of her release from the mental commitment, the court's group-home coordinator stated that Mary would be more appropriate for the girls' probation house, but that program too rejected her in turn.

Probation officers often also encounter resistance in stressful casework situations from another intraorganizational source, the court's intake department; Mary's is a case in point. When a judge learned that Mary was suffering from hepatitis and heroin withdrawal, he ordered that intake issue a mental petition, initiating commitment proceedings. But the judge only learned of Mary's condition during a hearing on a charge of probation violation, after intake had refused to grant Mary's father just such a petition, which he sought on the advice of Mary's probation officer to gain her release from the regional detention home for emergency medical and psychiatric treatment. Both an intake counselor and the intake supervisor had originally denied the mental petition on grounds of insufficient cause, despite the probation officer's impassioned appeals that he was extremely familiar with the case, that Mary was at the time an escapee from a mental institution, and that Mary's need for treatment was urgent.

In denying support to probation officers, both intake counselors and directors of court-operated residential programs are of course responding to their own distinct imperatives. Intake's purpose is to divert from formal judicial consideration those complaints which do not warrant that level of attention; intake counselors select matters to be set for court with reference to their interpretations of law and procedure. The court's group and foster home coordinator must be careful not to alienate group houseparents and foster parents, given the extreme difficulty of recruiting and retaining them. Decisions of probation house directors to refuse or expel certain children are swayed by the pressures of managing resistant groups of residents. Despite these competing pressures, it betrays a lack of administrative coordination for the intake, residential, and probation units to issue casework decisions at cross-purposes with respect to the same individual clients, since, after all, those units are subject to the same structure of judicial authority.

Bridging Political Boundaries

Imagine then the problems of coordination when agencies in different political jurisdictions are called on to collaborate in mutual cases. In an early stage of Jerome's case, the Department of Social Services placed him in a foster home which, though under contract to them, was physically located just across the county line in an adjoining jurisdiction. Jerome would come and go from this foster home as he pleased, visiting friends in his home county for days at a time in obvious disregard of his probation rules. Although his whereabouts were well known, it took almost a full month for the police to pick him up, because each of the neighboring police forces disclaimed responsibility for executing the detention order.

Mary's case illustrates even more vividly how political boundaries, though "merely" social constructs, are nonetheless real in their consequences. Although the scores of offenses Mary had allegedly committed all fell within a twenty-mile radius of each other, they covered four different local jurisdictions in several different states. Officials of the adjoining jurisdiction in the same state wanted to keep Mary in detention and process her charges under criminal law, but Mary's probation officer was able to pursue an alternate strategy of mental commitment because—through an accident of geography—the alleged felonies all occurred in other jurisdictions. Mental institutions cannot accept for commitment people accused of felonies; Mary's "home" court was able to proceed with mental commitment because no felony charges were pending in that court; when the probation officer informed the neighboring court of Mary's mental commitment as a fait accompli, the other court nolle prossed all outstanding charges. In Jerome's case, neighboring counties each tried to disclaim jurisdiction; in Mary's case, they both tried to claim it.

Interpenetrating Agency Domains

Even more significant than confusion over jurisdiction as an aspect of disorganization in the court's task environment is the absence of domain consensus with the other community agencies that have major responsibility for child welfare—the public schools and the Department of Social Services. As a result of this domain confusion, probation officers often wind up assuming the displaced role of seeking basic shelter, nurturance, and education services for children who are so hard to serve that more directly qualified agencies are either unwilling or unable to do so.

Issues of domain consensus arise because welfare and educational agencies define their competencies and responsibilities in narrowly specialized ways, while the problems of children are often diffuse, ambiguous, and synergetic. This problem is related to processes of social change. Interagency understandings about mutual responsibilities, which evolve gradually, are periodically upset by federal laws which redefine and reallocate administrative responsibilities. Deliberately vague language in enabling legislation translates into incomplete and inconsistent implementation by federal, state, and local administrators; in this way, problems of interagency and interjurisdictional coordination derive in large measure from conflict avoidance in national politics and the fragmentary linkages among different levels of government. This generalization is perhaps best illustrated by disruptions in relations among juvenile courts, schools, and local welfare departments created by the Title XX Amendments to the Social Security Act (P.L. 93–647) and the Education for All Handicapped Act of 1975 (P.L. 94–142).

In general, providing foster care for children without fit parents is clearly within the domain of the Department of Social Services, while special education for educationally handicapped students is within the schools' domain. But do these domains encompass particularly unruly children? DSS claims its foster homes cannot accommodate uncontrollable children, while the schools distinguish between "serious emotional disturbance," which is recognized as a type of educational handicap, and "social maladjustment," which is not. Public Law 94–142, which extends the right to a "free appropriate public education" to "all handicapped children" in "the least restrictive environment," expanded the public schools' domain to involve the out-of-home placement of children for educational purposes. But such terms as "appropriate" and "least restrictive" are defined only vaguely, nor is the schools' domain delimited when reasons for placing educationally handicapped children are partly or primarily noneducational.

What does this domain confusion mean to children like Michael and Jerome, who are not only uncontrollable but also in need of special education and foster care? By the time of Michael's first contact with the

39

court, his involvement with both the foster care unit of the Department of Social Services and the school office responsible for providing contract services to educationally handicapped students was already of long standing. Michael had been in the custody of DSS since an early age due to his mother's abandonment and his father's drunken beatings; the schools had diagnosed his visual handicap after having earlier misdiagnosed him as educably mentally retarded. Yet a judge felt it necessary to assign the case directly to the court's diagnostic team to coordinate and monitor these other agencies' efforts, because, as he sensed, the mutual recriminations between Michael's different caseworkers were also of long standing. The contract services worker considered Michael "socially maladjusted," while the DSS worker considered him "emotionally disturbed" and hence eligible for an additional range of special school placements.

The court's intervention in this case prodded both agencies into action. Shortly after the diagnostic team met—in much shorter time than the normal course of procedure—the schools convened an eligibility meeting to reconsider Michael's diagnosis. Based in part on the testimony of the court psychologist at that meeting, and on an awareness of the judge's interest and the pending return to court, Michael was certified emotionally disturbed. On the strength of this finding the search for placement could begin. The court's diagnostic team worker, Michael's DSS worker, and Michael's contract services worker all joined this search actively, even though it proved futile. When Michael was committed the first time, he moved further into the court's domain; both DSS and the schools disengaged from subsequent placement efforts. DSS automatically terminates custody of children committed to the Department of Corrections. Upon Michael's return to the community, the schools assigned him to a private day-school offering special education and claimed absolution from further placement responsibilities because his educational needs were thus being met.

At least initially though, the court was able to involve the public schools and DSS more actively in Michael's case. In Jerome's case, the court could coax those agencies into only limited participation, and only by itself assuming primary responsibility from the start. Jerome's mother was dead, his father mentally disabled in an accident, and his sister—the sole responsible adult—was seeking relief of his custody so she could escape her spouse's abuse; yet DSS brought lawyers into court to argue that Jerome was too "criminal" for their custody and that they had no foster care facilities available for him. Still, while refusing to assume custody over Jerome, DSS agreed to provide temporary shelter until the court could arrange long-term placement.

The schools also disclaimed responsibility for Jerome. They had placed him in a self-contained class for the learning disabled, based on the marked disparity between his aptitude and achievement and on diagnosed problems with his visual-motor coordination. But they refused to attribute his constant classroom disruptions to any emotional disturbance that might be considered an educational handicap. A school psychologist reported, "Jerome's academic difficulties are due not only to his learning disability but his emotional instability as well"; the court psychologist, finding "depression" and "chronically unresolved conflicts," recommended placement for Jerome in a residential program that would provide "structure, support, and consistency"; Jerome's social studies teacher wrote, "he desperately needs a more enclosed, structured environment with clear, consistent rules"; the teacher of a small alternative school for children under court supervision, who had accepted Jerome into her program when the regular public school would no longer have him, declared that "the County Public Schools are unable to administer to Jerome the kind of academic, emotional, and social help that he so desperately needs"; the head learning disability specialist at Jerome's regular public school urged, "Jerome needs a strictly controlled, consistent environment in which his behavior is constantly monitored, and he also needs long-term, individual and group counseling or psychotherapy."

Yet after reviewing this body of testimony, an eligibility committee of the schools' contract services office found that "the County Public School learning disabled program is appropriate for Jerome's needs at this time," although nonetheless agreeing to pay tuition costs for any state-approved private placement to be arranged by the court for noneducational reasons. When the court's first attempt at placement ended unsuccessfully, Jerome's probation officer felt constrained to keep him under court supervision primarily to forestall the schools from discontinuing payments for his special education.

Manifestly, eligibility decisions by DSS or the schools' office of contract services are judgments about the merits of individual cases. At the same time, however, they are also definitions of organizational domain. It is instructive to compare the eligibility decisions made about Michael and Jerome because they illustrate the ad hoc nature of this definitional process. In Michael's case, the court was able to pressure both DSS and the schools to accept its interpretation of their proper roles; in Jerome's case, paradoxically, the court could induce those agencies to deliver the services they controlled only by acceding to their denials of basic responsibility. In one important respect, however, the interagency relations involved in these two cases were alike: the various agencies worked out an agreement about dividing their responsibilities through informal processes of mutual accommodation in the course of routine bureaucratic procedures. These two cases, then, obscure the full extent of the domain confusion because they were settled without recourse to formal interagency confrontation. In this respect, these cases differ from the set to follow.

4

Crusading for Placement against Contentious Evasion: Rose, Harold, Henry, Joseph

Behold the chronic anomaly of probation officers drawn into others' domains by the predictable vagaries of their own casework: Rose's probation officer seeking tips from Rose's teacher about strategies for appealing a special education-eligibility decision; Harold's probation officer personally interceding with school supervisors to allow their subordinates to testify against the schools' own official position at an impending formal due process hearing; Henry's probation officer attempting to coordinate treatment plans of the schools and the Department of Social Services (DSS)—the former alleging child abuse and refusing to contribute the tuition costs of residential placement, the latter unable to contain Henry in local group homes because of severe emotional disturbance; Joseph's probation officer submitting his own personal religious beliefs to intensive inquisition by Joseph's pastor, a fundamentalist zealously mistrustful of civil authority, in an effort to weaken the family's stubborn resistance to public services.

Consider the litigiousness of public officials as step by step, unwittingly but inexorably, these ventures into unchartered domains lead to confrontation among representatives of kindred agencies. Rose's probation officer, for an administrative hearing conducted by the schools, assembles a coalition of expert witnesses to appeal the denial of special education eligibility; Harold's probation officer finds himself in casual attire opposing the school's due process specialist in a formal six-hour appeal hearing before a special examiner; Henry's DSS worker enlists a county attorney to file a motion in juvenile court against the schools, even as they deny the court's jurisdiction in a case headed for appeal to circuit court; Joseph's probation officer, at a judge's direction, subpoenas top school officials to defend themselves against possible findings of contempt.

In broad profile the cases of Rose, Harold, Henry, and Joseph resemble the cases presented earlier. They are cases that test the limits of advocacy. The problems of these children are serious, multiple, and diffuse, ambiguous in nature and transcending the specialized domains acknowledged by particular agencies. To procure services from other agencies for these children, their probation officers must improvise roles as interagency "moles." In contrast to the cases previously presented, however, the desperate dilemmas posed by these cases do not yield to interagency accommodation but rather erupt into open conflict. Thus even more dramatically than the previous cases, these reveal defended organizational boundaries. Given the ambiguous nature of these children's multiple problems, the contradictory directives of federal law, the indeterminacy of eligibility categories, and the uncertainty of clinical diagnosis, the eruption of conflict in some cases such as these was inevitable. The divergence of particular agency mandates created in part by vague and inconsistent federal statutes renders formal administrative channels ineffective for resolving the issues of interagency dispute which arise in these cases; rather, it is these cases—and others like them—which forge the informal ad hoc channels of interagency accommodation.

Reaching Out to the Periphery

Rose, Harold, Henry, and Joseph all grew up in families of meager means and low status, integrated only tenuously into the central institutional complex of society. Both of Rose's and Harold's parents were high school dropouts; both sets of parents were separated, the women becoming single parents. Rose's mother subsisted on food stamps, welfare, and sporadic support payments. Harold's mother was unable to maintain a fixed address, moving her large family from motel to motel sometimes as often as every week. Henry never knew his natural parents nor his natural siblings, since the children were all placed for adoption after the parents were imprisoned for robbery. His adoptive parents—the fifth set of foster parents he had lived with in six years—soon separated; his adoptive mother remarried and soon separated again.

By contrast with the others, the very intactness of Joseph's family served to obstruct his integration into the larger society. Though both high school graduates, Joseph's parents were deeply suspicious of secular institutions. The father, employed in the same menial job for over twenty years, insisted on working the night shift, a refuge of occupational marginality which nonetheless enabled his family to afford a modest mobile home. The family's strong allegiance to a fundamentalist religious congregation further served to isolate Joseph from civil society.

Probation officers strove to overcome the social marginality of these young people by extending to them full rights of education and the other public services to which they were entitled—despite both the contentious evasion of service-providing agencies and the lack of parental cooperation. Paradoxically, the ultimate strategy available to probation officers for pursuing this integrative goal involved removing these children to residential institutions.

Rose and Henry were placed on probation for family problems. Rose's mother petitioned the court to compel her daughter's return from a runaway house in a neighboring jurisdiction where—by Rose's account—she had gone to escape the mother's beatings. Henry's adoptive parents sought their son's placement in a psychiatric hospital for having stolen some equipment the stepfather had brought home from work—an episode they claimed was part of a chronic pattern. By contrast, Harold and Joseph were placed on probation because of the danger they posed to the community: both were fire-setters. Harold admitted setting fire to a pair of dumpsters behind a restaurant and was a suspect in other fires. Joseph's crime was more serious still—setting ablaze an apartment he knew to be occupied by a single elderly lady, a neighbor who had befriended him. When placed on probation, Rose was sixteen, Henry thirteen, Harold only ten, and Joseph fourteen.

In enforcing their clients' entitlement to services, probation officers and others often act out of personal commitment exceeding professional obligation. Rose's radically vacillating behavior in a wide variety of group settings alternately exhilarated and exasperated authority figures. Expressing regret over the decision to expel Rose despite an earlier period of good progress, the director of a residential institution reflected that "on the whole, we have grown very fond of this very angry young girl," even though Rose was expelled for "behavior . . . absolutely of the most aggravated nature ever witnessed by our staff." Noting that some people developed intense dislike for her, Rose's probation officer explained what made him like her: "She was always straightforward with me, which I gather she wasn't with all people, and I felt sympathy for her home situation, as the family scapegoat."

Harold had the irresistible appeal of a cute, needy little child. This image was captured by the court's placement coordinator: "He's like a seven-year-old, sitting in his mother's lap in the courtroom." Harold's probation officer explained his own emotional involvement:

> He's really a hungry kid, and he needed a lot. And he was so
> needy that you couldn't help the kid—I couldn't. He'd say things
> like, "Well, I always liked my other counselor better than you

anyhow," just those obvious things to get you hooked in to say, "But I really like you."

A psychologist's assessment, while more analytic, was consistent with the probation officer's observation:

> Harold alters his feelings of anger and rejection for fear that they might provoke familial and social rejection if expressed openly. His feelings are transformed in such ways as to attract attention, support, and nurturance instead of reproval and condemnation. He conveys his sad plight by his physical appearance, facial expressions and by not speaking. . . . Harold's depressed moods enable him to elicit nurtural responses from others.

Empathetic understanding of the delinquent's situation necessarily entails a process of interpersonal bonding. Even when occasioned by new trouble, the quest for such understanding at once draws and builds on that process. Thus Joseph's reluctance to apologize to his pastor for an untoward incident binds his probation officer closer:

> Now, what can I say? He's afraid, he's ashamed. The kid has a conscience. You know, he's not a criminal; he's a brain-damaged kid, who's functioning on a very low level. He has a conscience— he knows right from wrong. He's frustrated with life and his lot in life. He knows that he's different. And the more I'm with Joseph, the more I accept that.

In the probation officer's account, this quality of personal caring is crucial to casework success:

> It's interesting, all the people involved in the treatment team have personal concerns for Joseph, not just a professional dispassionate interest. You begin to read about Joseph's case and you get hooked. You begin to see that there is something redeemable about this kid, and you know—shoot—if this kid is given enough opportunity he can succeed. . . . I think Joseph responds to the knowledge that people care about him. But I think that also shows a lesson for almost every kid we treat, that we have to show somewhere along the line, even the worst cases, that we really do care about these people, and show it in concrete ways.

Resistive Parents

In reaching out to secure for children the services to which they are entitled, probation officers must often exert special efforts to overcome the evasion, deception, and overt defiance of parents. The first step, sometimes the most challenging, is simply to locate the parents. It can be difficult to get parents to appear at court hearings, to say nothing of appointments at the probation office, school, mental health center, or other agency. Occasionally, as in Harold's case, it is impossible even for the probation officer to go to the parent's residence, if the parent moves so frequently and surreptitiously as to keep the place of residence unknown.

Harold's court file is littered with returns of legal notices undeliverable to his mother. For mysterious reasons of her own, she moved constantly from one seedy motel to another, back and forth across the county line. Harold's probation officer spent hours each week over a period of several months just trying to track her movements. She did not enroll Harold in kindergarten until he was seven, and she skipped numerous meetings she was required to attend with school officials. When successfully summoned to school one day to take Harold home early for disciplinary reasons, she created an angry scene in the front office. She failed to attend psychological counseling sessions in clear defiance of a specific court order. She even forfeited disability payments for which she was clearly eligible because she chose not to complete her application to DSS.

Probation officers also had to track down Henry's and Rose's parents. Two weeks after a judge ordered Henry into the custody of the Department of Social Services for that agency to arrange out-of-home placement, the DSS counselor had to petition the court to compel the parents' cooperation because they had refused to answer or return her numerous calls. Notice mailed to Henry's mother of the hearing to consider that petition was returned to the court "addressee unknown." A year and a half earlier the parents had failed to respond to the schools' repeated requests to evaluate Henry's special education needs. When Henry was finally placed despite the parents' lack of cooperation, they disappeared again. Staff at the residential institution, Henry's DSS counselor, and his probation officer were all unable for a while to contact either of Henry's parents, who had since separated, to arrange the home visits which were an integral part of the institution's program.

Rose's mother also eluded caseworkers at times, while at other times she and her ex-husband each actively undermined case plans for Rose. The mother was supposed to supply clothes and other provisions for Rose's placement in a wilderness school, but when the probation officer drove out to her house as arranged to pick these up, all he found was an apologetic note nailed to the front door pleading her lack of funds. She was supposed to contribute toward Rose's support at the wilderness school, but failed to make the payments. She was supposed to attend a parents' group conducted by a community worker employed by the wilderness school, but claimed that she had no means of transportation—even though she lived on a bus route and the worker offered her a lift most of the way. She was supposed to arrange transportation from a local drop-off point for Rose's home visits, but failed to do that either.

Integrative Gestures

Rose's probation officer effected exceptional countermeasures to compensate for the mother's breaches of responsibility. He secured an emergency loan from the court's "heart fund" to purchase the clothes and provisions Rose needed. After numerous exhortations and warnings to Rose's mother about the support payments she owed, he took the virtually unprecedented step of bringing her to court on a criminal nonsupport petition. He arranged local transportation for some of Rose's home visits and got DSS to do so for the others.

Rose's father too evaded his parental responsibilities. He was often late in his child support payments to his ex-wife. He did however intrude on Rose's court-ordered treatment; his intrusion occasioned the most dramatic countermeasure taken by Rose's probation officer. Rose had a habit of running away from the wilderness school. On one of these runaways she called her father for help. Instead of reporting the runaway or arranging her return to the placement, he drove half a day to bring her to his home in a neighboring jurisdiction, harboring her in the apartment of an older sister. Learning of this, the probation officer went to the apartment, but Rose escaped through a rear window. Undaunted, the probation officer returned with the local police to take Rose into custody late that Saturday night, unexpectedly projecting his workaday authority into the heart of the weekend's liminal respite.

That Saturday night raid convinced Rose of the constancy of the court's purpose and marked a turning point in her acceptance of the placement, inaugurating a period of progress in her treatment. Rose's mother then did her part to undermine that progress by persuading Rose, during an extended homestay over the Christmas holidays, to quit the wilderness school. Rose's behavior deteriorated so rapidly after the holidays that the school expelled her. Within a week of moving back in with her mother, the mother turned around and kicked Rose out of her home.

Even more far-reaching as a gesture of integrative intervention than the Saturday night raid was the gesture made by Joseph's probation officer. While Harold's, Henry's, and Rose's parents retarded the societal integration of their children by passive evasion of governmental authority and abdication of their parental responsibilities, Joseph's parents

retarded their child's societal integration by active defiance of governmental institutions and resistance to yielding any parental powers. To
engage Rose more tightly within the sway of central societal institutions,
her probation officer had to sacrifice the privacy of his own weekend to
reach out across the temporal divide of the weekly cycle. To engage Joseph in the realm of secular institutions, his probation officer had to
sacrifice the privacy of his own religious beliefs to reach out across a
spiritual divide. Joseph's parents harbored a profound distrust of government and of public services—a stance reinforced by the fundamentalist
religious and political views of their pastor, the most influential person
in their lives. When they flatly refused to speak with Joseph's probation
officer, the officer devised the strategy (approved by a judge) of winning
their trust by working through the pastor.

The pastor was a most powerful figure, heading one of the area's largest and wealthiest congregations. The American flag which he always
wore on his lapel—and which adorned the tie of every student in his
church school—signified defiance of government no less than allegiance
to country. Regarding government as the cause of society's problems, the
pastor believed that it was not possible for true Christians to work in
government and, conversely, that only true Christians could help those
in need, while the government could not. When Joseph's probation officer first approached the pastor about Joseph's case, the officer immediately found his own personal and religious background as well as his
official role open to inquisition: "Why are you here? Why are you a
probation officer?"

Could it be providential, as the probation officer himself would suggest, that he just happened to be a devout member of a particular evangelical sect, whose religious activities commanded the pastor's respect
and acceptance? Perhaps no other probation officer on staff embraced a
religious attitude as genuinely compatible in at least some respects with
the pastor's. At the end of their first meeting, pastor and probation officer
prayed together.

As they continued to meet over the next few months, the pastor
gradually moderated and then reversed his attitudes toward civil authority. When he expressed his concerns about the "godless" treatment of
children by public agencies, the probation officer described the available
network of services. They discussed the needs of Joseph and his family.
At first the pastor insisted that his church academy could provide for all
of Joseph's needs; the probation officer could only convince him to arrange psychological counseling through a charitable Christian association. As the months passed and Joseph's behavior deteriorated, the
pastor revised his position; from the court hearings he attended on Jo-

seph's behalf, he also grew to respect the judge. At the end of this period the pastor presented an appeal to the court which stands in dramatic contrast to the belligerent and confrontational attitude he had brought to the first hearing: "Judge, I'm here because I love Joseph, and I know that I can't provide services, and I know that services need to be provided. And I trust in the court, and I trust in you, and I trust in the school system that they can do it."

The pastor's conversion had the effect on Joseph's parents that the probation officer and judge had hoped for. Like the probation officer's initial meeting with the pastor, his initial meetings with the parents became inquisitions into his own religious beliefs and practices: "Where do you go to church? What kinds of hymns do you sing? Do you read the Bible?" But following the pastor's lead, they became more responsive. "When the pastor said, 'Trust him, he's OK, I've checked him out,' it was like a flower opening up. The family just opened right up and said, 'Yes, we'll work with you.' "

Parents Neglectful and Abusive

Joseph's parents harbored darker reasons than they professed for guarding their distance from public authority. As Joseph's probation officer eventually learned, they abused their son. Psychological and neurological tests had consistently shown Joseph to be mildly mentally retarded and brain damaged. His parents attributed this to a hypoglycemic coma Joseph had suffered during infancy and to prenatal medical treatment (pregnancy was not diagnosed until the seventh month, four months after Joseph's mother had undergone general anesthesia and numerous X-rays in connection with major surgery); but a subsequent CAT-scan indicated that the brain damage resulted instead from blows to the head—blows possibly delivered by Joseph's father in rages against his infant son. For her part, Joseph's mother sexually abused her son regularly on nights when her husband worked.

The traumatic experience of parental abuse or neglect was common to Rose, Harold, and Henry as well as Joseph. Rose spent six months in the custody of DSS Protective Services when she was seven, while her parents were separated due to alcoholism-related problems. The mother forced the father to leave home permanently seven years later, after discovering his sexual abuse of their two oldest daughters. School officials in two different jurisdictions, meanwhile, suspected the mother of physically abusing Rose. The mother was enrolled in a program for abusive parents in one jurisdiction. Some months before the incident that brought Rose to the court's attention, school officials were sufficiently alarmed by bruises on Rose's hand and face to make a referral to Protective Services, but the investigator accepted the mother's claim that the wounds were self-inflicted. Rose alleged that her mother's continued beatings precipitated the runaway that led to her court involvement.

Harold's mother also was reported to Protective Services on several occasions for neglect. Harold was repeatedly picked up walking or hitchhiking along a busy highway on his way to school when he was a mere second-grader. Overburdened by her other children, his mother gave him to her sister to raise when he was a toddler of two and a half. He lived with his aunt for over four years; during this period, the aunt too was reported to Protective Services, which did not find physical abuse but did find that he was denied the opportunity to play with children.

The full extent of physical and emotional abuse inflicted on Henry, while considerable, is not even known. As a ward of a neighboring department of social services, Henry had lived in five different foster homes before he was finally adopted at age six; his next-to-last set of foster parents punished him by starvation, isolation, and placement on a radiator. His face bears permanent scars where he scratched himself to vent his distress during that stay. His adoptive parents did not learn of this abuse until after the adoption; he was scapegoated as the disruptive influence in both of his adoptive mother's short-lived marriages. When the court removed him from his adoptive parents' home at their insistence, workers at the juvenile detention home found serious bruises on his shoulder, apparently inflicted by his stepfather. As a consequence, the court awarded Henry's custody to DSS; DSS counselors were never able to secure real cooperation from either parent, least of all from the stepfather.

Sharing and Shirking Interagency Responsibilities

Even after awarding Henry's custody to DSS, the judge kept him on probation. DSS was assigned responsibility for arranging—and financing—appropriate residential placement. The probation officer was responsible to monitor the progress of Henry's case, to assist the DSS worker in securing necessary cooperation from the parents and from other agencies, and to enforce Henry's cooperation with the arrangements made for him. Both the DSS counselor and the staff of the residential institution that eventually accepted Henry used his probation officer to stay better informed about the parents' situation. The probation officer returned Henry to court for violation of probation when he proved disruptive in the short-term DSS placement, and the court was instrumental in making the public schools do their part to make possible long-term placement.

What Role for DSS?

It is not surprising that DSS assumed primary responsibility for Henry's case, given the lack of a suitable home environment. What requires explanation is how that agency avoided major responsibility for the other cases.

The court did eventually award Rose's custody to DSS, but only after the court's own probation staff had already arranged long-term placement. The role of DSS was limited to providing local transportation and short-term foster care when Rose's mother was unwilling or unable to receive her daughter's monthly weekend home visits. DSS avoided more basic responsibility for Rose through a combination of their own resistance, the initiative of Rose's probation officer, the contingencies of funding availability, and the vagaries of the judicial process.

DSS could not disclaim responsibility for Rose because of any criminal activity on her part, since she was before the court only as a "child in need of services" (CHINS) for running away. Had DSS Protective Services found substance to the complaint against Rose's mother of physical abuse, that agency would have had to assume responsibility; both the school guidance counselor and the probation officer considered the rejection of that complaint to be cursory and mistaken. Even so, the probation officer would have asked a judge to award Rose's custody to DSS for foster care placement on several occasions, had not other means of arranging placement materialized instead. A court-operated probation house agreed to accept Rose right before the final court disposition of her runaway complaint; when that placement expelled her for disruptive behavior, a judge unexpectedly returned her there to dramatize his disapproval of the termination procedure. Rose's probation officer was able to obtain correctional funds for private residential placement; he sought—and received—DSS support for that arrangement in the ironic form of an official statement that that agency was unable to provide placement.

The probation officer had received much less cooperation in other cases, when asking DSS actually to provide service. Intake counselors at the DSS central office often rejected his referrals. He fared better with DSS intake counselors whose office was located down the hall from his in a community center, but they later reported being excoriated by the foster care supervisor for accepting some of his referrals when the foster care unit was already so overloaded. Nor did the supervisor hesitate to complain to the probation officer directly.

In a case that had come to court shortly before Rose's, a county attorney engaged by DSS subjected the probation officer to tense protracted cross-examination in contesting the appropriateness of a referral, despite the initial judgment of that agency's own intake counselor that the referral was proper. In that case, the judge finally ordered DSS to take custody; but the probation officer's vindication was Pyrrhic, since certain revelations during the course of the testimony were psychologically devastating to the child.

Rose's placement was already effected; the probation officer was seeking relief from the responsibility of overseeing her monthly home visits and providing money for clothes and supplies. The probation officer provoked the wrath of the foster care supervisor by failing to consult her or notify her in advance of the court hearing when he successfully requested a judge to transfer Rose's custody to DSS. The DSS foster care unit expected probation officers to alert them about possibly impending referrals and summon them to court when custody was decided, in part because of the lead time required to make foster care provisions; most probation officers routinely complied with this expectation. Rose's probation officer however knowingly violated this interagency understanding, opting to forestall the possibility of their contentious evasion in Rose's case.

By contrast—in what each regrets in retrospect as a mistake—both Harold's and Joseph's probation officers chose to abide DSS evasion despite recognizing the need for family services, out of a sense each had at the time that under the circumstances DSS involvement would be pointless.

In Harold's case, it is unclear whether his mother was giving the slip to DSS or the agency was giving the slip to her. Her constant moves back and forth across the county line enabled the departments of social services on both sides of that boundary to disclaim jurisdictional responsibility for her family—even though Harold's school made several complaints of parental neglect, and Harold's mother was eligible for disability benefits as the result of a stroke. When the diagnostic team met to consider the issue of Harold's living situation, no representative attended from DSS. The team reiterated the need for Protective Services to investigate the family and urgently recommended residential placement for Harold.

Corrections funds happened to be available at the time to pay for Harold's placement, although such was not always the case; scarcer than public welfare funds for the purchase of private institutional care, corrections funds would inevitably run out at a certain point in the fiscal year, so in Harold's case—as in Rose's and Joseph's as well—the contingency of timing in the placement decision helped absolve DSS of responsibility.

In Joseph's case, DSS was represented at the first diagnostic team meeting to consider placement; against a majority of team members, the representative argued—successfully—that removal from home was not appropriate, since the parents seemed concerned and responsible and had enlisted their church's support for a plan of community treatment. DSS was not represented at the subsequent team meeting, convened months later after parents and pastor had joined in the opinion that placement was necessary, but once again corrections funds were available at the time.

If the court were not dependent on DSS for financing the purchase of institutional care, what was to be gained from involving that agency in these cases at all? Both Harold's and Joseph's probation officers, each weighing that question alone at different times, considered the same factors and decided that the trouble exceeded the benefit. DSS was reluctant enough to accept court-involved children in general; when the children were court-involved because of arson charges, that reluctance became fierce. In any event, the division of labor between probation officers and DSS workers in cases they shared was always vague: at best, the obligation to consult an additional party would complicate casework; at worst, the probation officer could lose control over the case, since DSS operated its own network of short-term placements and might oppose the probation officer's choice of long-term placement. Finally, how much could a DSS foster care worker be expected to accomplish under an even greater caseload burden than that of the probation officer?

Despite all these considerations, both probation officers look back on the decision not to involve DSS as a mistake. In the short run, little was to be gained. But even with the children in institutional placement, it was important to attempt long-term improvement in the family situations, by whatever means available, however long the odds.

Children beyond Control

Whatever the role of DSS should have been in any of these cases, the fact remains that no agency was able to control these children—in home or school, community or residential institution. Their parents complained that Rose, Harold, and Joseph each ignored curfew and ran away frequently. Henry started stealing from his various foster and adoptive parents at a very young age. At first his thefts were expressive rather than malicious—he would steal food to hoard in his room. Gradually however he stole more valuable items, including blank checks which he used fraudulently. Even when his parents caught him, he lied about the thefts and displayed no remorse. He fought constantly with his stepsiblings. During a home visit from a residential institution, he sexually molested his three-year-old niece.

He exhibited similar behavior at school—stealing, arguing with teachers, and fighting with students. In the fourth grade he was expelled from a parochial school for stealing the nurse's watch; he was often kept after elementary school to prevent him from terrorizing younger students on their way home. Even as his parents' complaint against him was pending disposition in juvenile court, the high school expelled him for fighting and other disruptive behavior.

The others also suffered expulsion from school for similar reasons. Starting in junior high school, Rose was in trouble for truancy, walking out of class, fighting, unprovoked assaults, and racial slurs; in one series of incidents, she shook down some handicapped students for money. Harold's serious school problems started as early as kindergarten, when his teacher noted his difficulty playing with other children. His teachers and bus drivers constantly complained of his fighting, profuse obscenity, tantrums, destruction of property, and runaways from school.

Joseph's school behavior fit the same pattern. Periods of good conduct were punctuated by angry episodes of physical assaults, violent threats, defiance of authority, disregard of his own personal safety, profanity, and vandalism. This pattern repeated itself not only in a succession of school settings but also in the streets, on a job site arranged by a work program, at a social center operated as a vocational rehabilitation service, and even in church-sponsored social activities. After completing his first term of probation, Joseph returned to the court's attention for vandalizing his trailer park and impulsively taking a school bus. In school, at the job site, and at church socials he exhibited a tendency to kiss other boys and make awkward sexual advances to both boys and girls. Not surprisingly this behavior evoked vicious teasing from schoolmates, neighborhood children, and children in his church. Despite the pastor's sympathy and patience, Joseph provoked periods of banishment even from church activities.

These children proved no less unruly in residential settings than in the community. By escaping school grounds and demolishing a car that happened to be parked nearby, Joseph earned his expulsion from a well-regarded out-of-state special education center in much less time than it had taken the public schools' office of contract services to arrange that placement under pressure of a court order.

Rose's stay at a court-operated probation house was even shorter. She generated intolerable tension in that residential program by flaunting house rules and flying into frequent rages. She spread feces on bathroom towels and trashed her room. Refusing at first to eat, she later adopted the habit of throwing up after meals. She made suicide gestures and carved her boyfriend's initials into her hands with a wall tack. During a sleepwalking episode, she threatened to kill two staff members. The following week she made threats which seemed genuine against two other staff members.

Even the staff of a private wilderness program, despite a financial incentive to keep Rose and a more tolerant and caring attitude toward her, were finally forced to admit she was unmanageable for much the same reasons. Although she exhibited good behavior for a period of her stay, she disrupted the program by leading runaways, staging such suicide gestures as drinking water sealant and overdosing on cold medicine, verbally abusing staff and residents, flaunting rules, and fighting. In the final incident precipitating her expulsion, she threw a chair at a fellow resident who was pregnant, striking her in the stomach (fortunately causing no permanent injury).

Harold and Henry caused serious trouble not only for private residential institutions but even for state training schools. During a stay at a private facility, Harold led several runaways during which he and his companions forged trails of larceny and breaking and entering across a number of different states. The placement staff tolerated these runaways for eight months; however when they demanded payment for additional counseling and security as the condition for keeping Harold after an off-campus arson episode, the state chose to place him instead in a training school for younger children. He lasted there only a few months, fighting constantly with the other children and openly defying authority (in an extreme instance, defecating in public). Although still only thirteen, he was transferred to another training school which indiscriminately drew together all the most troublesome inmates from the other state juvenile institutions.

Even there he continued the same pattern of verbal and physical aggression, although over the next two years his fighting became less frequent. This degree of progress earned him placement in yet another private facility. Despite professing to like that facility—which was a much more pleasant and supportive institution than any state training school—Harold was expelled almost as soon as he arrived for threatening and assaulting staff and students alike, and for demolishing his roommate's possessions after a fight. Once again he was returned to a state training school.

Henry too was prone to violent outbursts; controlling his anger was an explicit goal of the treatment plan in each of his residential placements. Although he made progress toward this goal, his progress was unsteady and lapses cost him expulsion from two community group homes. Still his official troubles derived from the fights others picked with him as much as from the fights he picked with others. He was able to complete a two-year program at a residential institution where, despite at least one incident of assaulting a staff member and persistent "problems with acceptance of authority and peer relations," the staff felt he had matured sufficiently to return to the community. Yet his stay in the short-term placement originally arranged by DSS to shield him from parental abuse ended precipitously when he threw a fellow resident against a wall, holding her neck and banging her head against the wall. And his stay at the community group home to which he graduated from the two-year residential program ended more tumultuously still.

As usual he was verbally abusive and threatening to others; he engaged in frequent angry confrontations with one resident in particular. From the first he was especially disruptive in the public day school where he went for special education; indeed he was admitted to a psychiatric ward for several weeks after attempting to jump off a moving school bus and later crawling around the floor of his classroom. Nonetheless, the group home staff felt he was making a genuine effort to work on his problems and saw improvement in his behavior for about six months, until his attitude and behavior began to deteriorate. Staff members claimed that they lost the ability to talk Henry into calming down during his outbursts. Tension mounted over Henry's repeated monopolization of the house telephone. Henry stole some items from a parked car—his first theft in years. When another resident urinated in his shampoo, he retaliated not only in that resident's soda but in the house's apple juice as well. Several days later he ran away from the group home, and staff decided not to readmit him.

He moved into a girlfriend's house, where for six weeks he continued to receive annoying phone calls from certain residents of the group home. He took his revenge by returning several times in the same day to indulge in an intoxicated spree of physical assaults against those residents—and staff members who attempted to get in his way, one of whom suffered a fractured nose in the fracas. The court detained Henry on these assault charges, and reassigned DSS his custody to arrange another residential placement out of the community. During a routine detention review hearing several days later, Henry persuaded a judge to transfer him to a nonsecure holding facility from which he promptly fled. Within a month, police responding to an urgent call apprehended Henry in the midst of yet another fight, this time with his new housemates. In short order the court committed him to the state Department of Corrections, where Henry found himself facing troubles of an even greater order.

Influenced by the nature of the committing offenses, the state's Diagnostic Center assigned Henry to the training school for the most hardened and violent juvenile offenders—even though Henry's aggressive tendencies were primarily verbal and he had never been committed to a correctional institution before, his long history of residential placements having been occasioned as much by concern for his own safety as for that of others. Henry appealed this assignment himself, as did his parole officer and even the judge, but to no avail. The initial hazing and harassment Henry encountered from other inmates at the dreaded training school confirmed his worst anticipations. In a state of intense anxiety, he reported to his parole officer after the first ten days that other inmates regularly punched, slapped, and pushed him and patted his backside; that they had forced him to pull down his pants and bend over in front of them; that they were threatening to extort his personal belongings and canteen purchases; and that one other inmate had burned him on the arm with a cigarette. He reported also that the staff's response was to look the other way, admonishing him to fight for himself. Other inmates on the parole officer's caseload confirmed Henry's report, and the supervisory counselor confirmed the incidents of harassment by inmates.

The parole officer relayed Henry's allegations and her own observations in the form of a memo routed through her immediate supervisor to the court director; she also showed a copy to the judge. The court director in turn forwarded the memo to the regional administrator of the Department of Corrections, triggering both an internal investigation of the state training school and an investigation by the local Department of Social Services. The parole officer was not surprised that her actions caused friction between the court and the Department of Corrections; she was however surprised by the considerable friction they caused within the court itself.

Discord within the Agency

Who was responsible to act in this case, and what action was appropriate? Who had the authority to decide? Aside from the domain confusion between the court and the Department of Corrections, who had responsibility and authority within the court? The parole officer? The judge? The court director? When children are beyond control or are in need of services that fall outside established categories of service provision, issues of authority and responsibility arise within agencies as well as among them.*

---

*Recall that the particular juvenile court which served as the setting for this research is unlike most other juvenile courts, where the chief judge exercises absolute control over the staff. Because the operations of this court are jointly supervised and funded by the county government as well as by the state, the court director does not report exclusively

In reporting Henry's complaints about the state training school to her superiors at the court, the parole officer unwittingly precipitated serious recriminations by the court administration against her own conduct. Not that anyone questioned the legitimacy of her concerns; rather, her "fault" was to pursue those concerns with the judge as well as with court administration, since the court director felt that the matter was properly his responsibility and that the judge's response preempted and undermined his. His strategy was formally to refer the parole officer's memo in redrafted form through established channels to the Department of Corrections, while informally playing on the court's good relations with the department to achieve Henry's transfer to a more suitable training school. Meanwhile however the judge—who had already failed in his informal attempt to have Henry's assignment changed—decided to act more urgently, ordering Henry returned from the training school for a review of his commitment to the Department of Corrections.

Differences in role help explain these differences in strategy. The court director was responsible for managing relations with the Department of Corrections and aware of informal paths of influence within the department. The judge was responsible for Henry's immediate welfare and aware of similar complaints raised publicly by judges in years past against that very training school. At any rate, the court director was embarrassed before officials of the Department of Corrections by his ignorance of the judge's action. The parole officer's supervisor criticized her for failing to respect the administrative chain of command and specifically enjoined her from speaking further about Henry's case directly to the judge; when the parole officer protested this injunction to the chief judge, he in turn reprimanded the parole supervisor and the other administrators involved. The parole supervisor had also intercepted messages between the investigative unit of the Department of Corrections and the parole officer concerning Henry's allegations, and instructed her to seek administrative guidance in responding to their inquiries. Similarly, the court administration had reserved the right to

---

to the chief judge. Judges, the clerk of the court, and her deputies are state employees reporting to the state supreme court; all other employees, in Court Services, work for the county, which is reimbursed by the state for half of their salaries. Court Services are subject to oversight by both the county executive and the state Department of Corrections. Although according to the state legal code all court employees serve at the pleasure of the chief judge, all county employees are covered by a merit system. This dual system of authority blurs lines of accountability and control; probation and parole officers are directly responsible to fulfill judicial orders with respect to particular cases, yet their immediate supervisors in Court Services are the ones who evaluate their job performance.

decide whether the allegations should be reported to child protective service officials, even though according to a clear and explicit section of the state legal code parole officers are personally liable for failure to report such allegations to those officials. The passage of time without decision of this issue placed the parole officer in a very uncomfortable position, until the Department of Corrections notified the proper authorities of the allegations in her memo.

Rose's uncontrollable behavior in the court-operated probation house also produced intraagency conflict over the issues of responsibility and authority. Even before Rose's behavior began to deteriorate dramatically, her probation officer had met several times with the probation house staff to discuss her lack of adjustment to the program. When her behavior became even more bizarre and menacing—so that staff members began to take her threats seriously—everyone could agree that she needed to be removed to another placement. But where? And when? How immediate was the danger of her staying there? Who was to decide: her probation officer, who needed time to find someplace else for her to go? the probation house director, concerned with the safety of his staff and residents? the court's director of residential services, on call in case of emergencies? the judge who had ordered Rose into the probation house originally?

These issues first surfaced when, after the sleepwalking incident in which Rose threatened a pair of counselors, the probation house staff decided to send her "home" for a weekend visit. Rose's brother was still hospitalized in serious condition as the result of an auto accident the week before, and the staff hoped that the opportunity to see him might reduce her level of stress. But where was "home?" Rose did not get along with her mother, who in any case was keeping a round-the-clock vigil at the hospital. For these reasons the probation house director, in consultation with his supervisor, decided instead to send Rose to stay with her older sister. This decision upset the probation officer, who knew Rose's mother would disapprove. He questioned the director's authority to defy the mother's wishes, asking him to request the mother's permission or at least to consult the judge. The director refused, citing a release the mother had signed authorizing him to act in Rose's "best interest" for the duration of her stay. Despite the probation officer's inability to influence this decision, he could not escape its fallout: Rose's sister called him in the early hours of the next morning to complain that her mother was trying to take Rose away.

Less than a week later, when Rose's behavior upon her return to the probation house seemed even more disruptive and threatening, the probation house director—again in consultation with the director of residential services—decided unilaterally to release Rose altogether. Rose's probation officer was already arranging a new placement, but it would take at least a week. Rose's case was due back in court within two days; the judge had affirmed that day to the probation officer that he wanted Rose to stay until then in the probation house. But the probation house director judged that Rose posed too great a danger to others. Although failing to get the court's intake office to issue a petition initiating an involuntary mental commitment hearing against Rose, he invoked the possibility of such a petition to persuade Rose's mother to take Rose home instead. Again the probation officer's objections were in vain; nonetheless his sleep was again interrupted in the aftermath of that decision, when Rose's mother phoned him to complain that she could not control Rose either. In court two days later the judge reprimanded the probation house director for releasing Rose without a judicial order and returned Rose to the probation house pending her transfer to the next placement.

What Role for Community Mental Health?

One of the reasons the court's probation house was reluctant to keep Rose was her CHINS (noncriminal) status. Unlike delinquent residents of the probation house, who were subject to secure detention or even commitment to the state Department of Corrections for violation of a court order if they were disruptive or uncooperative, CHINS offenders were immune from secure confinement under revisions to the state legal code mandated by the federal Juvenile Justice and Delinquency Prevention Act of 1974. These code revisions deprived the probation house staff of credible threats for coercing the compliance of CHINS offenders.

Was Rose "mental?" In the neighboring jurisdiction where Rose's family lived until she was sixteen, the juvenile court refused to pursue complaints brought by parents against children for family problems, so in that jurisdiction Rose would not have been court-involved at all. The juvenile court in the neighboring jurisdiction referred all such complaints to the community mental health centers. Rose had participated in therapy for several years at such a center before moving out of that jurisdiction.

Despite the urgency with which the director of the probation house felt it necessary to remove her, Rose clearly did not qualify for mental commitment. A month before the incidents that precipitated her removal, the probation house arranged an emergency psychiatric evaluation for Rose at the community mental health center in response to a suicide gesture and self-inflicted injury. The psychiatrist found Rose "alert, cooperative and oriented in all spheres," with "no evidence of a thought disorder or serious depressive illness."

Yet as Rose's probation officer complained in a court report written in support of a recommendation for judicial action, "part of the difficulty in this case was (and is) the lack of any precise diagnosis of Rose's problem." For example a psychologist from a community mental health center, evaluating Rose at the request of the court, concluded from the extreme scatter of her subtest scores on the WISC-R (Wechsler Intelligence Scale for Children—Revised) and results of the Bender-Gestalt test that Rose suffered some form of neurological disorder. However a neurologist who conducted a follow-up examination could find no evidence of such disorder.

With the exception of Joseph, whose family's religious politics led them to seek pastoral counseling instead, the other children had also received psychological treatment before they ever became involved with the court. Harold had been a patient for several months in the Children's Partial Hospitalization Program at a community mental health center, which offered him weekly individual and group therapy, and monthly family therapy with his mother; the center offered his mother weekly individual therapy as well. Harold's attendance at therapy sessions had been sporadic, his mother's almost nil. When Harold then became involved with the court, both mother and child were judicially ordered to attend the mental health center as a condition of Harold's probation. Harold's attendance improved; his mother's did not.

As for Henry, soon after his adoption his mother brought him to the pediatric center of the county health department for a psychological evaluation because of problems at school; as a result of that evaluation she put him into counseling, at first for a brief period through a prepaid health plan, then for two and a half years with a private psychiatrist. She and her second husband first sought the court's intervention for the explicitly professed purpose of obtaining public funds for the long-term psychiatric hospitalization of her son. As a ward of DSS, Henry did spend several weeks under observation in the psychiatric ward of a public hospital, followed by outpatient psychotherapy. His psychiatrist was considering hospitalizing him further at the time of Henry's runaway from the community group home.

Joseph too received extensive psychological treatment, once his probation officer managed to overcome the zealous resistance of Joseph's parents and their pastor. When the probation officer was finally able to convince the pastor that his church academy alone could not provide all the services that Joseph needed, the pastor arranged psychological counseling for Joseph through a charitable Christian association. Later Joseph and his parents became intensive long-term patients of the community mental health center, although Joseph's father defied court orders by generally refusing to accompany his wife to their sessions.

Despite the extent of these treatment efforts, however, psychologists exerted their greatest influence on these cases not as healers but as gate-keepers, through the testing and evaluation they performed for various public agencies: the court, the schools, the mental health centers, DSS, and the Department of Corrections. The court primarily used psychologists employed and supervised by the community mental health centers, but located at the courthouse to work with court-assigned cases. The schools and the Department of Corrections employed their own psychologists. Rose, Harold, Henry, and Joseph were each tested repeatedly by various agencies, as part of every axial decision concerning their treatment.

Situated Diagnosis

Psychological diagnosis is the generalized medium of exchanging cases among the network of child-serving agencies and institutions, a medium fluid enough to circulate both argument and agreement. Diagnosticians tend to endorse nuances of interpretation which serve the conflicting, narrowly focused specialized interests of their own particular agencies, while at the same time adhering to professional norms of courtesy and deference toward colleagues in other agencies. The written reports they produce are typically technical and incoherent, yet in a certain perverse sense they are remarkably successful examples of applied social science research, lending an aura of scientific legitimacy to a determinately haphazard system of decision making and indeed—whether as cause or effect—mirroring in their very illogic the irrationality of that system.

The progression of psychological reports about Henry from ages ten to seventeen illustrates the natural history of a diagnostic subject's career. From the first a psychologist at a public pediatric center urgently recommended psychotherapy not only for Henry but also for his adoptive mother, who seemed not to understand that Henry's behavior problems had emotional causes rooted in his traumatic early childhood experience. Two months later however, a psychologist working for a prepaid health plan that would have had to bear the cost of providing treatment found the need for only "a few sessions with Henry and his mother." Rather tautologically, this psychologist assigned Henry a diagnosis of "Other—personality disorder, 301.89—stealing, attention-getting behavior with early deprivation"; his judgment was that "despite

Henry's history, he does not appear seriously disturbed." Only four months after that a school psychologist, again citing Henry's feelings of "insecurity" and "vulnerability" arising from early childhood, "highly recommended that he become involved in intensive psychotherapy," as well as suggesting behavior management programs at home and school.

Two and a half years later another school psychologist, while continuing to find Henry "anxious" and "insecure," began to shift emphasis to problems of impulsivity, anger, and aggression. She recommended a school program for the emotionally disturbed for Henry; while reiterating the need for psychotherapy, she also raised the possibility of residential placement because of Henry's home situation and his need for "intense structure." Three and a half years after that, barely even alluding to Henry's early childhood deprivation, a staff psychologist for the Department of Correction emphasized instead Henry's impulsivity and lack of insight and complained that "he accepts no blame for his actions"; the psychologist recommended that "current emphasis must be placed firmly on consequences of his misbehavior." Psychological evaluations are ostensibly based on clinical findings derived from the administration of standard instruments measuring intelligence, achievement, personality, and perceptual and motor skills. Yet a half century of research, from Paul Meehl to John Monahan, has proven the uncertainty of such diagnosis as a technology for predicting dangerousness. Even if that technology provided a more solid basis for formulating treatment recommendations, the typically abstruse and elliptical style of presenting clinical findings would tend to make them incomprehensible to such lay users as probation officers and judges, to whom they are couched in "another language." What are such users to make, for example, of the following outcome of a Rorschach test, characteristically presented without explanation or analysis: "There were no human responses. Animal responses vastly predominated. Designs 4, 8, and 9 produced no responses."

Given the genuinely ambiguous nature of children's cases and the uncertainty of the clinical technology, it is understandable that so many diagnoses are tentative and indeterminate. Are these children vulnerable or threatening, dependent or dangerous? Rose "presents an interesting contrast of very immature, child-like behavior and of very 'tough' streetwise behavior"; "in much the manner of a younger child, Joseph tends toward impulsive, overt expression of his feelings and does not anticipate the potentially dangerous consequences of his actions"; Harold exhibits both anger and fear of rejection.

It is understandable too that different diagnoses may be contradictory.

A school psychologist finds that Harold's projective drawings give "no indication of highly significant emotional disturbance"; yet according to the same examiner a scant five months later, projective testing occasioned by a teacher's "additional concerns about his emotional development . . . makes more apparent Harold's significant difficulty in adapting to new situations. Harold tends to react impulsively." The psychologist goes on to observe that "at times his acting-out behavior may be attempts to manipulate people around him." Yet within less than half a year a psychologist with the community mental health center writes that "it would be simplistic to label a functionally retarded young man's attempts to adapt to pervasive conditions of deprivation and rejection as manipulation. Harold, given his cognitive deficits and social conditions, is over-adapting."

Such differences of interpretation, though common, can alter planned courses of treatment, as they did for Joseph. From the very outset of the case, Joseph's probation officer favored out-of-home placement; but because he could persuade neither Joseph's parents nor the pastor to accept his opinion, he solicited support from various psychologists. The court psychologist, an M.S. working under the auspices of a community mental health center, found Joseph to be "a dependent and immature youth who functions in the Mentally Deficient range of intelligence" with "perceptual-motor problems" and "severe" emotional difficulties," "evasive and secretive," lacking initiative, "impulsive" and lacking controls. She recommended "a structured, therapeutic residential setting." A Ph.D. psychologist from that same community mental health center, evaluating Joseph six weeks later for possible outpatient therapy, concurred with both the diagnosis and the recommendation:

> Joseph presents as an emotionally and physically immature youth with multiple difficulties including mental retardation, organic impairment, and a severe emotional disturbance. Joseph unquestionably needs to be involved in an intensive treatment program where he could learn more appropriate ways of expressing himself. It is strongly felt, however, that this treatment should be conducted in a highly structured, therapeutic, residential setting which would also provide for Joseph's educational needs.
>
> If Joseph were to become involved in outpatient treatment, we would be gravely concerned that the sensitive and powerful feelings addressed in therapy would find expression in the community. Outpatient treatment is contraindicated as it may increase the risk of acting out in the community.

Finally, a psychiatrist from that same mental health center evaluated Joseph separately on an "emergency" basis, with results nearly identical to those of his colleagues:

> It is strongly advised that complete neurological examination as well as psychiatric observation be done preferably on an inpatient basis because of his potential danger to the community because of impulsive behavior and poor judgment. It also appears that treatment in a more structured (residential) environment would be the treatment of choice for this young man because of his acting-out behavior.

Joseph's probation officer knew however that not even the combined weight of these impressively consistent expert opinions was sufficient to overcome the resistance of Joseph's parents to placing their son out of home, especially since a DSS counselor and one of the court's family counselors endorsed the plan offered by the parents and the pastor to work with Joseph in the community. The probation officer thus appealed to yet one more psychologist, an Ed.D. affiliated with a Christian counseling service who had begun to see Joseph at the pastor's behest. With the parents' consent the probation officer sent the other psychologists' findings to this counselor, pointedly signaling the official response he was looking for:

> The immediate issue is treatment modality. [The Ph.D. psychologist] has recommended residential placement. [Joseph's parents and pastor] feel that placement at the church academy is the best choice at this time.
>
> You will note that [the psychologist's] concern is that counseling might relax Joseph's emotional defenses to the point where dangerous behavioral problems injurious to himself and/or others might occur. . . .
>
> It is my feeling that the issue of community-based or residential treatment should be explored.

The psychologist from the Christian counseling center was not obliging in his response. While demonstrating understanding of the other psychologists' findings, he essentially endorsed the position of Joseph's parents and the pastor. "My interpretation of Joseph's WISC-R and Bender-Gestalt tests, which I [also] administered, basically support the findings of [the M.S. psychologist], which indicate that Joseph appears to be neurologically damaged and learning disabled." Yet he suggested that Joseph's behavior could be controlled in the community with psychotropic medicine: "Joseph is responding quite well to drug therapy."

And while deferentially acknowledging the others' prescription for residential placement, he respectfully emphasized the advantages of keeping Joseph in the church academy instead:

> Joseph is in need of individualized, self-paced, multi-modal instruction specifically designed to remediate severe sequencing and short term memory deficits. This instructional program is being provided at the church academy and if the Court so chooses to place Joseph in a highly structured, therapeutic, residential setting, I would strongly recommend the continuation of the ACE curriculum.

This countervailing expert opinion was sufficient to block Joseph's removal from home to a residential placement, at least for the moment. The probation officer's casework strategy was not totally refuted, however; by marshaling a preponderance of psychological evidence supporting placement and by forcing the issue to the point of conscious decision from the case outset, the probation officer succeeded in creating a presumption that Joseph's return before the court would indicate a need for placement. Still, this episode demonstrates psychologists' power as gatekeepers: their expert endorsement is necessary—if not sufficient—to effect out-of-home placement for children under court supervision.

This episode also demonstrates the *situated* nature of psychological diagnosis. Psychologists are made well aware of the particular treatment options under active consideration for the children they evaluate. Despite the indeterminate quality of psychologists' diagnoses, their reports to the court almost always conclude with clear and confident recommendations for some type of educational program, mental health counseling, court supervision, residential placement, or other treatment. Influenced by case circumstances, these recommendations are more definitive than the diagnoses on which they are ostensibly based. The contents of these reports clearly express the situated nature of their production. They generally start by recounting the nature of the presenting problem from the perspective of the parent or official agent who arranged the testing. They summarize the child's social history, based primarily on a review of official records; in many reports the current situation and social history are presented at greater length than the clinical findings.

The results of other psychological evaluations about the same child also help situate a diagnosis; although the divergent interests staked in competing diagnoses entail the potential for considerable conflict, at the same time a report to the court provides a medium of professional deference which serves to contain that conflict. Thus even while opposing the consensus among psychologists from the mental health center about the need to place Joseph, the psychologist from the Christian counseling center affirmed his respect for their findings and opinions. In general, psychologists go out of their way to avoid discrediting their colleagues' findings even when those findings contradict their own. In reporting their own findings to the court, they recast others' so as to lend credibility to both sets. Discrepancies in findings—if not ignored—are never attributed to testing error, as Rose's case illustrates.

A court psychologist, administering the same IQ test to Rose as had a school psychologist four years before, registered a significant drop in Rose's score. Although indicating that Rose exhibited considerable resistance to the testing situation, the psychologist interpreted the measurement result as a troubling deterioration in intelligence, explicitly denying that Rose's resistance could have depressed her score more than marginally. Based partly on the wide scatter of subtest scores from that IQ test, the court psychologist detected an organic disorder, leading Rose's probation officer to arrange a follow-up neurological exam. Although the neurologist administered with opposite results the same Bender-Gestalt test on which the psychologist had also based her inference, and could find no evidence of organic disorder, she respectfully acknowledged the psychologist's report in concluding, "I suspect that Rose is a child with neurological dysfunction." Unlike the psychologist, however, the neurologist emphasized the effects of emotional disturbance. Meanwhile a school psychologist who evaluated Rose's eligibility for special education soon thereafter found primarily "family dysfunction."

Which expert was right? Were Rose's learning and behavior problems the results of low intelligence, neurological disorder, emotional disturbance, or family dysfunction? On just such an arcane set of clinical distinctions, impervious to objective resolution, hinged Rose's eligibility for special education—and with it, funding for "structured therapeutic residential placement." Such a clinical conundrum precisely mirrors the policy conundrum embodied in the Education for All Handicapped Act of 1975 and the Title XX Amendments of 1974: the clinical as well as the statutory grounds of casework determinations are indeterminate and contradictory. The parallels between the policy confusion and the clinical confusion suggest an intriguing question: is the one cause or effect of the other? How can politicians and bureaucrats establish clear terms of public policy if psychological experts cannot agree with one another on the terms of a clinical diagnosis? Conversely, how can clinicians resolve ambiguities of public policy through the production of situated diagnosis?

Interceding between Strata of the School Bureaucracy

Did Rose—or Harold, Joseph, or Henry—require special education? Would the schools be partly responsible for placement in residential institutions providing such education? Agency perspectives are not monolithic. Just as Rose's probation officer clashed with the court's own probation house staff over Rose's removal from their facility, so did schoolteachers and their supervisors oppose school administrators over the issue of educational placement. The divergent pressures on line workers and administrators produced disagreement within the school bureaucracy over these students' needs. In each of these cases, the urgency to coordinate the schools' actions with those of other agencies compelled the court to intercede in the schools' internal differences. Teachers, guidance counselors, school psychologists, and principals agreed that the school programs in which these children were enrolled could neither educate nor control them. Yet the administrators who determined eligibility and purchased contract services for special education refused to approve residential placement for them. Even though teachers and others who had to work with these children in the schools bore the brunt of this refusal, they looked to the court's probation staff to challenge it.

Rose was denied eligibility for services as an emotionally disturbed student, even though she had already been receiving such services for several years in a neighboring jurisdiction. Although eligibility determinations are not binding across jurisdictions, there is a presumption in favor of honoring them. But the psychologist at Rose's new high school felt that Rose's history of truancy would disqualify her from special education placement, since school division administrators tended to interpret truancy as an indicator of "social maladjustment." School officials, perhaps seeking to escape the considerable paperwork entailed by applications for special education, talked Rose's mother into enrolling her for regular classes instead. The attempt to mainstream Rose failed in short order. According to Rose's guidance counselor, "She was unable to cope with the loose structure of regular classes and was absent 70 percent of the time." In the rare classes she attended, she would not accept direction and talked back to teachers. Ironically however, by interrupting the continuity of special education services, this failed attempt caused the presumption of eligibility for such services to lapse.

With Henry as with Rose, school division administrators denied what seemed to be the obvious facts of the case. For months before the court's first involvement in Henry's case, school officials had been complaining to his mother about his disruptive classroom behavior and discussing plans for residential placement. The probation officer's very first day on the case, the school guidance counselor reported that Henry could not stay in regular classes because he needed a supportive and confrontational residential environment. An eligibility committee had already certified Henry as emotionally disturbed. Yet the assistant principal of Henry's school still urged the probation officer to lobby the area office in support of the school's recommendation for transferring Henry to a public special education center pending residential placement. When Henry's DSS counselor first took the preliminary paperwork to that center, the center's principal shook her head and declared that Henry did not belong in her program at all. She agreed to state that opinion at a forthcoming meeting of the schools' contract services committee, but at that and other administrative hearings the opinion she stated was precisely the opposite.

A school psychologist gave discrepant reports to different audiences about Henry's test results, indicating her anticipation that school division administrators would resist her findings. Her written report concluded:

> Due to the severe anxiety which seems to be distorting and confusing Henry's perceptions and verbalizations and his uncontrollable impulsivity, it is recommended that he be placed in the program for the emotionally disturbed. Intense structure, one-to-one instruction, and psychotherapy seem necessary if Henry is to progress academically and socially and emotionally. The possibility of a residential placement may have to be explored.

Yet testifying about her findings in court, before the schools' eligibility committee had met, she hedged her expectations of that committee's formal decision. She told the court that her "testing doesn't show conclusively that he is emotionally disturbed" and stated that she "didn't know if the committee would find him eligible." She suggested an alternative explanation for Henry's school problems, that "family instability was very detrimental to Henry." The school social worker, in her written report of the family interview, was similarly careful to emphasize that it was the parents who were requesting residential placement.

As it turned out, Henry's parents and the line school officials seemed to get what they wanted: not only did the eligibility committee certify emotional disturbance, but the contract services committee approved Henry's transfer to a public special education center and encouraged Henry's parents to continue seeking psychiatric hospitalization for him, promising to contribute special education tuition funds. However this promise proved to be much more conditional than it seemed; when Henry's parents discovered that their insurance would not cover the costs of psychiatric hospitalization and turned to the court for help, the schools not only retracted their promise but denied they had ever made it. The school policy at the time was to pay the entire cost of residential placement or to pay nothing at all: consistent with the letter of the Education for All Handicapped Act, they would pay the entire cost of a placement arranged for educational reasons, but refused to contribute the tuition costs of a placement arranged by other public agencies for noneducational reasons, even for a child certified as emotionally disturbed. Of course this policy served financial purposes as well as strictly constructed legal ones: paradoxically, the schools incurred the least expense for special education services in the most exclusive psychiatric hospitals, when they had only to supplement private insurance coverage.

School division administrators in fact even dragged their feet on arranging Henry's transfer to the public special education center, so that Henry's guidance counselor again had to enlist the probation officer's support for hastening that transfer. Claiming a "sudden deterioration" in Henry's behavior, the school suspended him; his probation officer placed him in the court's detention home for violating his probation by getting suspended. Henry was to be detained until the transfer to the special education center could be effected, after spring break. Meanwhile the detention home staff discovered bruises on Henry's body which seemed to indicate child abuse, leading to the reinvolvement of DSS in Henry's case and curtailing the period of his attendance at that special education center.

Harold's probation officer was drawn even more dramatically into the internal conflicts of the school bureaucracy. Harold had been assigned to a program for the mildly mentally retarded in a regular public elementary school before be ever came to the court's attention. Half a year into Harold's period of probation, school officials—from Harold's classroom teacher to the principal—began to complain urgently about Harold's disruptive and assaultive school behavior. In conferences at the school and in a formal letter, the probation officer pressed them in turn to apply for a private program of special education:

> Harold's continued inappropriate behavior seems to indicate that more intense intervention is necessary. My hope is that a day program can be found for him that would focus both on his educational and emotional needs. . . . If a day program cannot be found, residential treatment may be necessary. It is my opinion

that at this time a day program would be the best treatment modality because it would not deprive Harold of the familial support that a youth of his age so depends on.

Five months later, in the culmination of the process set in motion by that letter—and just as the school year was drawing to a close—the schools' contract services committee finally approved a private day program for Harold. By that time, however, serious new arson charges had been filed against him, indicating a compelling public safety need for placing him out of home. Unsuccessfully, the probation officer requested an administrative review committee of the schools to approve tuition payments for residential placement. Since that approval was necessary to arrange long-term placement, the probation officer sought to overturn the schools' position from within.

In pursuit of this objective the probation officer improvised a masterful strategy combining a whole gamut of tactics from cajolery to confrontation, invoking personal contacts, playing on school officials' personal feelings, shifting the situational context of psychological and educational diagnosis, and exploiting formal adversarial procedures. Anticipating difficulty with the school division administration, the probation officer had recommended that a judge refer Harold's case to the court's diagnostic team to explore the need for residential placement. Knowing that the schools had failed to perform the new battery of tests required by their own procedures for the triennial review of Harold's special education status, the probation officer arranged for new tests in connection with the diagnostic team referral. Not only would the later tests supersede the earlier ones, but they would be conducted for an audience inclined to accept the need for residential placement. Both the school psychologist and a psychologist working with Harold at the community mental health clinic reported to the diagnostic team that Harold required residential treatment.

However the probation officer made his boldest inside move as he prepared the formal appeal to a special hearing officer of the schools' refusal to collaborate in Harold's residential placement. He knew that Harold's classroom teacher, the school psychologist, and the school principal—each of whom had at times pressured him to help remove Harold from their school—agreed with the need for residential placement, but that their immediate supervisors in the school administration would be presenting the schools' case against such placement at the formal appeal hearing. Basing his pleas in part on Harold's vulnerability and attractiveness, the probation officer personally interceded with those supervisors to permit their subordinates free expression of their opinions at the appeal hearing, even though those opinions challenged the schools' official position.

Bureaucratic Timetables out of Alignment

By the time the formal hearing was convened to appeal the schools' denial of Harold's eligibility for residential placement, Harold had already spent two months at a placement arranged by his probation officer. In fact, his probation officer had arranged his admission there and secured correctional funds to cover all noneducational costs by the time the schools were just getting around to finding Harold eligible for a private day program. Rose and Henry had each also spent several months in residential institutions before the schools finally agreed to pay their tuition costs; in each case the schools were just beginning to consider eligibility for special education as the child departed for the placement. Whether correctional funds or Title XX funds covered the noneducational costs of placement, the funds could be used only temporarily—if at all—to cover tuition costs as well. The schools' decision-making process lagged so far behind that of other related agencies as to disrupt their operations.

Difficulties of coordinating related casework services often take the form of the misalignment of related agencies' bureaucratic timetables. The schools operate under the presumption that every less restrictive educational alternative must be exhausted in turn before considering residential placement, while the court and DSS often work with children who seem to need more decisive and timely intervention. When casework crises erupt from the sudden or severe breakdown of children's internal and external controls, probation officers and DSS workers respond by attempting to arrange residential placement quickly. Yet the schools process applications for special education very slowly, partly because of the variety of diagnostic tests required and the multiple stages of decision and review, partly because of the volume of applications and the limit to available resources. They nevertheless resent having to make determinations about educationally handicapped children already placed by other agencies without their participation.

Recall the alacrity with which Rose's probation officer had to remove her from the court's probation house to a private residential placement, a wilderness school. The probation officer was able to effect that placement before he had even secured funding for it: the wilderness school agreed to take Rose for a week without reimbursement because they happened to have an opening in a new group for which Rose seemed appropriate. To obtain the necessary funding, the probation officer then had to exploit a procedural loophole. He applied for correctional funds, which at the time could be granted only after the schools had agreed to pay tuition costs; he was able to win a waiver to this precondition by arguing that the application was unavoidably being filed during the summer.

Henry also had to be removed to a residential institution precipitously. While the schools prepared to effect his transfer to a public special education center, his behavior at the short-term community placement arranged by DSS deteriorated so rapidly—culminating in an assault on a fellow resident—that DSS hastened to find a Title XX placement almost as soon as Henry finally got to transfer schools.

The issue of providing special education tuition for Joseph was settled before his actual placement only because it took such a long time to find a placement willing to take him, and because Joseph's judge and probation officer forced the issue in court. A year and a half after Joseph's first term of probation had ended, the probation officer received a call for help from Joseph's mother—a remarkable gesture in view of her initial distrust of the court. No longer feeling that the church academy could control their son, Joseph's parents had applied for special education services to the public schools. The schools found Joseph to be mildly mentally retarded—a diagnosis that usually rules out residential placement—making him eligible only for a special program in a regular public school. Although to no one's surprise that program proved unsuccessful, the schools had failed to inform Joseph's parents of their right to apply for residential placement on educational grounds. The probation officer relayed the parents' request for help to the judge in chambers. After contacting the schools' contract services committee on Joseph's behalf himself to no avail, the judge suggested that the parents petition the court to guarantee the services to which their son was entitled. In the hearing on the merits of that petition, the probation officer testified in open court that the schools were acting very slowly in this case. The judge ordered him to subpoena top school administration officials to the next hearing and to request the county attorney to represent the court.

5

The Litigiousness of Public Agencies

In Joseph's case, the county attorney represented the court against the schools. In Rose's case, the probation officer did not even notify DSS of his plan to have them assume Rose's custody, in order to avoid cross-examination by the county attorney representing that agency against the court. Understandably in this litigious age, the county attorney's office manages to stay busy representing the legal interests of county agencies. What calls for explanation is why so many of the county attorney's efforts on behalf of some county agencies are wastefully directed against other county agencies.

For their part, the schools retained a high-priced legal firm billing hundreds of thousands of dollars each year to represent them against citizens and other agencies alike, an expenditure of tax monies attracting an annual lead article in the metropolitan section of the region's major newspaper. Despite the interest shared by the court, DSS, and the schools in the welfare of their common clients, workers in those agencies could not settle issues of casework responsibility and authority solely through the exercise of their good offices. Instead they found it necessary to refer those issues to increasingly formal and adversarial arenas of conflict resolution.

Were the schools responsible for residential placement? Rose's and Harold's probation officers contested this issue in the schools' arenas. The former had a judge appoint a private attorney to serve as Rose's guardian ad litem in a school administrative review hearing. The latter appealed his case against the schools one level beyond that, to a formal due process hearing conducted by a private attorney specially appointed as a hearing officer. The other probation officers contested this same issue in juvenile court. Joseph's probation officer subpoenaed top school officials to answer possible charges of contempt; a county attorney represented the court against the schools' attorney. Henry's case did not end in juvenile court, where a county attorney represented DSS against the schools' attorney, since the schools argued to the circuit court that the juvenile court lacked jurisdiction over that case.

Was placement necessary on *educational* grounds? Were these children "emotionally disturbed" or "socially maladjusted?" Was it possible to distinguish the effects of a child's home environment from those of the educational environment? Why was placement appropriate in extreme cases for "emotionally disturbed" students but not for "educably mentally retarded" ones? And what were the educational rights of children placed residentially on noneducational grounds? Even assuming the schools could be required to provide appropriate special education services, who besides the schools was qualified to decide which services were educationally "appropriate?" Although adversarial proceedings between kindred public agencies are costly, the ambiguity of children's diffuse problems, the vague and contradictory mandates of public law, the easy exhaustibility of agency resources, and the uncertainty of clinical diagnosis all combined repeatedly to force the schools, DSS, and the court to the point of litigation to settle—if only in an ad hoc fashion—issues such as these.

Niggling Distinctions Intensely Disputed

It is the indeterminacy and inconsistency of federal law which infuses these niggling issues with such fateful consequence. These cases demonstrate the difficulties of applying the federal definition of *emotional disturbance* to determine eligibility for special education. They demonstrate also the difficulties of coordinating casework services among agencies that derive their mandate from the Education for All Handicapped Act—with its presumption against institutionalization and its lack of provision for educationally handicapped children institutionalized for noneducational reasons—and agencies that derive their mandate from the Title XX legislation—with its encouragement of institutionalization but its prohibition against assuming tuition costs.

Consider the definition of *seriously emotionally disturbed* contained in the regulations for the Education for All Handicapped Act, P.L. 94–142:

> (i) The term means a condition exhibiting one or more of the following characteristics over a long period of time and to a marked degree, which adversely affects educational performance:
> (A) An inability to learn which cannot be explained by intellectual, sensory, or health factors;

(B) An inability to build or maintain satisfactory interpersonal relationships with peers and teachers;

(C) Inappropriate types of behavior or feelings under normal circumstances;

(D) A general pervasive mood of unhappiness or depression;

(E) A tendency to develop physical symptoms or fears associated with personal or school problems.

(ii) The term includes children who are schizophrenic. The term does not include children who are socially maladjusted, unless it is determined that they are seriously emotionally disturbed. (34 C.F.R. sec. 300.5)

As members of the schools' special education eligibility and contract services committees interpreted this definition, it specified three basic criteria of eligibility: a child's handicap had to be *emotional*, not attributable to other "intellectual, sensory, or health factors"; it had to be *educational*, "adversely affect[ing] educational performance"; and it had to be distinguishable from social maladjustment. This last condition was hardest to establish. A set of internal guidelines employed by the eligibility committee suggested:

Making the distinction between the socially maladjusted and the seriously emotionally disturbed is often very difficult. Exhibiting the following characteristics is generally considered indicative of social maladjustment:

—lack of anxiety and guilt combined with apparent sincerity and candor

—inability to forego immediate pleasure for future gains

—insightfulness about the needs and weaknesses of other people and adeptness at exploiting them

—tendency to reject authority

—inability to profit from experience

—high degree of impulsiveness

Many of these characteristics may be exhibited in varying degrees by the seriously emotionally disturbed student. In the socially maladjusted student, these characteristics are pronounced; and they occur apart from other "symptoms" of psychopathology.

Essentially, as eligibility officials all emphasized, this distinction rests on inferences about a child's character. Although the behavioral symptoms associated with these two diagnoses overlap, *social maladjustment* in contrast to *emotional disturbance* is referred to in modern clinical parlance as a *personality disorder*. The emotionally disturbed are analogous to the "deserving poor": unwilling victims of forces beyond their control (albeit forces that are psychological rather than economic), and thus potentially redeemable. Intrapsychic conflict and the capacity to take the role of the other render them amenable to help, as opposed to the socially maladjusted, who are willfully impervious to treatment, manipulatively and remorselessly antisocial.

Was Rose, for example, emotionally disturbed? Her probation officer applied to reestablish her eligibility for services as an emotionally disturbed student as soon as the eligibility conferred by her old jurisdiction had lapsed, when the attempt to mainstream her in a new high school failed. To avoid the considerable delay of waiting for a school psychologist to perform the necessary testing, the probation officer requested the court psychologist to evaluate Rose instead. However the results of that psychological evaluation were damning. An IQ measured in the "mentally deficient" range and signs of possible neurological damage indicated that her problem had other than an emotional basis, violating one of the basic conditions of eligibility.

Other aspects of the report were damning as well. The psychologist characterized Rose in a way that suggested her problem was primarily one of character disorder; such phrases as "rigidly defended," "guarded," "impulsive," and "adept at superficially verbalizing what others want to hear" all pointed to social maladjustment. The eligibility committee ruled that "Rose is an intellectually low-functioning child whose behavior is the product of dysfunctional family situation. Her learned patterns of behavior are seen as adaptations which have worked for her in her previous environment. They are not seen as evidence of emotional disturbance."

In preparing the appeal of this decision, the probation officer followed several strategies. He asked a judge to appoint a guardian ad litem to represent Rose at the schools' administrative review hearing, putting the schools on notice of the court's interest in the case. He also managed to exclude the court psychologist from the review proceeding. He arranged a neurological examination for Rose, as the court psychologist had recommended; the neurologist found no evidence of any organic dysfunction, but did note that she suspected "severe emotional problems."

To establish Rose's characterological "deservedness" as an emotionally disturbed student, the probation officer enlisted the support of a special education teacher who had worked with Rose during her tempestuous stay at the court's probation house. Not only did this teacher document Rose's behaviors during that stay as indicative of emotional disturbance, but she also explained to the probation officer the schools' guidelines for interpreting the statutory definition of emotional disturbance. This "inside" knowledge enabled the probation officer to coach officials of the wilderness school that had since accepted Rose about how best to express their observations in support of Rose's eligibility.

The savvy orchestration of these testimonials succeeded. Along with the daily logs of Rose's behavior and the termination summary from the court's probation house, the schools' administrative review committee found in these materials rationale for paying Rose's tuition at the wilderness school. One influential member of that review committee found especially compelling the accounts of Rose's sleepwalking episodes, in which she took on a different identity, and the letter from the special education teacher at the probation house.

Although Harold's deserving nature was incontrovertible—the factor that may well eventually have decided the issue—his probation officer had to pursue the argument for special education tuition money in a residential placement one step farther than Rose's along the schools' appeal process. Initially out of concern about Harold's school problems, the probation officer had prodded officials of Harold's elementary school to request special education services. But by the time the schools finally got around to approving a private day school for Harold, several new arson charges convinced the probation officer of the need for residential placement instead. He therefore appealed the schools' decision to an administrative review committee, but that committee affirmed that "residential placement is not warranted for educational reasons," forcing the probation officer to request a formal due process hearing before a private attorney appointed as a special hearing officer.

The probation officer was not prepared for the formality of that hearing, or even the formality of attire of the various participants. He showed up dressed casually in a tennis shirt, anticipating a brief meeting. All others in the room wore dark business suits, and the hearing lasted six and a half hours. Nor had the probation officer anticipated the procedural issues that would confront him—issues that proved to be crucial.

Did the probation officer have the authority to represent Harold at all, instead of Harold's parent? The probation officer argued that he represented the court, which had officially taken custody of Harold in order to arrange residential placement.

Wouldn't the probation officer agree to waive the "rule on witnesses," allowing only one witness at a time to be present in the hearing room? The probation officer had not even been aware of this prerogative, but he shocked everyone by refusing to waive it. Even though he had secured in advance the permission of school supervisors for their subordinates to testify against the schools' official position at this hearing, he felt that those subordinates—whose support he needed—would testify more freely under the protection of confidentiality. This protection undoubtedly made a difference, since the appeal hinged on nuances of expression. The school psychologist, for example, had indicated in a written report to school officials only that Harold needed continued mental health counseling; yet to members of the court's diagnostic team soon thereafter, she had indicated a need for residential placement.

The schools based their official case on four contentions: that Harold's problems derived from the instability of his family—his mother's frequent moves—and not from his educational environment; that Harold was not emotionally disturbed but rather educably mentally retarded (as a result, incidentally, of cultural deprivation rather than cognitive deficiency); that a private day school was the appropriate educational placement; and that residential placement was too restrictive for educably mentally retarded students. The probation officer responded that it was impossible to separate the effects of a child's educational environment from those of his home environment. He asked the program coordinator of Harold's residential institution to explain why Harold required a residential program, and why a separate day program also operated by that institution would not meet his needs. He also elicited predictions by Harold's therapist and by the teacher, principal, and psychologist from Harold's elementary school that Harold would inevitably fail in a private day program. By cross-examining the director of the schools' contract services committee, he exposed the inflexibility of the schools' policy never to approve residential placement for an educably mentally retarded student without trying a day program first, which he could claim amounted to an insistence on setting Harold up for a predictable chain of failures. Finally, the probation officer criticized the schools' reliance on outdated diagnostic evaluations of Harold, especially since more current reports were available through the court's diagnostic team.

Even the due process specialist who presented the case for the schools later admitted she felt foolish arguing that Harold needed residential placement only for "noneducational" reasons. For his part, the probation officer felt overwhelmed by this specialist's legal expertise. Yet his arguments prevailed: the special hearing officer ordered the schools to pay Harold's tuition at the residential placement.

Making a Judicial Case out of It

In Harold's case as in Rose's, then, a probation officer was able to use the schools' own appeal process to get school division officials to redefine a child's educational needs in accord with the court's definition of the child's noneducational needs. The schools' own administrative procedures provided the forum of adversarial confrontation for reconciling the divergent particular interests and statutory mandates of these mutually dependent agencies. By contrast, in Joseph's case as in Henry's, the forum shifted to juvenile court.

The juvenile court's broadest mandate is to serve the "best interests" of the child; as part of that mandate—and as recognition of the court's increasingly focal position within the network of child welfare agencies—the court is responsible to ensure that children receive services to which they are legally entitled, if necessary by ordering other agencies to provide those services. This aspect of the court's mandate creates the potential for involving the court in interagency disputes.

In Joseph's case, the judge's resolve to subpoena top school officials provided sufficient incentive to resolve the dispute. When Joseph's probation officer relayed to him the parents' request for help in overcoming the schools' refusal to purchase special education services for their son in a residential placement, the judge was already concerned by the number of similar requests, influencing his decision to invoke the court's power to enforce entitlement to services. Joseph's parents had themselves resisted applying for assistance from the public schools until they could no longer deny the need to do so; the public schools' assignment of Joseph to a program for the educably mentally retarded had provided no relief from Joseph's educational problems. The schools, choosing to regard Joseph as "socially maladjusted," had not even made the parents aware of their right to apply for residential placement on educational grounds. Although Joseph's IQ level and neurological handicap suggested alternative explanations for his educational difficulties, the dependence on psychotropic medication to control his behavior during the past several years was compelling evidence of emotional disturbance as well. And after all, before the recent period of emotional deterioration, Joseph had managed to make educational progress in the church academy.

The school division officials subpoenaed to defend their denial of residential services to Joseph comprised a chain of command extending just short of the school superintendent himself. The county attorney questioned them closely about the content of Joseph's school records, and in the courtroom the judge literally read them the applicable sections of the legal code. In anticipation of the court hearing to which they had been subpoenaed, the school officials had convened the schools' contract services committee, which agreed to provide residential placement for Joseph. The head of that committee later confided to the probation officer that although personally he had not opposed providing such services to Joseph, prior to the court's intervention he was under direct orders to deny them. To ensure that the schools acted to arrange placement for Joseph as expeditiously as possible, the judge placed Joseph on probation and set up a series of review hearings to monitor the schools' progress.

Whose Ground Rules?

Is the juvenile court powerful enough to compel kindred agencies to work together toward their common purpose, despite the divergence of particular mandates instituted by vague and inconsistent federal statutes? In Joseph's case, the schools acceded to the court's authority; in Henry's case, they did not.

There was actually less interagency disagreement in matters of judgment about Henry's treatment needs than in many other cases. The schools readily agreed, for example, that Henry was seriously emotionally disturbed; the only focus for dispute was finding an appropriate placement for him. Yet in the wake of clashing bureaucratic timetables, this dispute erupted into litigation so abruptly as to cast conflict over principles of interagency authority and responsibility in unusually pronounced form. Rather than observing procedural niceties by arguing the educational grounds of Henry's residential placement, DSS insisted instead on the schools' obligation to provide special education for children placed residentially on noneducational grounds. The juvenile court asserted its authority under the state legal code to enforce this obligation on the schools. The schools invoked federal law in turn to deny not only that obligation, but the court's very authority over the matter at all.

The issue doubtless expanded in scope because of the confused and reactive manner in which it came to be litigated. Henry's DSS counselor originally returned the case to court on a petition to compel the parents' cooperation with her placement efforts; with Henry out of their home, the parents were refusing even to return her calls. When she asked the judge's help in securing cooperation from the schools' contract services committee as well, the judge ordered the head of that committee subpoenaed to the next hearing, at which Henry was to be represented by a guardian ad litem. Since the schools' attorney appeared at that hearing, the guardian ad litem asked for still another continuance so that a county attorney could represent DSS. Recognizing that as a matter of legal procedure the court could not order the schools to provide services on a petition against Henry's parents, the guardian ad litem also suggested that the county attorney file a petition on behalf of DSS claiming Henry's entitlement to special education services. In hindsight, the county attorney feels that it would have been more effective simply to emphasize the educational grounds for placing Henry; however, having received the case only at the last moment, she pressed instead the more expansive claim of the schools' obligation to children placed on noneducational grounds.

Although the scope of the issue litigated may have been inadvertently broadened in this way, the need for litigation in Henry's case was inescapable. In the midst of the various continuances, Henry's behavior in a short-term community placement deteriorated so suddenly and dangerously that DSS hurriedly transferred him on its own to a wilderness school downstate. They would be able to use Title XX funds for up to six months to cover all the costs of that placement, educational as well as noneducational, but the Title XX coverage would then elapse unless the schools assumed tuition costs. Thus the funding arrangement was jeopardized by the schools' normal torpor in processing contract services applications; by choosing to appeal any funding decision beyond the full set of administrative steps to the various levels of courts, the schools could easily stall long enough to abort the placement, as in fact they had already done in several other DSS cases.

Meanwhile Henry's case was contested on the schools' administrative front all the way to a formal due process hearing, in which the lone DSS counselor opposed a team of the schools' experts armed with their various diagnostic reports in support of Henry's assignment to a public special education center. The schools' representatives argued their case, and the special hearing officer decided it, purely on educational grounds. The schools claimed that while their own center could meet Henry's educational needs, the wilderness school selected by DSS deemphasized education and was "not especially geared to the medical, emotional, or psychological treatment of seriously emotionally disturbed students." According to the DSS counselor, she had selected that placement in consultation with the school psychologist among others precisely because of the nurturing environment it offered; according to her also, some testimony by school officials flatly contradicted previous statements they had made to her informally. At any rate, the special hearing officer upheld the schools' placement decision, while noting: "The criteria used by a Juvenile Court Judge, however, may be, and undoubtedly is, different from that used by a hearing officer in making a placement. The hearing officer is charged with determining the educational aspect of child placement, not with other factors that may bear upon a court ordered placement."

The hearing officer had not yet issued this decision—the due process hearing had just been held—when Henry's case finally returned to juvenile court with all lawyers present for disposition of the petition claiming entitlement to services. The schools' lawyer argued that the juvenile court lacked jurisdiction over the matter, since the schools' process of administrative review took precedence, as subject to review by circuit, state, and federal courts; although it was the juvenile court's responsibility to ensure that children received services required by law, when it came to education it was the schools' prerogative to determine which services those were, according to standards of educational appropriateness. The county attorney responded that the schools were required to provide special education for Henry wherever DSS placed him, and that the court had to intervene to prevent the schools from stalling until the expiration of Title XX coverage. The juvenile court judge construed the intent of the education act as the county attorney argued and affirmed the court's authority to enforce entitlement to services, ordering the schools to fund Henry's placement.

The schools appealed this decision to the circuit court, where the argument followed the same general lines. Claiming that the juvenile court judge "exceeded his authority," the schools cited *Scruggs v. Campbell* (630 F.2d 237 [4th Cir. 1980]): "both the federal and state statutes contemplate broad judicial review at the conclusion of the administrative action. . . . the Act contemplates exhaustion of administrative remedies." Henry's guardian ad litem countered by citing *North v. District of Columbia Board of Education* (471 F. Supp. 136 [D.C. Cir. 1979]), concerning a multihandicapped child whose situation raised the same basic issue as Henry's:

> The defendants contend . . . that while plaintiff's *emotional* difficulties demand this residential placement, his *educational* needs can be met by . . . a special education day program. They argue further that plaintiff's emotional well-being is the responsibility of the D.C. Department of Human Resources and that they, the Board of Education, can adequately discharge their duty to provide for his education by a less restrictive placement, that is, by a day program. (139)

Noting a regulation for the Education for All Handicapped Act indicating the legislative intent "to assure a single line of responsibility with regard to the education of handicapped children," the judge in *North v. District of Columbia Board of Education* interpreted that act to mean that the board was responsible for residential placement.

Besides citing this case, Henry's guardian ad litem invoked the section of the state code empowering the juvenile court to enforce entitlement to services. He also invoked the broadly stated "purpose and intent" of the juvenile court code chapter:

> This law shall be construed liberally and as remedial in character; and the powers hereby conferred are intended to be general to effect the beneficial purposes herein set forth. It is the intention of this law that in all proceedings the welfare of the child and the family is the paramount concern of the State and to the end that this humane purpose may be attained, the judge shall possess all necessary and incidental powers and authority, whether legal or equitable in their nature.

The circuit court judge (himself a former chief judge of the juvenile court) was well aware how broadly this mandate was granted and had always taken it most seriously. He upheld the juvenile court judge's decision.

Keeping Agreements Ad Hoc

The outcome of all this litigation was merely to reproduce in Henry's particular case a general policy agreement established several years earlier between the state Departments of Education and of Welfare, as expressed in an interagency memorandum which stated in part:

> The school division of legal residence shall pay the approved reasonable charges for special education and related services specified in the individualized education program for a handicapped child placed by other public agencies in approved private sectarian schools when such placement is not primarily for special education purposes. The placing agency shall be responsible for the payment of board, room, treatment, and other necessary services as required.

It is surprising, given the existence of this directive, that Henry's case came to be litigated at all. Essentially, the local school division—a legal entity largely autonomous of the state Education Department—chose to disregard the directive. The local director of special education services formally challenged it by claiming that it violated the schools' statutory obligation to choose the "least restrictive" educational alternative; pending a requested formal response to that challenge—which never came— the schools simply ignored the state-level agreement. Still, it is remarkable that that policy agreement did not enter into the legal arguments raised in Henry's case. The various judges involved were not even aware of its existence. The schools' attorney did allude to it, but only to claim that it imposed a condition of assuring the least restrictive educational placement, in effect presenting it as precisely the opposite of what it really was.

The issues raised in Henry's case were significant, for they highlighted basic inconsistencies in federal law. The Title XX legislation was intended to facilitate institutional placement of children, while the Education for All Handicapped Act was intended to discourage it. True, the latter act was also intended to encourage the provision of needed services. But while the Title XX legislation specifically prohibited local welfare agencies from subsidizing tuition costs, the Education for All Handicapped Act failed to contemplate the need for placing educationally handicapped children in residential institutions for noneducational reasons.

A state-level interdepartmental administrative agreement attempting to resolve these statutory inconsistencies was evidently not binding on local agencies; would the judicial ruling in Henry's case establish a significant precedent? The issues were to the point, given full scope in their expression, and fully articulated in written motions and case law precedents. Moreover the judicial ruling was not shrouded by the confidentiality of the juvenile court, since the case was appealed to the circuit court, a court of public record. However, just as the existence of an administrative policy at the state level failed to obviate the need to litigate an ad hoc disposition for Henry's case, so did the clear articulation of broad issues in that case fail to produce a precedent generalizable to others, since for reasons that were not purely accidental the resolution of that case was never clearly stated or defined.

Henry's case lacked the sense of an ending; more precisely, the ending was as confused and ambiguous as the case itself. Three months after the circuit court hearing, Henry's guardian ad litem had to prod the judge to issue a decision because Henry's Title XX funding was about to expire and the schools were still refusing to contribute tuition costs. The judge issued his ruling without immediately indicating his reasons, deferring them until a later time. Soon thereafter, however, the schools' attorney communicated to the judge that the parties themselves had reached a compromise, making the reasons moot. Yet in a significant deviation from the standard practice, no order was ever drawn up expressing the terms of that compromise. The schools were willing to incorporate into a new order the terms of the order issued by the juvenile court judge and upheld by the circuit court judge. However they insisted that that original order be vacated, something the county attorney representing DSS saw no need to do; this difference was never settled. But the schools did send a letter to DSS promising to start paying tuition costs not only for Henry but also for other educationally handicapped children similarly placed in residential institutions under DSS custody. Still claiming concern over possible liability for collaborating in placements more restrictive than educationally necessary, the schools saved face by declaring submission "under protest" to the directives of the state Department of Education in consenting to these payments. In the press of other cases, Henry's circuit court case was never formally closed. The judge never indicated the reasons for his decision, and no order was ever entered. The schools were more willing to settle on an ad hoc basis by assuming tuition costs in all disputed cases than to allow the establishment of a single precedent or to accede to the authority of the juvenile court.

Opposing the Department of Corrections

Three and a half years later the juvenile court's jurisdiction over Henry's case was appealed yet again to the circuit court by another public agency. Once more, kindred agencies had recourse to the extreme of litigation to settle a dispute, wastefully deploying government attorneys to represent one agency against the other. Once again litigious activity produced only an ad hoc resolution. This time, the governmental actors were state rather than county employees; it was the Department of Corrections (DOC) which claimed that the juvenile court judge had exceeded his authority; and it was the state attorney general's office which represented that agency, although they were equally responsible under other circumstances to represent the juvenile court judge as well. Litigation served not only to satisfy a grudge, but also to delimit confused boundaries of overlapping responsibility.

The Department of Corrections challenged the authority of the juvenile court judge to rehear the disposition of committing Henry to DOC, after the allowable period for vacating commitment orders had elapsed. The grudge held by DOC officials against Henry's probation officer and the judge seemed natural enough. After all, both of them had challenged Henry's initial assignment to the "toughest" state training school by the DOC Reception and Diagnostic Center; nor was Henry's assignment the first one the probation officer had challenged. The probation officer had then embarrassed the superintendent of that training school and his direct supervisor, the department's assistant youth services director, by formally reporting Henry's allegations of staff negligence in response to physical harassment and intimidation by fellow inmates, precipitating an internal affairs investigation by the department itself and a protective services investigation by the local DSS. By having Henry transported

back from the state training school for rehearing the commitment disposition—and by then returning Henry's custody to DSS for private
residential placement—the judge lent credibility to those allegations.
Moreover, these provocations recalled to DOC officials embittering criticism by a previous chief judge of the juvenile court, who had deplored
conditions at that training school a decade before in outspoken testimony before the state legislature.

But this case also revived an even more fundamental interagency tension. Who—state or local authorities—were responsible for the most
dangerous committed offenders? This was an axial issue in demarcating
the juvenile court's jurisdiction. Just after the Second World War, even
before the court's mandate was clarified and consolidated in the state
legal code, the Department of Public Welfare—DOC's precursor—
insisted that local juvenile courts be required to accept back those
committed offenders who were judged unsuitable by the state for their
training schools; the state Council of Juvenile Court Judges was first
organized around this very proposal, successfully preventing its adoption. Still, down to the present day, decisions about when to discharge
committed offenders from the training schools have always been contentious, with DOC generally pressing for early discharge—often within
four months of arrival—and the local jurisdictions resisting this form of
"dump." In a notorious recent case, DOC staff was held liable on grounds
of negligence for the personal injuries sustained by victims of a particularly violent crime perpetrated by an ex-committed offender whom DOC
had discharged directly back into the community without arranging for
aftercare supervision by the local court—and indeed without even notifying the local court—despite a documented need for continued surveillance and treatment.

In Henry's case, paradoxically, DOC was arguing to retain custody
rather than relinquish it. The real issues, however, were control of the
discharge decision and responsibility for the committed offender in the
community. Even if DOC lost its challenge to the juvenile court judge's
jurisdiction, it stood to gain a clear statement absolving it of that responsibility. The specific points of contention indicated the extent of interagency dispute and confusion. The state legal code authorizes court
judges to rescind commitment orders within sixty days, but not after
that. But when did the sixty days toll? There was always some lag between the date of commitment and the date of transporting the committed offender to DOC's reception and diagnostic center. The state was not
responsible to reimburse local detention homes for holding committed
offenders during that entire period, and if a child successfully appealed
commitment the state was not responsible for local detention costs at

all. Henry's lawyer had first filed, but then withdrawn, an appeal to the circuit court of Henry's commitment. Did the local court's authority end with the date of commitment or with the date of withdrawing the appeal?

DOC claimed to have sole authority over the decision to discharge a committed offender. Why then, asked the juvenile court judge, did he have to sign a form accepting responsibility for aftercare supervision of every offender discharged from state training schools? DOC claimed that according to the highly publicized recent judgment against them, they could again be held liable for any injuries to victims Henry might inflict during the course of new crimes. But the judge had signed the order transporting Henry back to the community; in any event, this was not a case of unsupervised direct discharge but rather of transfer to a private residential placement certified by DOC among other agencies.

The status of DOC's appeal to the circuit court was similarly confused. What was DOC's standing in the case? Appeals of juvenile court cases to the circuit court are trials de novo. To appeal the award of Henry's custody to DSS for private residential placement instead of commitment to DOC, the state attorney general representing DOC would have had to subpoena witnesses to prove all over again that Henry was even guilty of a crime. Yet no such subpoenas were issued. The more proper legal action would have been to file a writ of prohibition, seeking to prevent the juvenile court judge from rescinding the commitment order after more than sixty days. If however this course had been pursued, the juvenile court judge, as a party to the circuit court proceeding, would have been entitled to representation—also by the state attorney general.

This confusion was never dissipated, nor were the basic interagency issues even tested. Just before DOC's appeal could be heard in circuit court, the course of events made the case moot. Henry's probation officer, after a frantic search, had located a private institution willing to accept Henry. Aided by the patience of staff and visits from his probation officer and DSS counselor, Henry successfully managed to complete a rocky thirty-day trial. He professed to like it there. Yet, as so often in the past, he could not control outbursts of belligerence, leading in short order to his expulsion. His probation officer was forced to return him to court for violation of probation; reluctantly, the judge had to commit him once again to DOC.

The judge could offer only one consolation—a promise that Henry would not return to the same training school to which he had originally been assigned. The judge had won this concession from DOC's director of youth services, with whom he had discussed Henry's case in detail. The various investigations into conditions at that training school established no official wrongdoing. But there were prima facie questions about how those investigations were conducted. Training school staff members were present at all interviews with inmates, and the report of the DOC internal investigation was never divulged, even to court staff. At any rate, the judge struck up a pleasant personal acquaintance with the director of youth services, and they could both agree that assignment to a different training school was in Henry's interest. Officials at the DOC reception and diagnostic center, under orders from above to assign Henry to a less restrictive training school, preserved some measure of discretion by assigning Henry to the high-security cottage there.

The practice of kindred public agencies expending precious legal resources to contest the division of their common responsibilities, as wasteful as it seems, was nonetheless as inexorable in Henry's case as it was in Rose's, Harold's, and Joseph's. It was wasteful to have recourse at all to formal adversarial methods to determine bases of cooperation; such methods were all the more wasteful because they did not even yield generalizable principles of agreement or necessarily even clarification of differences. Still they were necessary in these four cases to create the possibility for ad hoc settlements.

For Henry, the litigious contention between the juvenile court and DOC made possible an outcome—assignment to a less restrictive training school—which was all his probation officer or judge originally sought in their informal appeals to DOC officials. For Rose's, Joseph's, and Harold's probation officers, adversarial confrontations with the schools similarly improved their personal relations with school eligibility and contract services officials; all those probation officers drew a common lesson that working through a network of personal contacts toward ad hoc casework objectives would be more productive than formal confrontation.

Harold's parole officer parlayed long-standing good personal relations with caseworkers at the DOC reception and diagnostic center into an exceptionally favorable placement for Harold. Harold had already spent two years in a training school for the most troublesome committed offenders to which he had been transferred when still only thirteen; the length of stay attests to the difficulty of his adjustment there. Soon after his return to the community on parole, however, he was implicated in an act of arson, for which he was committed a second time to DOC. Neither the parole officer nor the judge could suggest an alternative. Yet the parole officer made a point to attend the meeting of Harold's assessment team at the reception and diagnostic center. Portraying Harold as primarily a needy child rather than a delinquent one, and conjuring the realistic prospect that Harold could learn to spend a lifetime in total institutions, the parole officer advocated assignment to a private residential placement instead of another training school. His advocacy succeeded; the staffing team referred Harold's case to the special placement coordinator at the reception and diagnostic center. Knowing how overworked that placement coordinator was at the time, the parole officer volunteered to do the legwork—lobbying the admissions director, sending copies of voluminous case records, and accompanying Harold to a series of interviews—to effect Harold's placement in a well-respected facility.

Pressing Advocacy to the Limits

The parole officer's success in persuading the DOC reception and diagnostic center to approve private placement for Harold was remarkable since Harold had already been through a training school; funds for such special placements were exceedingly scarce and usually reserved for first-time committed offenders whose offense histories were not thought to warrant training school stays at all. Yet while the parole officer's personal efforts made a dramatic difference, their success was dependent on favorable contingencies—chief among them the availability of special placement funds at the time Harold's case happened to come up for consideration. When available, those funds were expended rapidly; much of the time they were simply not available.

All the more poignant, then, that Harold's original probation officer had failed in a similar attempt to maintain Harold in a private placement as an alternative to commitment just before Harold first entered a training school. At that time the necessary funds (from a different source) were not available, although Harold would have been more likely to benefit from an alternative to commitment then than later. Still, the failure of the probation officer's attempt is instructive, since it produced a precise measure of the limit to DOC's valuation of Harold's best interests.

For eight months Harold had made progress in the private residential placement his probation officer had battled the schools to help support, even though Harold had tested the placement staff's patience by masterminding several runaways and had involved fellow residents as collaborators in break-ins and larcenies along the way. Yet the staff could not tolerate a runaway episode culminating in a dangerous act of arson. Harold's probation officer was roused from his sleep for several hours on his birthday night to receive reports of the episode and to arrange Harold's return to the court's own juvenile detention home. His ensuing efforts to avert commitment failed. The placement staff was willing to take Harold back if additional resources could be arranged to provide him more intensive counseling and surveillance; at the probation officer's request, they presented their conditions as a formal proposal to DOC. (DOC provided the noneducational funding for such "community special placements" under regulations worked out jointly with state Title XX administrators, although local courts were responsible for arranging the placements and monitoring the courses of treatment.)

What extra resources did the residential facility require by their own reckoning to meet Harold's needs? At the minimum, an additional full-time staff member to work with Harold one-on-one for at least six weeks, at a cost of $500 per week; optionally, two additional hours a week of psychological counseling, offered in brief daily periods, and parent training for Harold's mother in her own home. DOC's supervisor of community special placements rejected this proposal as inappropriate and too costly: "if Harold does need the intensive supervision and structure reflected in . . . [the] proposal, then his placement in one of DOC's central juvenile institutions is what is apparently being described."

Like Harold, Rose also undermined the special efforts of her probation officer by spoiling a period of encouraging progress in residential treatment, exposing the limits of the possibilities for advocacy. Having skillfully persuaded the schools to contribute support necessary for Rose's placement in a wilderness school, the probation officer had also persuaded Rose to give that placement a chance, signaling his resolve by bringing the local police in the midst of a weekend night to foil her runaway attempt. Rose then achieved several months of good progress until, encouraged by her mother, she insisted on returning home to stay several months before the placement staff or her probation officer felt it would be appropriate to let her do so. Undaunted, she forced the wilderness school to expel her by engaging in deliberately disruptive and dangerous behavior.

This left the court with only a single pair of treatment options for her, diametrically opposed but neither desirable: emancipation or commitment to a state training school. Feeling that Rose's serious emotional problems still required attention, and realizing that her mother was neither willing nor able to provide supervision or support—and perhaps frustrated by Rose's defiance of his authority—the probation officer favored the latter option. Through her recalcitrance, Rose had transformed her probation officer's advocacy into a recommendation for commitment.

However as things stood it was not even legally possible to commit Rose to a state training school, since as a CHINS offender she had never been convicted of any criminal act. Therefore the probation officer brought her back to court not only for probation violation, but also on the rather obscure criminal charge of having made threatening phone calls to a staff member of the court's probation house (from which she had previously been expelled) five months earlier. Disagreeing with the probation officer's position, his supervisor—who was responsible to initial every official casework document—favored the former option. The supervisor added an unusual note to the end of the court report written by the probation officer: "Judge—[The probation officer] and I have talked about this case and have agreed to disagree. I simply feel her age and the level of her criminal involvement do not justify incarceration." Essentially agreeing with the probation supervisor, the judge found Rose guilty as charged, assessed a $100 fine, and terminated all involvement by the juvenile court in Rose's case—returning Rose's custody to her mother, instructing the court's intake department to reject any future CHINS complaints from Rose's mother, and warning Rose that she would be treated as an adult for any future criminal complaint.

Under the circumstances, Rose's attorney could interpret the court's disengagement as a victory. Besides Rose's rebellious attitude, her "advanced" age—just six months shy of eighteen years—precluded the possibility of finding any further private residential placement for her. The passage of time of course poses a compelling limit to the court's efforts. Since the juvenile court's jurisdiction over children only extends until age eighteen (at least in this particular state), it was not unusual for juvenile court judges to emancipate children of Rose's age. Joseph too earned his expulsion from a private residential placement, upsetting special casework efforts made on his behalf. But it is an indication of the extraordinary limits to which the court was willing to press advocacy in Joseph's case that Joseph's own attorney argued for the court to remain involved, and that Joseph's probation was extended to his twenty-first birthday.

Joseph's probation officer had subpoenaed top school officials into juvenile court to hear the judge read them the law to compel the schools to find a private residential placement for Joseph. Despite the pressure of regular review hearings to ensure their compliance and monitor their progress, the search took school officials seven months. Encountering rejections from every approved school placement within the state, they extended their search nationwide. By the time they finally found a school willing to accept Joseph, they had been making inquiries of unapproved schools as well, requesting them to consider not only accepting Joseph but also submitting to the certification process leading to state approval. Yet barely had Joseph finally entered a well-regarded out-of-state placement than he slipped away from campus and trashed a parked car, causing the school to expel him. Returning to the community, he was reassigned to a private day school where he had done well during the wait for a residential placement. However less than two months into the first full semester after his return, he was expelled from that school too for assaultive behavior. Joseph was already nineteen by that time; his probation officer, discouraged, summarized his casenotes with the comment that "conventional probation is ineffective." Hoping that the judge would release Joseph from probation, the probation officer returned the case to court.

At the least, the probation officer was seeking the judge's guidance about the purposes of continuing court supervision. The probation officer had insisted that Joseph and his parents begin individual and family counseling at the community mental health center. The schools were supposed to provide special education until Joseph turned twenty-two, but what were they to do if Joseph, who was old enough to wield veto power over his own Individualized Education Plan, refused to cooperate? The probation officer had already referred Joseph's case to the state agency of vocational rehabilitation, the Department of Rehabilitative Services. What more was he supposed to do?

Yet the court psychologist, reviewing a variety of old diagnostic evaluations, was concerned about Joseph's emotional, neurological, and educational problems and felt that continuing court supervision was necessary for both surveillance and support. Joseph's lawyer also asked the court to ensure the provision of needed services: prevocational counseling, homebound educational instruction, and mental health counseling. (These services had all been suggested to the lawyer by the probation officer.) The school's attorney politely challenged the court's authority to order homebound instruction, but offered to have the schools evaluate the appropriateness of such instruction. The judge ordered Joseph's probation extended through his twenty-first birthday, for the purpose of coordinating and monitoring these various services and of ensuring participation in mental health counseling by Joseph and his parents.

Forging Channels of Accommodation

The probation officer was essentially left to his own devices in ensuring the cooperation of other agencies. This challenge led him to reconceive his casework strategy not only for Joseph but also for similarly difficult "kids who fall between the cracks." The strategy was to share the burden of advocacy for such children, "to get them hooked in so deep with other agencies that [other caseworkers] can be their advocates." This could be done—indeed could only be done—by creating a network of personal relations among line workers in different agencies.

Joseph's probation officer took the initiative of forming an ad hoc task force to coordinate services for Joseph, including as members the head of the schools' contract services committee, Joseph's therapist from the community mental health center, the court psychologist, Joseph's vocational rehabilitation counselor, the adult mental retardation case manager who was to inherit primary casework responsibility for Joseph upon his release from juvenile probation, as well as Joseph, his parents, and their pastor. Besides their common interest in Joseph, the various caseworkers on this task force were soon united by a sense of common frustration with normal administrative barriers to interagency coordination and a sense of common satisfaction in the innovative nature of their joint venture.

With so many different agencies involved in Joseph's case, the probation officer felt the task force was necessary, among other reasons, to prevent caseworkers from duplicating efforts or working at cross-purposes. The probation officer, for example, wanted the mental health therapist to address the major family problem of sexual abuse, but the therapist at first refused to believe that incest was happening; the therapist was especially suspicious of any such information originally provided by the pastor. The schools and the Department of Rehabilitative Services agreed that Joseph needed some form of vocational training, but each agency felt the other should provide it. Who would provide a sheltered living situation for Joseph when he moved away from his parents—the community mental health center or the adult mental retardation center?

The first step in resolving such issues was to share information. The probation officer had worked with Joseph for six years before forming the task force, and Joseph's pastor had worked with the family for years before that; half the caseworkers on the task force had never even met Joseph's parents or the pastor. The task force provided a forum for aligning particular casework objectives and strategies; it also provided a forum for involving Joseph and his parents in the case planning process. Thus it helped define the responsibilities of both servers and clients. Not incidentally, it provided a forum for Joseph's father to express open resentment of government interference in his family's life, an act of catharsis which the caseworkers found useful.

By convening the task force intermittently, about half a dozen times over a two-year period, the probation officer was able to hold the various agencies to their responsibilities much more effectively and efficiently than by returning the case to court. Since it was apparent that Joseph would continue to require services as an adult, a major objective of the task force was to make the transition to adult services as smooth as possible for him, to maintain continuity of casework. Just as the juvenile court judge stretched statutory limits by extending Joseph's probation until his twenty-first birthday, task force members persuaded the Case Management Center for mentally retarded adults to accept Joseph's case two years before they had to, when he was only nineteen. At one time, however, when the case manager began to express doubts about eventually assuming primary responsibility for Joseph, the task force reconvened to exact a renewed commitment from her. Similarly, Joseph's vocational rehabilitation counselor seemed indifferent in her commitment to Joseph, slow in finding training opportunities for him, and absent from several task force meetings. In the name of the task force, Joseph's mental health therapist successfully appealed to a rehabilitative services supervisor to have Joseph assigned a new vocational counselor.

Before long the various task force members were routinely prodding Joseph to attend the others' sessions as well as their own. The mental health therapist, for example, came to respect and appreciate the pastor's services to Joseph's family, and encouraged Joseph's participation in church activities. The church afforded Joseph and his father a valuable opportunity to be of service to others, assigning them a "bus ministry" which entailed regularly transporting people to church functions. When Joseph was suspended from church activities for making homosexual advances at a church social (after a girl had spurned his invitation to dance), his probation officer coached him on how to approach the pastor for reinstatement. About half a year later, both Joseph and his father were again suspended from church activities because the father had defied a ban against Joseph's presence on the church bus, where once more Joseph had made homosexual gestures. This time, after several months had elapsed to let passions subside, the probation officers personally appealed directly to the pastor to reinstate Joseph's father. Ironically, Joseph's case had come full circle. Years before, the probation officer had invoked his private faith in appealing to the pastor for allowing the family's participation in public services; now, in his public role, the probation officer appealed for allowing the family's renewed participation in the church.

To What Effect?

Joseph's probation officer, despairing of Joseph's chances to stay out of serious trouble in the community, always seemed to have contingency plans for placing him in some private psychiatric treatment facility or mental hospital. Yet Joseph managed to avert institutionalization in weathering periodic crises, including episodes of assault and vandalism.

He never did anything terribly dangerous, and he started showing signs of maturity. One month when Joseph was almost twenty, the probation officer complained in his case notes, "basic skills lacking—emotional maturity 13–14"; yet the very next month he noted, "Joseph always makes his appointment by himself. I am encouraging more independent choices, away from parents." Joseph gradually began to present himself in a more coherent and understandable fashion. On his own initiative he found—and did well in—a succession of fast-food jobs. He passed one section of a pretest for the General Equivalency Diploma (GED), though he would never be able to earn that certificate. Most strikingly, he and his mother gradually were able to discontinue their sexual relationship; with assistance from the task force, he was preparing to move away from his parents' home into a semi-independent living situation.

The other children did not all experience similar encouraging progress. Just like Henry, Harold had been rescued from a state training school by the efforts of his probation officer to arrange instead a private residential placement, but he ruined this chance in short order by behaving disruptively despite professing to like it there, and was again returned to a training school.

Harold and Henry disappointed the more hopeful expectations of their probation officers; Rose disconfirmed the gloomier expectations of hers. True to form, after encouraging Rose to quit the wilderness school, Rose's mother kicked Rose out of the house within days of the judicial order restoring Rose's custody to her. Rose reached out to professional helpers with whom she had forged close personal bonds. She first went to live with her former special education teacher, leaving after several months because of a fight. She then sought out the director of the wilderness school, who had since transferred elsewhere. This woman arranged for Rose to live in a nearby trailer and participate in a program through which she earned her GED. Not long thereafter, Rose married a local auto mechanic.

Of course none of these stories is finished. Given the nebulous and protracted passage to adulthood, it is never even clear how to mark the end of adolescence. Of all the uncertainties and ambiguities of probation work, none is more mysterious or unsettling than ultimate case outcomes. In initialing the termination summary of Rose's probation, the probation supervisor wrote out a comment for no other apparent reason than to give voice to his own musings. The document bearing that comment was to be filed directly away with Rose's other records; the only person who might ever see it was Rose's probation officer. Yet the comment was appropriate not only for Rose's case, but also for the others as well: "A great deal of effort that may have been worth something."

2

Technology, Culture, and Outcomes

6

Normal Casework

Very few cases are manifestly as stressful for the juvenile court as those of Larry, Michael, Mary, Jerome, Rose, Harold, Henry, and Joseph. While straining the limits of the court's organizational competence, these cases reveal the full disorganization of its task environment. The very resourcefulness and commitment that these children's probation officers display as individuals betray a basic lack of resources, commitment, and organization on the systems level. Many desperate dilemmas of individualized casework derive from basic institutional gaps and cross-purposes. The children's stubborn problems are multiple and ambiguously diffuse, yet agencies with overlapping domains insist on defining their responsibilities and competencies in narrowly specialized ways. Judges and probation officers wind up assuming child welfare responsibilities contentiously evaded by different agencies, jurisdictions, and levels of government—evasion not merely sanctioned, but actually prescribed by the vague and contradictory provisions of federal law. Even when expressly litigated on issues of general principle, disputes about interagency coordination are only settled on terms of narrowest accommodation. The ad hoc interagency arrangements which probation officers are forced to improvise in these cases attest to the unresolved—and indeed irresolvable—nature of these endemic systemic disputes. The network of child-serving agencies seems no less remote and fragmented to probation officers than to children and parents; to procure needed services from other agencies for their clients, probation officers must adopt casework strategies of "problemization." The apparently inordinate discretion probation officers exercise in fact reflects not their power, but rather their essential powerlessness; that discretion is effectively bounded by systemic disorganization and resource scarcity.

Not only the court's task environment is disorganized. Probation officers cannot count on agreement for their case plans from the court's own judges, intake counselors, or residential directors. To some degree, the court internalizes the disorganization of its environment; intracourt tensions mirror the court's external conflicts. Intake counselors are more concerned than probation officers with legal technicalities, while residential directors are most concerned with maintaining control over their own programs. Judges must attend to the claims of parents and lawyers. Quite properly, then, the court is not a monolithic agency. Yet contributing to the court's internal tensions is a reflexively critical institutional self-consciousness. Court workers tend to share some of their clients' frustrations with systemic disorganization, further alienating those workers from their colleagues. The incompleteness of the court's technology contributes to (and in turn is partly sustained by) the incompleteness of its culture; in a reflexively self-critical institution, the very notion of "success" is ambivalent and uncertain.

In many respects, of course, the "special" treatment accorded Larry, Michael, Mary, Jerome, Rose, Harold, Henry, and Joseph is dialectically antithetical to the practice of "normal" casework. Caseloads are ordinarily crowded, so that the time and emotional energies that probation officers lavish on their special cases inevitably detract from their already limited attention to normal ones. While cases receiving every possible effort reveal the full extent of systemic disorganization, normal casework imposes organization on the task environment. While special cases inspire probation officers to improvise innovative dispositions, in normal casework they make do with the limited range of routinely available ones. While case advocacy attempts to penetrate defended organizational boundaries, normal casework abides those boundaries.

Yet it would be a mistake to conclude that cases attracting special advocacy constitute only token efforts by probation officers. For there are important continuities between such cases and more normal ones. After all, in testing the limits of advocacy, probation officers attempt to stretch—or at least loosen—the normal channels of interagency accommodation. In their challenges, meanings, gratifications, and disappointments, these special cases are not so much *atypical* as *prototypical* of more normal ones, as the story of a single case whose processing abided bureaucratic limits can only illustrate.

A Normal Case

Rashid's probation officer exerted little effort to avert Rashid's commitment to the state Department of Corrections, even though she felt that that commitment was not right. She believed that Rashid needed residential placement instead to treat his special education needs and emotional instability, for which the school system disclaimed any responsibility. Nevertheless, based on a realistic assessment of the forces arrayed against her within the court as well as without, she chose not to press her protest of the commitment.

Admittedly, Rashid—who had already spent two years in a private residential institution—got himself into trouble for repeated incidents of aggression following rapidly upon each other. But Rashid's companions and the other parties to those incidents seemed to receive milder treatment than Rashid, who was neither ringleader nor primary instigator. Indeed, it appeared as if Rashid might have been the scapegoat for an incident blown up by the press as a racial problem at his high school.

The charges Rashid accumulated within short order sounded considerably more ominous than his accounts of the incidents that produced them. Rashid claimed, for example, that he was only trying to calm a companion whom the police were in the process of arresting when the police turned on him, forcing him to defend himself; a judge assigned Rashid to probation for assaulting a police officer. Even before the court could finish processing that complaint, however, Rashid was found guilty of maliciously wounding a man in the course of an attempted robbery. There is no doubt that the victim received a severe beating with a stick; but Rashid disavowed robbery as the motive and denied any part in the beating, accusing instead one of his companions who harbored a grudge against the victim. Rashid's probation officer tended to believe him; in general, she felt that Rashid was too dull witted to have undertaken the behavior attributed to him. But his companions—whom the probation officer considered "slick"—made their versions of the story stick in court and got off lightly.

Finally came the incident at the high school: a girl accused Rashid of stealing $10 from her, and school officials later called in the police to break up a fight between Rashid and two of the girl's boyfriends. Rashid claimed that the girl was a drug pusher and that the trouble arose out of a dispute over a minor drug deal. But because he feared the pair of boyfriends, he brought a baseball bat to school the next day. Not only did that earn him an expulsion, it also attracted press attention as a sign of racial conflict. (Rashid's racial background was mixed; the girl and the two other boys were white). The court received yet two additional complaints against Rashid as a result of this incident—complaints of robbery and disorderly conduct.

Rashid's probation officer felt that the court also handled these complaints unfairly. The school principal initially brought complaints for disorderly conduct only against the two other boys, but when the court's intake officer realized Rashid was on probation—and when, despite that intake officer's prodding, the probation officer refused to file a probation violation—the intake officer took a petition for disorderly conduct against Rashid as well. (Had the probation officer's own office not been too busy at the time, they could have processed the principal's complaint instead of the Central Intake unit, averting the charge against Rashid.) All three boys were detained, but the other two were immediately bonded out of detention. After Rashid had spent the weekend in the detention home, his probation officer managed to gain his release too through a bond reduction. As it turned out though, this release proved to be only a further indignity to Rashid, for the very next day a different intake officer issued yet another order for his detention on the robbery charge. The pair of related charges against Rashid happened to be processed separately and at different times, so that even as the probation officer was pleading for a bond reduction on the one charge, the intake department had scheduled an appointment to receive the other. The probation officer could do no more than arrange for Rashid to turn himself back into the detention home rather than have the police bring him there.

Soon thereafter, for both the malicious wounding and the robbery, a judge committed Rashid to a state training school. To avert this outcome, his probation officer would have had to arrange another private institutional placement, which in turn would have required the cooperation of the public schools. But the schools, whose neglect of Rashid's documented special education needs in regular school settings may have contributed to his behavior problems, were intent on getting rid of him instead.

Without even notifying Rashid's mother (in violation of administrative due process), the school principal and his administrative superiors convened to transfer Rashid to a different school, whose administrators were not consulted either, and where Rashid soon got into further trouble. In the context of these events—and in the midst of Rashid's court involvement—the schools arranged a precipitous meeting to consider Rashid's eligibility for further private residential special education services. Despite the fact that Rashid had only recently entered the public schools from a residential special education program arranged by the public schools of a neighboring jurisdiction—and despite an evaluation by the schools' own staff psychologist which concluded that "Rashid is a learning-disabled youngster whose behavioral difficulties stem from these learning disability problems rather than from an emotional disorder"—the committee ruled that Rashid was emotionally disturbed and did not require residential services for his learning disability.

What is remarkable about the meeting to determine eligibility for educational contract services was that it took less than a week to arrange. The meeting was convened in such haste that neither Rashid's mother, nor the probation officer, nor even the school psychologist whose records were summoned knew about it. It normally takes school administrators two to three months to arrange such meetings, but in Rashid's case they managed to produce a decision in time to influence the court disposition, and so to preempt any appeal.

Rashid was committed to the Department of Corrections just three months after the start of his probation. His probation officer felt that he had received less of a chance than most other probationers. She thought that his completion of the two-year private residential program indicated a potential for rehabilitation, and she empathized with the personal problems that contributed to Rashid's troubles. In addition to his learning disability, Rashid suffered vision and health problems. He also experienced problems of racial identity; his parents were of different races and he was light complexioned. His white father abandoned the family when Rashid was six, and his mother was often drunk.

Rashid's case exemplifies the continuities as well as the antitheses between "normal" casework and "special" advocacy. Rashid's problems were no less special than anyone else's, nor did they command any less empathy from his probation officer. Yet Rashid was committed to the Department of Corrections in the course of normal casework. Only because she realistically assessed their futility did the probation officer refrain from special efforts to avert Rashid's commitment. She would have wanted to give him more of a chance, and she experienced deep disappointment in the case outcome. If Rashid's case claimed in fact little of her time, it was not for lack of caring on her part.

A number of factors conspired to seal Rashid's commitment. The judge, aware of how personal attachments could color judgment, felt that the probation officer was unduly optimistic about the prospects of residential treatment for Rashid. The receipt of many different complaints against Rashid in rapid succession created a sense that he was a chronic offender, impervious to any treatment the court could muster. His successful completion of the residential program meant that remedies less drastic than commitment had already been attempted on his behalf, warranting the court's recourse to a "last resort." The inability of Rashid's mother to supervise him properly also helped make him seem a poor risk.

Although the court appointed a lawyer to represent Rashid at his hearings, the level of representation provided was typically ineffective. By the time of the final hearing, Rashid's commitment was a foregone conclusion. The schools' resolve to rid themselves of him was peremptory. Although it is possible to appeal the schools' denial of services on an ad hoc, particularistic basis, the appeal process is protracted and the schools dictate its terms. The emphatic nature of the schools' response to the publicity generated by Rashid's behavior foreclosed any possibility of reversing their decision in his case. Challenging the schools' abuse of administrative due process would have presented the only opportunity for effective legal advocacy on Rashid's behalf, but no lawyer ever even contemplated such a challenge.

As Rashid's story illustrates, normal casework operates within a wide range of practical constraints. Probation officers must learn to ration their time, hope, and energies. Compounding the sheer logistical difficulties of managing crowded caseloads are the inevitable crises which demand their frenzied attentions, punctuated by seemingly interminable waits for court. Balancing their mutually inconsistent roles as helpers and enforcers, probation officers confront the natural reluctance of children to either seek help or accept authority. They must temper their grandiose goals of transforming children's characters with realistic expectations of effecting only barely perceptible behavioral changes.

Endowed with neither the expertise nor autonomy of judgment that characterizes professionals, probation officers also suffer a lack of organizational support. Their supervisors can offer little more than training in the mechanics of procedure, while enforcing paperwork requirements that are largely ceremonial. The court's administrators pursue strategies of opportunistic expansion without developing a distinctive or harmonious organizational competence. Nor do those administrators coordinate relations with other agencies in the court's organization-set, tacitly condoning their passive-aggressive practices and leaving probation officers to pursue the cooperation they need almost exclusively through the exchange of personal favors.

In the absence of either professional authority or a well-defined institutional ideology, probation officers depend on the unreliable support of judges and parents for the legitimacy of their case plans. The task of persuading these others to approve their decisions is complicated by the divergent role strains that differentiate the triadic positions of judges, parents, and probation officers. In part because they are defensive about what their children's troubles reflect upon themselves, parents exhibit ambivalence toward both their children and the court. Parents and probation officers struggle against each other to maintain control over the definition and treatment of children's problems even while disclaiming responsibility for those problems. Judges maintain a stance of impartiality toward probation officers and parents. They tend to be more legalistic than probation officers. Their policies are vague and inconsistent, partly as a result of the collegiality that governs their own relations. Parents can enlist the services of lawyers to promote their partisan interests; although legal reform has raised the hope of making the juvenile court more central as a societal institution, the practice of juvenile law remains marginal to the court's broader institutional purpose.

The incomplete technology of probation work leaves probation officers little recourse with difficult children except to seek their placement in residential institutions. Removal from home is the "normal remedy," which at least allows probation officers to spare most children from the "last resort" of commitment to state training schools. Yet placing children in residential institutions is itself a dubious recourse. The quality of those institutions is unevaluated, and the assignment of children to placements tends to be indiscriminate, governed in part by the informal referral channels available to particular probation officers. Although residential placement serves the casework purpose of "buying time," separating children from parents, friends, and school compounds their problems of adjustment by disrupting their ties to the communities to which they will eventually return.

This chapter and the next three explore how probation officers operate within the range of practical constraints that characterize normal casework. They explore how probation officers learn to respect limits of time, hope, and energy; how they develop networks of personal contacts to compensate for the irregularity of organizational support; how they seek to persuade skeptical judges and parents to legitimate their casework designs; and how they implement the "normal remedy" of residential placement. It is these constraints which establish the limits of what normal casework can accomplish.

Learning Limits

The probation officers I observed carried an average of forty-odd cases at any one time, a light workload by national standards. Yet even veteran probation officers routinely put in unpaid overtime, while it was not unusual for new probation officers to put in over fifty-hour weeks, even though their supervisors contrived to keep their caseloads only about half full. As the accounts of "special" cases demonstrate, the care of a single child can easily consume all of a probation officer's time. The scope of probation officers' duties and responsibilities is genuinely overwhelming.

Time Constraints

Probation officers organize their time around the schedules of judges, children, and parents. First priority, of course, is attending court and meeting deadlines on court-ordered social investigations. These investigations entail extended office appointments with parents and children, follow-up visits to home, school, and job site, arrangements for psychological or other evaluations, and requests for information from other agencies—in all, several days' work to be completed within a few weeks for each investigation.

In addition to these investigations, probation officers maintain a round of regular appointments with the children under their supervision, as well as with their parents. These appointments must be scheduled around the parents' work and the children's school and jobs. Thus, probation officers meet with working parents in early morning or early evening; they conduct office hours for children after school hours; they visit schools to see children and to monitor their attendance and behavior; and they visit children in the detention home or residential placements.

Their goal is to spend as much time with clients as possible, beyond the minimally required monthly contacts with both children and parents. The sheer number of cases, however, reduces the time that normally can be given to any one case, to say nothing of the tedious tasks which drastically lessen the amount of time available for "direct service" to begin with. A probation officer averages about an hour a day just driving from place to place on the job. Even more draining on the probation officer's time is the variety of administrative paperwork requirements: drafting the reports of social investigations, designing and periodically revising case plans, maintaining case records, submitting workload and other management statistics, keeping case files in proper order, and locating missing files for cases scheduled to return to court. Desk work can easily consume more time than seeing clients, which competes with such other administrative activities as meetings with supervisors, training sessions, and committee work. On the average, probation officers get to spend less than ten or twelve hours a week directly with their clients.

These demands would strain the organization of probation officers' time even if their plans were not always vulnerable to sudden disruption by casework crises and unexpected court appearances. To arrange a single residential placement requires days of work. Driving a child to and from a placement interview takes an entire day, and it is usually necessary to arrange a number of such interviews. Applying for funding can be even more time-consuming. Residential institutions considering a child's application require copies of the child's records; public funding agencies, including the Department of Corrections and the contract services committee of the public schools, require multiple copies of the records. By the time the court considers placement, a child has typically accumulated voluminous records, compartmentalized into separate file pockets. A probation officer can literally spend days duplicating, collating, and reassembling those records (rarely is clerical assistance available for that task). Assuming responsibility for coordinating the interagency agreements necessary for funding compounds the disruptive expenditure of time the probation officer incurs by deciding to seek residential placement for a child.

Even more disruptive of a probation officer's schedule, however, are calls to "put out fires"—unanticipated demands for immediate intervention in suddenly deteriorating situations. A child makes a credible suicide gesture; a school administrator complains that a probationer has defied the terms of suspension by trespassing on school grounds; hysterical parents describe a blowup at home; an official from another jurisdiction sends word of having picked up a child as a runaway; the director of a residential institution abruptly expels a child; a police officer reports a new offense or a serious violation of probation. The task of restoring a sense of normalcy, at least for the moment, supersedes whatever other activities the probation officer had planned.

Compounding the disruptive effects of these crises are the unscheduled court appearances they often entail. Any court appearance means an inordinate—and worse, unpredictable—wait for the case to be called into court; although the actual court hearing rarely takes more than fifteen minutes, the average wait in the crowded corridor outside the courtrooms is an hour and a half, with a standard deviation of an hour. Every so often, the wait kills an entire day. Probation officers can make some use of the waiting time, negotiating with clients, victims, cops, defense lawyers, prosecuting attorneys, and representatives of other agencies about recommendations to the judge; but for long durations, they have as little to do as the clients at whose side they wait.

Waiting for court occupies on the average a full morning or afternoon of the probation officer's week. The sacrifice of this much time is even more frustrating in relative than in absolute terms. As a humiliating indication of low professional standing, the probation officer's wait is usually longer than that of the other parties to court hearings because the probation officer waits on those others. The advance docket schedule is established, and the daily docket is called, around the convenience of judges and attorneys, at the expense of probation officers. Prosecuting and defense attorneys, and even police officers, can designate certain days as their only days to appear in court. Probation officers' attempts to rationalize their schedules in the same way repeatedly fail, precisely because the others' scheduling preferences take priority. Similarly, attorneys can schedule a number of different hearings for the same time— indeed, even hearings in different courts—secure in the knowledge that no hearings will start without them; conversely, when they appear at court, their hearings receive the priority of call (with allowance, of course, for the preparation time they need). Probation officers may also schedule more than a single hearing for the same day. But they do so at some peril, not uncommonly finding that their hearings have gone on without them (getting them into trouble with the judges), to prevent judges or attorneys from having to wait. In this respect, even defendants enjoy greater deference than probation officers.

Probation officers naturally curry personal favor from the clerks who call the docket, but cannot count on receiving preferential—or even equal—treatment in return. In a study I conducted of over five hundred prescheduled criminal hearings, probation officers delayed only 10 percent of their hearings through simultaneous involvement in other cases or tardiness for other reasons, while defense attorneys delayed 23 percent of their hearings, and prosecuting attorneys fully 49 percent of theirs; while the delays occasioned by probation officers lasted on the average under three-quarters of an hour, those occasioned by attorneys lasted two hours.

Probation officers often observe that casework "fires" tend to erupt in bunches. The laws of mathematical probability can begin to explain this observation. Assuming that the probabilities of individual cases erupting into crisis were discrete and constant over time, crises would tend to cluster to some degree merely as a consequence of random chance. Other forces, however, also contribute to the observed clustering of case crises. The disruptive effects of having to "put out a fire" in one case ramify throughout a caseload. It is risky to ignore certain cases while concentrating on others, since every case is potentially troublesome. Probation officers lament the existence of a vicious cycle: "If you're stuck in court, your kids get into trouble, and you spend more time in court." Moreover, the more "fires" raging in a caseload at any one time, the less the opportunity for working informally with people to keep any one of those cases in crisis from coming back to court.

Probation officers' normal commitments must be elastic enough to absorb the disruptions to their schedules caused by case crises or the receipt of many new cases at once. When they must curtail normal activity to make time for unanticipated tasks, they start by neglecting such nonpressing matters as processing paperwork, monitoring restitution, visiting children in residential placements, or meeting with parents. When their schedule contains no further slack, they must cancel probation appointments. Although some choose to sacrifice the children least likely to respond to their efforts, most instead skip seeing those children who seem to be doing best. This means forsaking the most enjoyable part of the job: "nice time," "getting to know children better," "enrichment activities." One therapeutically oriented probation officer identified this as a core frustration of probation work: "If kids are doing well, that's precisely the time you should be seeing them more often, to get at underlying issues. Instead, the way the job is set up, you stop seeing them."

In practice, then, probation work is primarily reactive. Too often probation officers seem to find themselves either waiting monotonously for court or driving frantically from one casework "fire" to the next, helplessly falling ever farther behind their plans.

> Basically, the probation system operates on the "squeaky wheel" principle—if the schools are bugging you about a kid, or the parents are bugging you about a kid, then you're going to be on the kid, and whatever you do, you're going to do a lot of it. The kid may be out doing all sorts of things, but if he's not being complained about, then nothing's going to happen, because we're a reactive system.

Grandiose Goals, Modest Expectations

The rush of probation work strains against the grandiose goals of juvenile justice. In contrast to the scarcity of time and the constraints—some routinized, others unpredictable—on the ability of probation officers to control their own time, these goals are expansive. At the least, probation officers are supposed to reduce repeat criminal activity by enforcing the written and signed rules governing each probationer's travel, curfew, personal associations, compliance with specific court orders, and respect for other forms of authority. Yet although these minimal goals are essentially restrictive or inhibitory, the deeper purposes professed by judges and probation officers are actually facilitative or supportive instead.

The most ambitious of these purposes are to effect growth and transformation, not just to control behavior but rather to build character: to make the child "understand" or "get a handle" on his or her problems, to learn "responsibility" and learn to "face reality"; to improve a child's self-image, so that "kids will begin to realize how important they are as individuals and grow in appreciation and respect for themselves"; to encourage children to realize their potential, "to be the best that they can be," turning them from "losers" into "winners"; to support the child in becoming more "productive," more of a "contributor to society," by supporting the child's achievement in school or at a job; in short, to foster "maturity." These purposes entail working not only with the child, but also with the parents, "teaching them to parent." The ultimate goal is nothing less than transcending the structural opposition of generations—"to teach the kids to earn their independence while teaching their parents to grant it."

This is not to deny the importance court workers attribute to "setting limits" or "providing structure." Lamenting the "permissiveness" of modern society which "creates kids who've never had any structure whatsoever," a judge declares, "our obligation is to provide that structure." A probation officer reports that children whose parents will excuse any sort of behavior express tangible relief when told they must abide a set of probation rules. Another judge explains:

> Most times the kid is involved in criminal activity it represents some type of crisis, either in the family or in his life. Or maybe he's just getting a taste of strange and more exotic things, or frightening things, and the sooner we can react and show him that that type of life-style is going to bring him an awful lot of hassles, a lot of change, and the community is going to react very swiftly, the easier it is to turn him around. The kid who gets into criminal acts has almost invariably been told and understands or wishes that he won't get caught, that there's nothing to it if he does get caught, and you have to change that opinion in his mind. . . . Most kids who are in trouble are under extreme peer pressure, and they need that ability to resist the peer pressure. If they don't get it from their parents we have to supply it.

Court workers assert that the immediate repressive goal of controlling children's behavior is necessary to the broader goal of developing character. In the words of a probation officer, "You exercise control to get their attention, and then you can do the work. You get them to *internalize* rules and limits." As a judge describes his conception of probation to an assembly of probation officers, "you become the surrogate parent— friend, confidant, and authority." Another judge speaks of the need to provide "friendly structure" and "friendly firmness," especially to teenagers who are immature: "The probation department can provide firmness and standards, whether by rapport or threat. Punishment is part of treatment." Yet another judge observes, "We as a court do not control crime, we negotiate emotional and family problems. We use our muscle to do that."

In the initial meetings with children assigned to supervision, probation officers usually explain how they reconcile the enforcement and counseling aspects of their role. While identifying their primary responsibility to ensure compliance with probation rules and court orders, they also volunteer to work on any problems the children bring forth, as long as the children behave properly. Yet this formulation cannot erase the strain between the adversarial and supportive aspects of the probation role. Speaking to a group of probation officers, a new judge describes the uncertainty of her attempts from the bench to clarify what children should expect from probation: "I want to say that the probation officer is someone to help them, someone to talk to; but in the next breath, I have to warn them about probation violations." Probation officers often comment among themselves about the diverse roles they are expected to perform in the courtroom. Depending on the number and types of lawyers who happen to be party to the hearing, the probation officer may wind up playing witness, prosecutor, or defense attorney—or all of those roles at once. "My people always assume I'm on their side in a hearing. I have to tell them not to assume that."

Whatever clarity of anticipation the probation officer can impart at the outset, the course of probation often proves ambiguous in its sense of an ending. A few children become so dependent on the support of their probation officers that they seek voluntarily to prolong their probation. More commonly, probation is extended on account of violations or new offenses. Some children manage to stay out of trouble even though they do not cooperate with their probation officers. Still others move away. Many find themselves in residential institutions as they leave probation. Many others, of course, finish successfully and on time. Probation officers generally reduce the frequency of appointments with their successful clients toward the end; despite the special efforts of a few to arrange ceremonial court appearances to mark the conclusion of successful cases, probation typically ends at best simply by winding down to a perfunctory form letter of termination.

The ambiguity of the probation role (along with normal variations in personality and commitment to work) helps define the different styles of probation work. There are cop types who emphasize surveillance, and social-work types who emphasize counseling; "cool operators" who guard professional dispassion, and "screamers" who demonstrate emotional involvement; workers "of the head" who spend more time in the office brokering specialized services, playing it "by the book" and keeping their paperwork in order, and workers "of the heart" who reach out to children by spending more time with them in the field, acting more as surrogate parents attending directly to children's broad needs, taking greater liberties with agency regulations, and ignoring their paperwork for months at a time.

Whatever style they adopt, all probation officers must learn to moderate their expectations of success. In negotiating with the child and parents the improvements in behavior to be sought, the probation officer is often the one who insists on defining progress in terms gradual and incremental enough to be attainable. In many cases, the first step in restoring some measure of parental control is persuading parents to drop unenforceable restrictions on their children's hours and associations. "The way you make parents feel competent is by breaking down behavior into small pieces." A probation officer claims to have found gratification in 90 percent of her cases by being able to recognize "little tiny" measures of success: getting a chronic class-cutter to attend two classes a day; getting a druggie to smoke dope only three times a week; getting someone to return home by two o'clock each morning, rather than staying out all night.

Even in cases where no progress is evident, probation officers can find consolation in the belief that they are "planting a seed" whose fruition may well be long delayed. As a probation officer reflects on one of his first, most frustrating cases, in which he finally sent to a state training school one of a pair of sisters to whom he had devoted nearly every Saturday morning over a period of many months:

> I like to think there was more good in all that, that they knew
> someone at some point in time cared about them; that in itself the
> process of caring, of being involved, did some good that you
> could never causally link to anything; that maybe it took effect at
> some later time, when they were older; and the fact that they did
> have somebody . . . giving them some good advice, encouraging
> them, and trying to get them to go straight . . . that I in some way
> contributed to their parenting, and gave them a base they could
> come back to in their later lives—I could never prove that, maybe
> it's wishful thinking, but it's a satisfaction. If you stay in this busi-
> ness long enough, maybe the whole satisfaction game is one of
> waiting—waiting until someone grows up.

In fact, probation officers lose track of most children soon after they stop working with them. The effects they have on those they do hear from are often surprising. Children considered "success stories" later get

into serious trouble as adults. Conversely, nearly every veteran probation officer has received heartfelt thanks many years after the fact from
former clients only faintly remembered or ones remembered as being
unresponsive at the time. Some veterans, perceiving their impact to be
minimal, consider their efforts worthwhile nonetheless for allowing the
natural processes of maturation a chance to work: "All you can do in this
business is buy time"; "you're trying to buy time and hope they grow up."

Hooking Kids

At once adversarial and supportive, combining grandiose goals with
modest expectations, the relation between probation officer and child is
ambivalent. Whatever shifting tenor that relation may assume, to engage
the child in the probation process at all requires overcoming the child's
natural reluctance either to seek help or accept authority. Before anything else, the probation officer must manage to "hook" the child. Applying a precept of family systems therapy, a probation officer explains:
"You have to get in there, and you don't go in there having any power.
You gain that power by going with the system and then at some point
going counter to the system. You support people, and at some point you
challenge them."

Initially, information about the child is all the probation officer has to
work with in attempting to build a relation and establish control; information remains crucial to the probation officer for strengthening the
relation and retaining control. Success in gathering information about a
child feeds on itself, since people are more willing to divulge information
the more the confidant seems already to know. Probation officers like to
impress children at their very first meeting by announcing that they have
been expecting them, having known about them for quite some time. In
the normal course of casework, probation officers cultivate a network of
sources about present and prospective clients: other children on the
caseload and their parents, school officials, other probation officers, and
sometimes police officers. They seek information from parents, with
mixed results. As the relation with a child develops, however, the probation officer becomes increasingly reliant for information on the child's
self-reports.

The child's willingness to reveal personal and even compromising information grows with familiarity. The probation officer is often the only
adult outside the child's home—or the only adult at all—willing to lend
an attentive and sympathetic ear. The child may be more willing to share
intimate concerns and confessions with the probation officer than with
a psychologist, a seemingly more forbidding figure because of superior
professional status. Indeed, by communicating attitudes of genuine car-

ing, probation officers are sometimes able to elicit accounts of such secret traumata as incidents of sexual abuse. Some children return to seek personal advice from their probation officer months and years after completing probation.

Probation officers employ a wide variety of techniques for getting children to open up. Workload permitting, they go out to children's homes instead of holding office appointments. One probation officer recalls how readily girls would confide in her as they sat cross-legged in their own bedrooms. Children appreciate such favors as rides to a job or school along the path of a probation officer's daily commute. Probation officers organize activity groups for recreational outings. A few children find a place to "hang out" at the probation office, doing their homework, helping with office chores, exchanging small talk with other children and with probation officers between appointments.

Other techniques for breaking through to children are more inventive. Over a series of meetings, one probation officer broke a child's habit of silence through mimicry: whenever the child turned his chair away to face one corner of the office, the probation officer would turn his own chair to face the other corner. Another probation officer, confronting a punk-rocker who similarly refused to talk, assigned the child to bring a joke to each meeting. In a parody of the ethnic jokes that the child brought in, the probation officer made up insulting "punk-rocker" jokes. The next session, the child retaliated with a repertoire of "probation officer" jokes fashioned in the same genre; his reticence vanished. The same probation officer would engage children in debate over styles of musical taste, by playing widely disparate types of music while driving them around in his car.

Still other techniques for overcoming children's resistance are even more dramatically insistent. A probation officer learned sign language to be able to communicate directly with a duplicitous child's deaf parents. Another probation officer conducted a number of initial meetings with an acutely withdrawn child under the child's bed, since the child refused to come out under any circumstances.

Overcoming children's initial resistance is obviously only a start. What bonds children most strongly to probation officers is support in situations of crisis or trial. The probation officer searches out a suicidal girl, staying with her and offering reassurance until effecting psychiatric intervention. The probation officer not only arranges medical care for a pregnant teenager, but gives up her evenings to serve as the girl's partner in childbirth classes; she rushes to the hospital at 4:30 one morning to coach the girl through labor and witnesses the birth in the delivery room. The probation officer uncovers parental abuse and finds emergency shelter. The probation officer is the adult "back home" willing to accept periodic long-distance calls from the runaway wanting to check in; the probation officer arranges transportation back when the runaway is caught or asks to return. The probation officer acts as legal guardian for the child facing deportation as an illegal alien. The probation officer helps the boy reconstruct the pattern of increasingly self-destructive behavior leading up to a near-fatal automobile collision. In a magnanimous gesture of physical self-debasement, the probation officer props up the boy who cannot stop vomiting in the holding cell after an arrest for public drunkenness.

The probation officer can do little before the fact to spare children from such trials. As one probation officer observes, "everybody learns the hard way anyway. . . . You figure time is really the cure for all kids." But as another claims, those children who develop close attachments to their probation officers may be willing to reform their behavior as a result.

> The kids know you're there. And when they finally start trusting
> you, when all the anger and the hate is worked through . . . that's
> when the kids will really make changes because they're making
> changes for you as much as they are for themselves. You can use
> that. You have to be careful that it doesn't become a dependency
> kind of thing. . . . But I've seen kids make some real progress
> that's lasted for years and years afterward, and it's because they
> were doing it for me, because they knew that I expected them to
> be able to function on a higher level than they were functioning
> and they didn't want to disappoint me. . . . And that's what it's all
> about.

Most children of course do not develop such close attachments to their probation officers. Some probation officers take forceful action to foster desired changes in children's behavior. In one case, a probation officer personally delivered a chronic truant each day to and from the alternative school he found for her, assuring that she would not leave by confiscating her shoes. A different probation officer, tired of waiting for a child to unlock the bedroom door each morning when the probation officer dropped by to bring him to school, finally removed the door.

For the most part, however, the probation officer can only attempt to persuade the child that change is in his or her own self-interest. Probation officers learn to avoid casting struggles of will with children in terms of winning and losing, since the motivation to change has to come from the children themselves. For some, this requires a triumph over their own will: "It's something I have to learn over and over again. . . . It's just

117

part of my nature. In times of stress, I slip into being authoritarian. . . . Then I have to pull myself up to being more rational."

"Providing the Tempo"

Yet recognizing the self-motivated nature of change does not diminish the significance of the role probation officers assign themselves—shaping children's motivation to change by making them feel anxious enough about the prospects of continuing in their old ways. "You have to make them feel more anxious about *not* changing than changing." One probation officer's description of the role is typical: "You manipulate their environment so as to raise their anxiety." The assumption underlying another probation officer's assessment of his caseload at a certain moment is instructive:

> The probation officers provide the tempo. Kids are coming in involuntarily. They are resistive. The probation officer has to provide the energy. You have to produce a crisis. Like now, my energy is low, so nothing is happening with my caseload. They're not getting any worse, but they're not getting any better either . . . except with one kid, who was picked up over the weekend on DWI [driving while intoxicated]. I've been trying to get him into alcohol treatment, but with no response. Now he's saying, "Gee, I'm a drunk—what can you do to help me?"

This assessment assumes that children need some sort of "crisis" to motivate them to reform their behavior, even if the probation officer must help manufacture one. This assumption is widely shared by probation officers.

The probation officer can appeal to the power of the court to help pressure the child to change. With recalcitrant children the probation officer's power to persuade is backed by the threat of coercive sanctions. However since that threat remains more formidable the less often it is actually invoked, probation officers hesitate to return children to court for violations of probation before first exhausting a graduated series of informal sanctions.

Their preference is to reinforce rather than supplant the parents' authority. They usually start by clarifying rules of proper conduct, negotiating explicit statements of appropriate behavior in the form of contracts between children and their parents, hoping to limit their own role to that of monitoring that contract. Sometimes the mere act of articulating or clarifying rules is sufficient to bring a child's behavior into line; in other cases, parents are able to exercise authority effectively with a minimum of encouragement, guidance, or support. When attempts to strengthen parental authority fail, or when the child flaunts the probation officer's authority by missing appointments, probation officers turn to the imposition of informal sanctions: making the child spend time in the probation office; setting earlier curfews; restricting the child to the house on weekends; assigning the child additional house chores. Unfortunately, many of these measures themselves depend on parental effectiveness for their implementation.

Probation officers return approximately half their children to court on charges of violating probation. Since it is impossible to supervise probationers who run away, chronically stay out all night, ignore court orders to participate in treatment, or repeatedly miss appointments, those behaviors automatically evoke such charges. In general, probation officers file a violation when they feel that they "don't have a child's attention" or that they want to get the child "unstuck." Some probation officers are especially prone to file a violation in the very beginning of a period of probation, to impress the probationer with their seriousness. Others prefer to wait, to build a more damning case before returning to court. If the primary purpose is to impress the child, the probation officer may want the judge to impose a fine or community service, to extend the period of probation, or simply to present a stern lecture.

Yet all probation officers recognize the necessity to limit probation violations, because in a number of respects it is a Pyrrhic tactic for "hooking" kids. In light of all the recalcitrance probation officers are forced to countenance, it is difficult to justify an emphatic response to any particular set of violations. Probation officers cannot expect judges to do much; as one reasons,

> I'd bring a kid back to court for not paying restitution and often the judge wouldn't do anything. What are you going to do? Fine him? He can't pay restitution; he's going to pay the fine? A kid doesn't go to school. What's a judge going to do? Lock the kid up? He's not going to be in school [if he's locked up]. Curfews? You can't bring a kid back every time he misses a curfew.

Moreover, court appearances for any reason are time-consuming for the probation officer, due to the waiting involved. Probation officers cannot count on judicial hearings to produce the desired impressions on probation violators, nor can they afford the time.

Thus the tactic of returning a child to court has its only real effectiveness in the form of a threat. Probation officers may docket a hearing on violations weeks in advance, but offer to postpone or cancel the hearing (which can be done until the last moment) if the child's behavior improves. There is always the risk that the child will call the probation officer's bluff—persisting in the disapproved behavior and forcing an anticlimactic hearing—but the genuine uncertainty about the judge's reaction provides some inducement for the child to reform. One probation officer describes his bargaining stance toward the child: "My chips are taking you back to court to talk to the man who doesn't know you. It's much more in your interest to talk to me who knows you, to form a relation with me, because if you want to disregard that, you're going down for a half-hour interview with a guy who's only seen you once before—and that's because he found you guilty of something. That's a risk on your part."

There may be another casework purpose to be served by filing a probation violation, quite apart from any judicial disposition of the violation itself. Merely by filing the violation, the probation officer can arrange the child's admission to a juvenile detention home. Although a judge must decide the next court day whether to continue the child's confinement, judges most often agree with the probation officer's recommendation about short-term detention. Even if the probation violator receives no other sanction, the probation officer can virtually count on effecting some degree of punishment in this form. Detention is obviously a more powerful way to "get a child's attention" than merely bringing the case back to court; some probation officers use detention in this way to establish their authority at the very beginning of probation, while others reserve this treatment for repeated violations. One probation officer describes how she used detention to effect a "miracle cure" of a "very depressed" girl who refused to get out of bed in the mornings or pick up anything from the floor of her room, a "real monster" both at home and at school:

> I issued a detention order for her, and she was gotten out of bed by the police. . . . When I saw her in detention she was a nervous wreck. She really hated it. I doubt she would remember the last time anyone really said no to her and was able to enforce it. She didn't like being cooped up, and she didn't like being one of those criminals, and she didn't see herself as one of those kids. She was shaking. She wanted out, and I just told her, "well, if you want out of here you have to come up with some reasons why you should be out in the community. You need to follow your mother's rules. . . . The bottom line is, you're going to have to do certain things or you're going to stay locked up." So I went away, and I said, "You think about it and make me a list of why I should rec-

ommend you get out of here." And she did—she made some contact with her mother, and she had a history of things she was
going to do. . . . And she never had any more trouble.

In especially exasperating cases, such as those of chronic runaways,
probation officers may feel their only recourse is to try to "wear the child
down" by returning him or her time after time to detention (perhaps in
a nonsecure facility, as prescribed by law). But detention as a short-term
punishment is another tactic yielding diminishing returns—less effective in practice than as a threat. Children adapt to the regimen of detention, so any "shock value" wears off after a day or so of their initial stay.
Prospects of detention cease being fearsome to "veterans" who have
learned to normalize the experience.

With recalcitrants, then, the threat of coercive sanctions provides necessary but hardly sufficient grounding for the probation officer's power
to persuade. With recalcitrants no less than with children who identify
strongly with their probation officers, it is necessary to develop relations
of trust. Success in achieving this trust is evidenced by the overwhelming proportion of children who consent to appear "voluntarily" for court
hearings at which their probation officers have informed them of their
intention to seek detention. Probation officers jealously cultivate repu-
tations for dealing with children in a "straight" and "up-front" manner.
Children and parents often leave juvenile court proceedings with questions about exactly what happened and with what effect. They depend
on probation officers for explanations, which probation officers strive to
provide as openly as possible. From the outset, they make explicit what
children can expect from "the system," the kinds of consequences they
can expect for certain types of behavior. "I try to be an advocate for
kids—dealing honestly with them, alerting them to decisions they have
to make, helping them keep their dignity in a lousy system." Probation
officers promise children inviolably not to surprise them in court, which
helps mitigate the resentment children feel when punished: not only
have they received fair warning, but they can construe the punishment
as the consequence of their own choice, according to terms identified in
advance. (A few children go so far when committed to state training
schools, for example, as to apologize to their probation officers for let-
ting them down.) Yet in presenting themselves as honest brokers between children and judges, probation officers in effect understate (to
themselves as well as to clients) their own discretion and the weight of
their recommendations as judicial agents. Paradoxically, the trust they
nevertheless enjoy as mediators complements and reinforces their authority to file violations.

Remaining Unhooked by Kids

Perhaps the most formidable obstacle to hooking kids is the probation officer's personal and professional need to avoid being hooked by kids in turn, despite the strong natural tendency for that to happen. Probation officers find themselves attached to many of the children with whom they work. They are thrust into parental roles with children who in fact or in effect have no parents of their own. In emergency situations, when it is impossible to find appropriate shelter for a child, the probation officer may bring the child home for short periods of time. Although exceptional, it is not unheard of for a probation officer practically to adopt a child.

However to survive in probation work beyond the phase of initial "burn-out," it is necessary to learn to conserve personal resources. Attending too conscientiously to casework obligations cuts deeply into personal time. Day in and day out, it is common for the probation officer to face such situations as attempting to comfort a girl resisting plans for an unwelcomed return home: "I was with her for an hour and a half at the foster home last night while she sat on the floor and cried. I felt sorry for her, but after an hour and a half I stopped being sorry and just felt tired and hungry and wanted to leave. It was nine o'clock and I hadn't eaten dinner."

The chronic tension between work demands and personal needs usually comes to a head a year or two into a probation officer's career, forcing the individual either to delimit casework involvement or to leave the job. A first-year probation officer reports: "I sat down and figured out one month that I had worked 232 hours but was only being paid for 160. I decided enough of that." Another probation officer recalls "getting fed up with it" after two years of similarly long work weeks; on the verge of tears, she confided that "I can't do it anymore" to her supervisor, who advised her she was "right on schedule" and would have to change the way she worked if she wanted to stay. She determined to observe a forty-hour schedule by reordering her weekly routine, seeing children primarily in her office or in school rather than in their own homes, and resisting intervention in clients' family "crises."

Substituting office appointments for home visits—a time-management strategy generally adopted by probation officers who find it necessary to limit their casework involvement—obviously entails the sacrifice of a certain intimacy with clients. Some probation officers, of course, opt to change jobs rather than curtail their level of involvement. A woman who gave up probation work after a year and a half explains: "My personality style is to get more involved than I should, and I don't think you can get really involved and do ... all the things you're supposed to do. ... There's too much to do, never enough time to do it." A man's desperate desire to get out of probation work after five years results from indecision about delimiting his professional involvement: "The hard thing is to maintain the proper balance between commitment and detachment. I'm always going in and out, back and forth between feeling 'I don't want to hear it, I'm burnt out, I want [some impersonal desk job],' and getting too close to cases—'Oh my God, what do we do?' "

Probation officers who stay on because they cannot find satisfactory ways to get out tend to "cruise" on the job, going through the motions with a lack of energy. One veteran probation officer confessed that she had to keep xeroxed copies of all the social investigations she wrote, because she would forget her recommendations almost immediately after submitting the written report to the court, and she would even forget the investigation subjects' names in the three days until the court hearing.

To disengage from unsustainable levels of involvement requires learning to separate clients' troubles from one's own, to moderate expectations of achievement, and to leave casework problems at the office. As a public official mandated to intervene in private, domestic affairs, the probation officer must take care to avoid being overwhelmed by a Pandora's box of children's and parents' problems. The realm of clients' private troubles is limitless, and there is no clear demarcation of the probation officer's public responsibility, since the social and psychological conditions underlying delinquency which define the purview of possible juvenile court intervention are also without bound. Supervisors and veteran probation officers caution new probation officers against accepting ownership over too broad a range of their clients' problems; as a new probation officer reports, "People tell me I get upset because I know too much about cases—things that go on with everybody's cases, but they don't know." Probation officers also learn the futility of efforts "to be all things to all people." "You can't handle this type of job if you take it all home or take it all personally. You can't solve all the problems that exist. Be thankful for the successes you do have."

Probation officers rationalize on professional as well as personal grounds their disengagement from unsustainable levels of involvement, claiming that by helping to dampen their "reactivity," disengagement not only helps preserve the objectivity of their decision making but also achieves clinical benefits. To reserve judgment about such crucial casework decisions as detention or removal from home, probation officers must constantly guard against the influence of parents, children themselves, and others. "Good p.o.'s can handle pressure and not react [in their] casework because of it, and that's really the key." This requires the insistent assertion of professional authority. "All people come in here wanting what they want, and you have to be able to say, 'I'm in charge, I know better than you do.' If you're not in charge, those people aren't going to get what they want out of the court."

In addition to asserting the independence of their judgment about axial casework decisions, probation officers resist more mundane attempts to undermine their professional distance in the form of requests for intervention in the day-to-day affairs of their clients. In general, probation officers see clinical benefits to resisting intervention on demand. They are wary of "feeding into" individual or family pathologies through overinvolvement, as they are of relieving individuals (parents or children) of responsibility for their own actions. New probation officers, who may be distressed when first finding themselves unable to respond to a number of different "crises" simultaneously, observe to their surprise how readily such crises tend somehow to resolve themselves unattended; veteran probation officers often make a point of waiting at least a day before responding to certain "emergency" calls, to avoid exacerbating tensions and to encourage the parties involved to take responsibility for devising their own responses.

7

Erratic Organizational Support

In relating to clients, probation officers assume professional and organizational roles rather than purely personal ones. Not only do they invoke "professional" status to avoid being hooked by kids even while attempting to hook them, they also operate as organizational actors, at once constrained and empowered by structures of administration and supervision. But the professional and organizational supports available to probation officers in the conduct of normal casework are limited, continually throwing them back on their own personal resources.

Although probation officers frequently refer to themselves as professionals, they cannot claim to satisfy the most stringent conditions of that status. Probation work appeals to no identifiable base of esoteric or specialized knowledge in the sense that law, medicine, or science do. Nor does it command high occupational prestige; probation officers commonly experience a degree of stigma in disclosing their occupation at private social gatherings, and many aspire to the "superior" status of lawyers or psychologists. Neither do they operate autonomously, accountable only to their peers; rather, they are subject to both bureaucratic and judicial supervision. Nor do they experience a feeling of collective identity. Probation officers often complain of how isolated they are even from colleagues in their own work unit, how unfamiliar with others' methods in the same job.

Ineffective Supervision

The training, skills development, casework consultation, and oversight that probation supervisors can offer are limited in scope. Probation officers receive neither training nor consultation about clinical casework issues at all. And since so many administrative matters are handled in an ad hoc manner, it is not even possible to provide complete training in organizational process. Discussing the need to initiate future probation officers more effectively, a group of probation officers characterized the substance of their own orientation as "Here's your caseload, do it." Probation supervisors can inform new workers of procedural mechanics and the range of services available through the established referral network. Beyond that, however, even the supervisors expect probation officers to let their own experience be their guide. Assessing the career prospects of his workers, a probation supervisor notes, "The ones who need direction don't make it; if you know what you want, you can learn to play the system." Probation officers concur: "It's a job where you have to be comfortable with ambiguities." New probation officers seek out more experienced colleagues for consultation about difficult casework issues as they encounter them. One explicit criterion for promotion to higher rank as a probation officer (expected after the first year on the job) is independence of supervisory guidance. In considering proposed changes to job definitions and requirements for the various ranks of probation work, the court's probation officers (a majority of whom themselves had master's degrees) unanimously objected to substituting a master's degree for a year's experience in probation casework.

Probation supervisors meet regularly with each probation officer to review the results of social investigations, case plans, and the progress of cases. These conferences help probation officers organize and focus their casework, and since probation supervisors are free from the emotional reactivity of direct involvement, these conferences add an element of dispassionate consideration to casework decision-making. Supervisors may suggest exploring alternative casework options or gathering additional information. They may, for example, encourage a probation officer to work more with a family before considering removal from home; or conversely, they may encourage removal from home, feeling that a probation officer's efforts are being wasted. Among other things, supervisors try to counter the effects of children "hooking" probation officers: mindful of aggregate workload levels, supervisors may pressure probation officers to close cases the probation officers want to keep active of children the supervisors consider either beyond help or unneedful of further court services.

Probation supervisors exercise casework oversight most directly through the requirement that they approve all probation violations and detention orders filed by their workers. Although supervisors routinely question such actions, sometimes finding them premature, rarely do they withhold approval from an insistent probation officer. Approval for probation violations is virtually automatic. Supervisors are more skeptical of detention—which according to legal statutes should be reserved for serious criminal offenders dangerous to themselves or others—in view of probation officers' natural tendency to employ detention as a punishment for recalcitrance. Even so, the statutory criteria for detention are vague enough to allow considerable discretion in any particular case. The primary supervisory strategy for controlling detention use is to track each worker's detention usage, publicizing that information within the probation unit.

Of course probation officers take their supervisors' suggestions seriously, usually—if perhaps only upon reflection—coming to agree with them. As a general rule, however, in instances of disagreement the supervisor must honor the probation officer's decision, since the probation officer answers directly to the judge, who reserves the ultimate authority of decision. The supervisor conducts the probation officer's annual employee evaluation, but all court employees serve at the pleasure of the chief judge. Even when denied a detention order through established administrative procedures, for example, the probation officer can appeal to the judge. Conversely, no supervisor can effectively buffer the probation officer against a judge's displeasure. Indeed probation officers are more directly familiar than their supervisors with various judges' casework preferences.

Although probation officers do not operate autonomously, and there is no body of professional knowledge or skills to inform their judgment, they learn through bitter experience to follow their own instincts. "I've found that . . . I should always trust my gut because I know the cases better than [my supervisor]. . . . The two or three times I've done what he's suggested rather than what I wanted, it didn't go right." The lore of probation work is replete with examples of disastrous disregard for the worker's better instincts. Despite misgivings, one probation officer let a boy off with only a warning for possessing marijuana at a probation appointment; two and a half hours later, the boy killed someone during an armed robbery. Another probation officer did not object to a new judge's unsure decision to release a boy to his parents, despite the probation officer's recommendation for emergency institutionalization, based on an urgent sense of the boy's distraught state; the boy committed suicide that night. (Judges too learn to trust their own convictions in similar fashion. One judge recalls serving as a guardian ad litem in a child abuse case during the early stages of his legal career, well before ascending to the bench. Stifling his reservations in deference to the unanimity of others, he agreed to return the child to parents known to have abused the child's sibling; six months later, the child was dead from abuse.)

Probation supervisors devote a major share of their energies to enforcing the expanding requirements for administrative paperwork, which they no less than their workers regard as superfluous to the task of probation. Case plans and narrative case summaries, the most time-consuming types of paperwork, are often completed long after the fact. It is not surprising to hear a probation officer returning from a two-week vacation in September resolving to tackle the paperwork put off since July. Many probation officers only get around to the paperwork on a case as they prepare to close it, since supervisors will not allow them to close cases unless the paperwork is complete. (As a result, the administrative closing of cases often lags significantly behind the effective closing.) Similarly, the triennial audit of case records by the state Department of Corrections stirs a predictable frenzy of past-due paperwork.

Paperwork only detracts from time spent directly with children. A few probation officers who manage to stay abreast of their records report that their casework is better organized or more oriented toward tangible goals as a result. Most others, however, regard paperwork as simply a nuisance: a case plan is a mechanical exercise to be finished as quickly as possible, then ignored. One probation supervisor inquired of his staff in unit meetings why "60 percent of case plans are nonsense." Privately the supervisor offers his own explanation:

> It almost doesn't matter what our analysis of the underlying problems is; the strategy is to work with the family and the school. Right now, I'm being lax in my review of case plans. I'm just trying to get people used to getting them in on time. But in a few months, I'll start to examine their rationality again, by asking probation officers to justify their objectives and strategies in terms of their analyses of problems. "If you see this as the problem, why is this your strategy?"

Though perceived as largely irrelevant to casework, paperwork represents a growing burden on probation officers' time. Over the period of a decade, the introduction of quarterly case plans and other forms of paperwork increased this burden fourfold by some estimates, or by about ten hours a week. Requirements to plan and document casework more fully reflect the increased formalism of juvenile justice, accompanying the emphasis in case law on greater due process for juveniles. More directly, however, the introduction of case plans and other forms of casework documentation results from the drafting and expansion by the state Department of Corrections of detailed minimum standards for the operation of local court service agencies. Although the promulgation of these standards has produced little appreciable effect on casework practice, it has imposed a measure of administrative overhead. The irrelevance of paperwork requirements to probation casework corresponds in large degree to the ineffectiveness of the state's oversight efforts, which are almost purely ceremonial in nature.

Ceremonial Oversight

The state Department of Corrections certifies local court service units on the basis of three-day audits conducted every three years by teams drawn from the staffs of other court service units, auditors who can look forward within short order to being the objects of similar audits themselves. The audits consist primarily of examining procedure manuals and case files, rather than observing actual operations. The court service unit under study itself selects the case files to be reviewed by the certification team; court service staff are not only allowed but even encouraged to review and revise these files to make them more presentable. The certification team judges the quality of the documentation more than the quality of the casework itself. Thus, for example, when the court service unit was found to be violating a requirement for at least monthly contacts with parents of probationers, probation supervisors instructed their staff not necessarily to make the contacts, but merely to include in their monthly casework narratives pro forma explanations for not doing so. Court service administrators learned from the certification team that no courts around the state were in actual compliance with that particular standard; in effect, the only requirement was explicitly to document and rationalize—however superficially—the failure to satisfy it.

In similar fashion, the certification team reviews a procedure manual frantically revised expressly for their benefit during the weeks immediately preceding the audit. This procedure manual is all but unknown to the court's own line staff. Each probation office is required to have its own copy of the manual; typically, that copy arrives hot off the press just ahead of the certification team. Probation officers are oblivious to many policies and procedures stated in the manual, some of which cannot reasonably be observed in practice, such as a general prohibition against transporting children in private vehicles.

The Department of Corrections also requires local court service agencies to report monthly workload levels. The state officials responsible for implementing the reporting procedures openly conceded that workload standards were established arbitrarily, that reporting policies would vary from one locality to the next, and that since the state did not have administrative staff to monitor the localities' reporting practices, the reports were essentially self-reports.

Administrative Drift

Assuring that the court fulfills even the ceremonial oversight requirements imposed by the Department of Corrections is a nonnegligible
task for the court's administration. As in any formal organization, the
dual task of administration is both internal and external—coordinating
the efforts of court staff toward a common goal, on the one hand, and
buffering environmental threats and uncertainties on the other. The
ceremonial nature of the oversight the court must satisfy and the unde-
veloped nature of the court's technology pose no less a challenge for
court administration than *institutional* leadership. As Philip Selznick
notes, "Leadership is most needed among those organizations, and in
those periods of organizational life, where there is most freedom from the
determination of decisions by technical goals and methods" (1957: 16–
17). As characterized by Selznick, "leadership in administration" is primarily an enterprise of establishing an institution's identity and integrity,
by defining and implementing institutional goals that are neither opportunistic nor utopian, in recognition of the institution's distinctive
competence.

In Selznick's analysis, the inability of court administration to articulate a meaningful set of organizational goals indicates an abdication of
leadership. Court administrators and supervisors labored individually
and in committee for hundreds of hours over many months, under the
guidance of a management consultant, to produce a set of "mission statements" that amounts to little more than a grand tautology; these statements are reproduced in table 7.1.

The vagueness and ambiguity of these statements serve an administrative purpose antithetical to institutional leadership—that of opportunistic growth. Court administration has been successful in its pursuit
of growth. Over the course of a decade, while the total population of the
jurisdiction served by the court increased less than 20 percent and the
juvenile population actually declined, the court's staffing level increased
two and a half times and its budget increased even more than that in real
terms, due to the addition of a full range of community and residential
programs. By refraining from identifying any distinctive competence for
the court, court administration has been able to play on ambivalent and
shifting public attitudes in seeking resources. In the seventies, court administrators could appeal to the social welfare ideology of federal funding sources for program expansion; in the eighties, administrators could
appeal instead to the law-and-order sentiments of state legislators.

The development of an outreach detention program illustrates the
opportunistic nature of this strategy for expansion as well as the ad hoc

Table 7.1 Agency, Subagency, and Division Mission Statements

The mission of the . . . Juvenile Court is to provide efficient, effective and equitable judicial and court service programs which promote positive behavioral changes for those children and adults who come within the court's authority, to act in conformance with orders of the court, the provisions of law as contained in the Code, case law, and Department of Corrections Minimum Standards, consistent with the well-being of the client, his/her family, and the protection of the community.

Judicial Administration Mission: To provide efficient and effective judicial services for those children and adults who come within the Court's authority to act, in conformance with the provisions of law as contained in the Code, case law, State Supreme Court policies, and the protection and well-being of the community.

Court Service Unit Mission: To provide efficient and effective Court Service programs for those children and adults who come to the attention of, or are referred to the unit, in conformance with orders of the Court, the provisions of law as contained in the Code, case law and Department of Corrections Minimum Standards, consistent with the well-being of clients, their families and the protection of the community.

Administrative Services Division Sub-Mission: To receive, process, complete and evaluate all fiscal, financial, budgetary, personnel and data management activity as required for the efficient operation of the Court Service Unit.

Probation Services Division Sub-Mission: To provide to children, adults and families community, social, rehabilitative and correctional programs and services that meet Department of Corrections standards and statutory and judicial requirements.

Residential Services Division Sub-Mission: To provide efficient, effective, accredited residential care programs and services to those youths and their parents who come within the Court's authority to act and who require such services.

SOURCE: Agency document.

nature of policy planning and implementation. Outreach detention was proposed to be a program of intensive supervision in lieu of secure detention. The court director acceded to pressure from various citizen groups and the regional office of the state Department of Corrections to seek such a program, even though his real interest was approval for a new secure detention home. He consented to establish an outreach program because he held the well-founded expectation that even with a full gamut of "alternatives" to secure detention, the old detention home would remain overcrowded. He consequently submitted a request for federal Juvenile Justice and Delinquency Prevention (JJDP) funds for three outreach workers. Just before the award of the grant, he received a call from the state agency responsible for disbursing those funds, explaining that the state was left with an embarrassing surplus and asking him to accept six workers instead of three.

The court director devoted several meetings with his probation supervisors to the issue of how to use these workers; at first, no one could think of a useful function for them. The six workers were assigned to work as a subunit of the court's intake department. In the early months of the program, they had so little to do that they fought each other for each new referral. Finally after anxious deliberation, the intake supervisor and outreach director came upon the idea of having outreach workers cover detention hearings for probation officers; not only would this give outreach workers something to do, it would also give them the opportunity to recommend judicial assignment of children to the program.

The program goal as stated in the original grant application, expressing the intention of the Department of Corrections, was to divert status offenders from secure detention. With the addition of three extra workers, however, the program assumed the capacity to serve many more youths than there ever were status offenders detained in the first place. The reasons judges found to use the program not only undermined the program's intended purpose but also created difficulties for the court's probation officers. Some judges developed greater confidence in the outreach workers, with whom they worked more closely on troublesome cases, than in the regular probation staff. Judges assigned criminal as well as status offenders to outreach detention whenever they felt a need for immediate, intensive supervision, or whenever they distrusted the performance of a probation officer. As a result, according to an evaluation I performed, the program failed to reduce the level of detention use; if anything, by subjecting children who would not otherwise have been detained to intensive supervision, it produced precisely the opposite effect. In the first year of the program's operation, over 40 percent of those children initially assigned to outreach subsequently experienced secure detention, while fewer than 30 percent of those detained in the first place were ever readmitted to detention.

For their part, probation officers could not rely on outreach workers to make the recommendations they wanted at detention hearings. Probation officers found it awkward to inherit the cases of children who had participated in outreach detention; the parents of those children expected greater frequency of contact than probation officers (whose average caseloads were about seven times heavier than those of outreach workers) were able to provide. Outreach workers also tended to convey unrealistic expectations about the types of services probation officers would be able to arrange.

As Selznick suggests, the sort of administrative opportunism evidenced by the addition of an outreach detention program has serious consequences in the form of institutional drift, the attenuation and confusion of organizational character. "Attenuation means that the sought-for distinctive competence becomes vague and abstract, unable to influence deeply the work of staff and operating divisions. . . . A confused organization character is marked by an unordered and disharmonious mixture of capabilities" (1957: 145). Other of the court's own specialized programs founded with federal grant monies similarly contribute to a "disharmonious mixture of capabilities."

The therapeutic orientation of the court's family counseling program, for example, conflicts with the correctional orientation of probation work. Modeled after a particular school of family systems therapy, the court's family counselors work only with parents, rarely if ever seeing the children whom probation officers supervise. Probation officers resent family counselors' principled insistence on keeping confidential the contents of their sessions with parents, even as the probation officers seek desperately to discover the sorts of information which parents withhold from them. Probation officers resent also that if the parents' refusal to cooperate with family counseling requires returning the case to court, the probation officer rather than the family counselor is responsible to do so. In seeking more immediate results from intervention, probation officers tend to confront parents overtly about problems of theirs affecting children's behavior, while such confrontation is counterproductive to the longer-term strategies employed by family counselors for reconfiguring family systems. In one instance of a probation officer and family counselor working at direct cross-purposes, the probation officer accused a father whose self-esteem the family counselor was trying to strengthen of being "a worthless alcoholic." Both workers recognized the son's need for alcohol treatment; the probation officer sought to convince the boy of his evenhandedness by recognizing that his father shared the problem, while the family counselor sought to alleviate the father's guilt over forcing the boy into treatment.

Problems of external coordination mirror internal ones. Just as court administration fails to produce a harmonious mixture of capabilities within the court, so it fails to produce a harmonious mixture of capabilities among the court and the other agencies within its organization-set. The juvenile court operates in a political context of vague and contradictory federal laws which induce related local agencies to defend parochially narrow definitions of their separate domains against the transcendence of common service ideals. A major challenge of administration is to buffer an organization against the institutional and technical threats and uncertainties of its environment. In the case of a juvenile court, the challenge is to develop administrative procedures for routinizing interagency exchange, through appeal to those ideals. Just as administrators inherit this challenge from politicians who choose to pass it down the line despite their more advantageous position for addressing it, so administrators tend to displace the task in turn to their workers on the line. Appearing before the court's probation officers, who had begun assembling on their own each month to identify and discuss issues of mutual concern, the court director responded to a question about interagency relations by saying he knew less than they about such issues. At a time when the schools were disrupting normal casework by routinely refusing to cooperate with the court or Department of Social Services in providing special education services to educationally handicapped children in need of foster care, the court director reported that the major concern of his meetings with school officials was the production of a slide show publicizing various joint school-court projects to civic groups; he was oblivious to any interagency conflict over special education.

Passive-Aggressive Relations among Agencies

Abdicating administrative coordination of interagency relations has consequences for organizational character as serious as those of abdicating intraagency coordination. As brokers of services and punishments, probation officers are dependent on a network of community agencies. Even without formal channels of interagency cooperation, probation officers must work in concert with school, welfare, mental health, and police officials among others. The absence of administrative coordination forces probation officers to develop their own personal contacts, through the informal exchange of favors, for conducting interagency affairs.

The formal behavior of other community agencies is routinely evasive or dilatory. To deny special education eligibility the schools are inclined to claim that students are socially maladjusted or chronically truant. Even if they do grant eligibility, the decision-process takes the better part of a year; it can take months for a school psychologist to produce an evaluation based on a single testing session. Guidance counselors have too little time for college-bound students to bother with nonachievers; school officials offer the latter group release from compulsory school attendance or participation in the euphemistically named "school furlough program." School attendance officers, required to report truants to the juvenile court, wait until so late in the spring that the schools can claim there is no longer any reason for attendance at all that year. Nor do the schools necessarily respond in a timely manner to probation officers' simple requests for attendance checks; in one instance, it took four weeks—until the end of a quarter—for a probation officer to discover that a new probationer had not attended school at all.

The Department of Social Services (DSS) is similarly reluctant to provide foster care for "delinquent" children. Chronically short of placement facilities, understaffed, and unable to retain experienced workers, DSS screens most stringently the "appropriateness" of children referred by the court. Even after agreeing with a probation officer on the futility of their patient attempt to keep an abused thirteen-year-old girl at home by working with her parents, a protective services worker went into court to argue that the girl was too "old" for foster care. Juvenile court judges have the unquestioned authority to order DSS to assume custody of children for foster care. Yet DSS asks probation officers to submit their referrals to the court's diagnostic team, where DSS representatives can dispute their appropriateness, before submitting them to the judges. Citing the lead time required to make foster care arrangements, DSS requests sufficient advance notification of impending court referrals; yet foster care supervisors and agency attorneys are likely to use this time to prepare arguments against accepting the referrals. They request continuances of certain hearings involving custody determination to gain still more time.

Judges often order probation for children even while assigning their custody to DSS for foster care placement, to ensure that DSS will not lose track of their cases. This concern is especially well founded for the many cases handled by new or part-time foster-care workers. It is not unusual for a child to languish in a detention home for months on end while the foster-care worker—beset daily by more urgent demands to arrange immediate shelter for other children—fails to exercise the concerted effort required to arrange long-term placement. Because the probation officer's role of instilling accountability is unstated, the combination of probation and DSS custody produces inevitable tensions over the division of responsibility and authority. One caseworker winds up doing most of the work, while the other may object to the choice of placement. Probation officers complain that the inexperienced foster-care workers seem to pursue only one placement possibility at a time rather than several, while the veterans may be such "movers" that they ignore the suitability of placements they arrange. Since their agency provides the funding, DSS supervisors in turn often object to the selection of a particular placement by a probation officer, even if the probation officer does most of the work. DSS commonly seeks relief of the custody of absconders or children who disrupt their placements, docketing cases for judicial review without necessarily notifying the probation officers involved.

Although judges may order children and parents into therapy, community mental health centers employ their own criteria in deciding which persons to accept into treatment. Therapists restrict treatment to motivated, voluntary participants, choosing to reject some adolescents who "act out" or exhibit "character disorders," or who simply do not fit into existing therapy groups. They also ignore court orders in prescribing courses of treatment. One therapist, for example, unilaterally excused a child from a judicially ordered program of drug counseling which the therapist considered "redundant." Another therapist refused to discuss parenting issues with a couple ordered into treatment while their child was removed to foster care; since the child was out of the home, the therapist insisted on dealing only with marital issues as the condition of accepting them as clients.

Even if a mental health center does eventually consent to extend services, it is only after an inordinate delay. The wait for an intake appointment runs at least six weeks; the waiting list for service is about six months long, and only parents who persist in their inquiries receive offers of service at all. "Emergency" treatment—for especially dire situations, or especially insistent parents—is available for short periods only. An official court referral form was not honored (probation officers quickly discontinued its use); indeed, probation officers advise their clients to conceal court involvement from mental health intake counselors altogether, so as not to retard the admissions process even further. It is common for a child's probation to terminate before treatment at a mental health center ever begins. In similar fashion, judicial requests for psychological evaluations and recommendations often go unanswered. An interagency procedure for designating certain of those requests as "emergencies" broke down when judges, realizing that they could get timely responses only by invoking the procedure, resorted to making all requests on that basis.

Public bureaucracies are passive-aggressive in defense of their organizational boundaries. This is a particularly effective strategic style, impervious to direct formal challenge. Even judges willing to engage the schools over the provision of special education services, for example, concede the issue of compelling service to be a standoff. Clinical diagnoses and eligibility determinations are conditioned by the larger politics of agency funding; as demonstrated by the "special cases" described in chapter 5, even broad legal challenges of restrictive policies yield only ad hoc settlements. It is impossible to routinize reversals of an agency's denials of service, since it is always extraordinary to overturn a diagnostic judgment exercised within an agency's own specialized realm of authority and expertise. Just when probation officers were beginning to attain some success in appealing special education eligibility decisions, for example, the schools adopted a new set of diagnostic guidelines, which they refused to reveal to outsiders. Under any circumstances, however, the incongruity of probation officers having to argue such diagnostic issues indicates how stubbornly each agency's official posture of evasion is entrenched.

Official Duty through Exchange of Personal Favor

Defended agency boundaries are permeable to the personal contacts of line workers linked by networks of informal exchange. Denied access through formal administrative channels to necessary resources controlled by related agencies, line workers develop interagency networks of personal contacts for the informal barter of information and services. Probation and police officers, school, welfare, and mental health workers are prohibited by rules of confidentiality from divulging information about mutual clients without formal permission by the clients themselves. Yet since each worker needs the others' information, personal networks form in part to exchange that information.

Each agency has its own strictures of confidentiality. Confidentiality is integral to the very founding purpose of the juvenile court as a separate, civil court not-of-record to shield juveniles from the full rigors of adult law. Confidentiality is similarly integral to the therapeutic technique practiced by mental health centers. Federal statutes—notably the Privacy Act of 1974—safeguard the confidentiality of individuals' welfare and educational records, as well as juvenile court and mental health ones.

Technically then, school officials should only divulge student information to probation officers on the basis of release forms signed by the students and their parents, and probation officers should protect the identities and records of their clients. Informally, however, probation officers and school officials exchange all sorts of information about children: their family situations, their hangouts, whom they date, what kinds of relations they have with their friends, whether they are suspected of using or selling drugs. To keep abreast of children's attendance, classroom performance, and attitudes, probation officers consult regularly with a range of school personnel, from assistant principals to school security officers to secretaries. Since this sort of information about students is often fragmented within each school, probation officers not only seek out a number of different sources, but also learn to identify the particular individuals best informed about student life. If the guidance counselor does not know what is going on, there is usually someone—a shop teacher perhaps—who does. A quick phone call from the school to report a class cut that day can help the probation officer make a powerful impression on a child. By the same token, the school might wish to know the nature of a student's court involvement if any. Many probation officers would guard the secrecy of this information, but others would respond to inquiries of this sort from trusted school officials.

Mental health workers as a rule are reticent toward probation officers with whom they share clients. The few therapists who represent an exception to this rule attract many referrals from probation officers, who may receive in return such assistance as casework consultation, calls alerting them to dangerous changes in behavior, informal handling of probation violations outside of court, and expert testimony when disputed cases must be returned to court. But most mental health workers guard the confidentiality of their therapeutic relations so jealously as to resist the attempts of probation officers even to check the attendance of court-ordered clients. All mental health centers require signed permission to release any client information; some centers will answer probation officers' inquiries over the phone on the basis of general release forms on file, while other centers require the presentation in person of release forms specific to each information request.

While the reticence of mental health therapists toward probation officers is unreciprocated, the reticence of police officers is not. Mutual distrust is as great a barrier to the communication between police and probation officers as concern for confidentiality. The unwillingness of either party to divulge information rests on a perception of the other's unwillingness to listen. Probation officers avoid cops they feel are only out to make arrests, while police officers avoid probation officers they feel only coddle criminals. Either party can gain the confidence of the other by disconfirming these negative stereotypes: police officers by showing interest in children's life situations and attempting informal responses before formally arresting children; probation officers by holding children accountable for their deeds in some manner, following up on police referrals and charges, and apprising police officers of case outcomes.

The cop and the probation officer are in positions to help each other. They can aid each other's investigations. The arresting officer can provide details of the crime for which a child is under social investigation by the court, as well as a child's history of informal police contacts. The police investigator can test the plausibility of a suspicion by running it past the probation officer. The cop and the probation officer can help each other exercise surveillance. The probation officer can warn of the return to the streets of a child who had been placed out-of-home; the cop can serve as "the eyes in the neighborhood, day and night," providing evidence of probation violations by reporting children seen in the company of certain others, in certain locations, and at certain times of night. The cop can also tip off the probation officer about investigations of possible new offenses. Perhaps most significantly, each can contribute "bits and pieces" of information—not only about crime and attitude, but also about family situation, peer group, school performance, and employment status—affording the other a more complete picture for evaluating the child's moral progress.

The informal favors probation officers exchange with members of other community agencies include personal services as well as information. County police officers, for example, often travel far out of their way to file charges at an outlying probation unit instead of the court's specialized intake unit, in order to circumvent the legalistic standards and preference for informal disposition they encounter at Central Intake. Members of the outlying probation unit will grant petitions to police complainants automatically, accepting their allegations for formal judicial consideration, while expediting the requisite information-gathering and paperwork as much as possible.

As another type of favor, probation officers encourage children to cooperate with certain police investigators in either confessing their own crimes or informing about others'; probation officers often help investigators get hold of children they wish to interview, by either arranging meetings at the probation office, bringing children to the police station, or riding along with the police to pick up the children. As yet another favor, probation officers help administer informal sanctions to children the police are unable to bring to court. A boy on probation exploited his after-school job at an old-age home to rob many of its residents, who were however too infirm to press formal charges; even without formal court action, the probation officer arranged to send the boy to live with an out-of-state relative. Probation officers have the authority to bring children to court for probation violations without legally compelling evidence of new criminal behavior.

Police officers may reciprocate with a variety of favors. They may honor probation officers' intercessions either by relaxing their attention to probationers who may be experiencing undue harassment or, conversely, by exercising increased vigilance over probationers suspected of continued criminal activity. Police investigators may consult probation officers about how to handle new charges. In the case of a marginal offense, the police officer may be guided by the probation officer's opinion about whether to pursue formal court processing at all. If requesting formal court processing, the cop may follow the probation officer's preference about requesting a detention order or not. If the child has committed a number of new offenses, the police officer may agree to file a formal petition on just one of them. In court the police officer may endorse the probation officer's recommendation to the judge about final disposition.

Serving detention orders filed by probation officers is the job of the police. Yet the tendency for the police to ignore "kiddie detention orders" is so strong that it is considered a personal favor for an officer actively to serve one. Some police officers nonetheless go out of their way to do so, even if it involves the detective work of tracking down children on the lam. Even less proactive searches are appreciated. One probation supervisor, understanding how formal requests might routinely be ignored, made a point of dropping in on the local police squad's weekly roll call to ask squad members simply to look out for certain missing children they might come across on their rounds. Police officers could also repay favors by agreeing to pick up runaways, returned by other jurisdictions, at the local airport or bus station.

The services that probation officers trade with school officials are analogous to the ones they trade with cops. Probation units offer favored treatment at intake to school officials seeking to bring children to court for truancy or other alleged offenses. Probation officers also lend informal support to the schools' own processes for maintaining order. When called to the scene of serious incidents at school, probation officers respond by talking tough to the students involved and advising school officials about the appropriateness of court action. They accompany probationers on their return to school after periods of school suspension. Most dramatically, they can help school administrators signal a "get-tough" attitude to the student body by helping remove from school two or three designated troublemakers at a stroke. School administrators are constrained by administrative due process procedures from removing students as quickly as they would like; however if those students are also on probation, probation officers can detain them any time on violations and attempt to place them out of the community. Probation officers can also endorse school administrators' petitions to have the court release children from compulsory school attendance.

Probation officers benefit indirectly from helping to tighten discipline within a school, since it makes it easier to control drug use and truancy among their probationers from that school. Probation officers also benefit more directly through the favors they can request for "deserving" probationers in return, such as a second chance before school expulsion, a shorter period of school suspension, a change in class schedule to accommodate part-time job opportunities, a transfer to a new school for a "fresh start," or admission to a special school program. Conversely, school officials may be more willing to bring criminal charges (such as assault or school trespass) against children whose probation officers request them to do so. Favored probation officers are more likely to receive more timely responses to their requests for information from the school.

Probation officers assist Department of Social Services (DSS) counselors too with court intake and the use of informal sanctions to control children's behavior. Despite inherent tensions between caseworkers when probation coincides with DSS custody, the establishment of good personal relations is mutually beneficial. Probation officers can help maintain order within DSS placements by threatening or actually filing probation violations. When children on probation run away from DSS placements, probation officers can issue detention orders to get them back. Pooling DSS and court facilities increases the range and supply of short-term placements; children awaiting longer-term placement can stay in the court's detention or less-secure shelter homes as well as in DSS group and foster homes. Although subject to abuse, the availability of detention is especially useful to DSS because that agency commands relatively fewer short-term than long-term placements. The different agencies' caseworkers can divide the responsibilities of making application and arranging placement interviews at various residential institutions, transporting the children to those interviews, and maintaining regular contacts with the children and their parents after placement. Probation officers benefit from the readier availability of DSS funds for residential placement. They also gain access to case history information. DSS refuses on grounds of confidentiality to release copies of its records under any circumstances or even to allow outsiders to inspect them. However DSS counselors will divulge the relevant contents of those records to probation officers in person.

Developing a network of personal contacts with workers in other community agencies, then, is essential to probation work as the only way to circumvent the evasiveness of those agencies' official policies. It helps to have someone nudge another agency into cooperation from within. New probation officers learn relatively quickly which types of referrals to various agencies are "appropriate," judged by the fit of agency capabilities to client needs; veteran probation officers experience greater success than newcomers in their referrals because they know people to contact in the various agencies. Various probation officers call on different persons within the mental health center: one knows the center director, risen from the ranks, from the days when he was a lowly therapist; another knows an intake counselor from graduate school; yet another knows a therapist from conducting a group for disturbed adolescents with her; still another gets the court psychologist to intervene. Although there is no single person to contact within the mental health center to expedite the intake process, unless the probation officer finds someone to help, the client's wait for mental health service may be interminable. Similarly, probation officers who have personal relations with school eligibility officials claim to get timelier and more sympathetic eligibility hearings for their clients. At the least, personal contacts can provide probation officers with knowledge of the guidelines and procedures internal to other agencies.

For this reason, it is necessary to cultivate personal friendships with workers in those agencies. As one probation officer puts it:

> You have to take the energy to develop those kinds of relationships with school personnel and then you'll find that they can be real helpful to you, even as far as testing a kid and having them pursue it and follow through. If they don't see you except maybe once every six months, you don't have that kind of relationship with them, they don't feel the need to go that extra nine yards to maybe process something for you. . . . You're talking about developing working relationships.

Another probation officer resolved to improve personal relations with DSS workers when correctional funds for residential placements were suspended, increasing the court's reliance on DSS. Although angered and frustrated by the repeated refusals by DSS to assume custody of his clients, he "went through a phase of going over there and shaking hands," with the desired effect: "seven placements out of seven." Still another probation officer, stressing the importance of hand-delivering documents and referral forms right away, relates a similar formula for success: "It was just those personal kinds of touches." This probation officer had especially good relations with the mental health center. "Again, it was the working relation. . . . I was down there all the time, and I knew all the people personally, and when I gave them a particularly difficult case they knew I'd be down there with them." The lesson she draws is clear:

> If they think that you're no good, than they're not going to do anything for your kids either. And it's the whole thing with all the organizations. You have to sell *yourself*. After you've sold yourself, then you can get whatever services you need for the kids—but if you yourself don't have a personal relation with those agencies,

you can forget it as far as your kids getting anything. Which is not the way it should be.

As this probation officer suggests, a system of performing official duties through an exchange of personal favors has serious drawbacks. This practice depends on the receptivity and good faith of individuals working in other agencies. As probation officers learn through bitter experience, they must be discriminating in their contacts since they cannot take trustworthiness for granted. "There were some [DSS] workers who worked real well with probation officers and some who didn't." It is only beneficial to share information with a school official "who knows how to use it"; some school officials harass students they discover to be court-involved. It is a common refrain that police officers sort themselves into "good" cops and "bad" cops. "A lot of the investigators seem to be really concerned with kids and want to help them; the cops who weren't kid-oriented I wouldn't give the time of day." "You know if I had a kid who came to me and wanted to talk to a police officer and confess to something, there are police officers I would send him to. . . . I [also] run into cops who . . . malign the kids I work with terribly. . . . I tell them 'be careful of this guy; he'll do maneuvers, he's sneaky, he'll be dishonest.'" Some cops are "hard," "uncaring," "officious," and "vengeful"; there are cops probation officers "wouldn't accept information from."

In other words, it is often impossible to work out an exchange of favors. Even when it is possible, conducting interagency affairs by exchanging personal favors defeats the twin purposes of bureaucracy—efficiency and impartiality—that are served by the impersonal application of stated rules to large numbers of cases. In principle, agencies should dispense treatment according to a client's needs rather than the breadth of the caseworker's network of personal contacts. The practice of casework favors is particularistic, violating the bureaucratic norms of universalism and technical rationality.

This practice also abridges client rights of confidentiality and due process. When services are requested on grounds of personal favor, there is no recourse to their denial. The informal exchange of personal favors among caseworkers from different agencies which characterizes "normal" casework tacitly affirms the renunciation of formal challenge to official policies of interagency evasion which characterizes the "special" cases described in chapter 5. Why don't probation officers insist that judges simply order DSS to assume custody of certain children, which judges have the clear legal authority to do, even if DSS does not want to? Because, replies a probation officer, "you can't do that too often . . . without losing working relations with those people."

Similarly, a probation officer who insisted on dealing with other agencies in an adversarial manner not only aroused the wrath of other agencies, but was considered a maverick by fellow probation officers as well. Because he enjoyed the judges' confidence and pursued arrangements for residential placement more energetically and skillfully than DSS counselors, he not only convinced judges to order children into DSS custody for placement, but also got them to designate the placements he had already arranged, usurping the prerogative of DSS. Rather than following the usual channels for appealing denials of special education eligibility, he had the chief judge intercede directly with the director of schools.

> I operated under the principle, do for your kids what you can, and other agencies be damned. I approached it as an adversary process, rather than as a cooperative process, because the cooperative stuff I found doesn't work. . . . I'm not liked, probably, by a lot of different agencies because of the way I abused their processes and went around them. . . . As to what damage was done longer on down the road by that attitude, I don't know. . . . I did not have a good reputation for dealing with other agencies. I was a troublemaker.

His poor reputation in this respect spread within the court itself. In describing their ways of relating to other agencies, a number of fellow probation officers made a point of explicitly contrasting their methods with his.

8

Seeking Skeptical Approval

Not only is the system of juvenile justice and child welfare fragmented, its ideology and technology are incomplete. Even with the cooperation of other agencies, the set of treatments available for children is limited, and probation officers must still gain the support of judges and parents for their casework strategies. For children who cannot stay out of trouble at home, in the neighborhood, or in school, removal from home to residential institutions is the only recourse. Just as probation officers depend on other agencies for the casework resources they need, they depend on judges and parents for the legitimacy of their designs. Yet judges and parents often operate at cross-purposes, and the support each offers the probation officer is wavering and uncertain. Judges' policies are vague and inconsistent, and their legal orientation diverges from the casework orientation of probation officers. Parents are defensive about their own contributions to their children's problems, and ambivalent not only toward their children but also toward the court. Tensions among probation officers, judges, and parents derive not only from these structural differences in attitude and orientation, but also from the incomplete technology of juvenile justice, constraining treatment decisions to the limited set of options available.

Judges as Uneasy Allies

Communications between judges and probation officers seem especially strained by comparison with their memories of the court's pre-*Gault* days, when a single judge (himself a former chief probation officer) worked with a small probation staff out of a single office. The judge was intimately familiar with the nature of probation work and the situations of the court's relatively few probationers. He would discuss the circumstances of a case with the probation officer before each return to court, to predetermine not just the outcome but also the dramaturgic staging of the hearing. By his own description, the judge operated from the bench as a "surrogate probation officer." A boy who had brashly refused to come to the office to sign his probation rules, for example, suddenly found himself in detention under order of commitment to the state Department of Corrections, an order rescinded several days later when the boy begged for a second chance.

Since the extension of due process protections to juveniles mandated by *In re Gault* (387 U.S. 1 [1967]) and related U.S. Supreme Court decisions, relations between judges and probation officers have grown more distant and formal. The judge reflected that he had grown increasingly removed from clients as well as probation officers during a career of over two decades, so that ironically he became more dependent on the probation staff even as the intimacy which bred trust in them diminished. Probation offices are now stationed away from the courthouse, and most new judges are unfamiliar with the nature of probation work as they ascend to the juvenile court bench. Judges generally refuse to discuss with probation officers alone matters that may arise in open court, even though very new judges may request private guidance from probation officers before hearings. Yet the need persists for probation officers to communicate informally with judges: to convey delicate information awkward to disclose before children in open court, such as a mother's desire to relinquish custody of her child; to clarify the terms of an order; to amend an order formally issued in court, as indicated by a change in circumstances. Although probation officers seek out judges in chambers for these reasons, the logistics of schedule and courtroom security make it difficult for them to do so. Probation officers feel that children's attorneys have readier access to judges than they do.

These barriers to informal communication strain the formal interaction of the courtroom, forcing probation officers to adopt oblique presentational strategies. They adduce evidence they know to be inadmissible as a way of expressing their suspicions about such matters as drug abuse and parental fitness. For dramaturgic purposes of impressing probationers, they may make recommendations that they expect—and hope—judges to reject. Thus they may recommend commitment, hoping to lend credibility to a disposition of suspended commitment. This strategy entails the risk that judges will honor the stated recommendations; probation officers' real intentions may not be skillfully enough cued or sensitively enough received, or else judges may simply choose to disregard them. Probation officers also practice indirect strategies of courtroom persuasion. One probation officer explained that she never hazarded debatable recommendations directly, but rather sought to influence judges to conceive her tacitly preferred dispositions as their own, guiding their decision processes in part by subtle eye gestures.

Communication lapses erupt into overt expressions of courtroom tension between judges and probation officers. Court hearings are usually occasioned by emotional disagreements among the parties. Yet in the press of the daily docket, judges expect the probation officer to facilitate the dispatch of a case by providing concise, cogent analysis of a problematic situation in support of recommendations compelling enough to provide the basis of consensus among the parties. Judges express exasperation with probation officers whose courtroom presentations are not concise and cogent, or whose accounts do not seem dispassionate enough to command assent. It is especially damning in a judge's eyes for a probation officer to report what proves to be inaccurate information. One probation officer, for example, irrevocably lost credibility with a certain judge by reporting that a child had a history of shoplifting—because this report was based on a reference in a psychological evaluation to an incident that turned out to have occurred when the child was only five years old.

Court hearings move so rapidly that, for their part, probation officers learn to speak up quickly to assure themselves a full say before judges issue dispositions. Each hearing is divided into phases of fact-finding and decision, but hurried judges may collapse these phases unexpectedly. The issuance and transmittal of judicial orders are similarly rushed, with the result that the orders as stated verbally in the courtroom may not accord with the orders as documented in the legal records. (Dispositions entered in the court's computerized information system may be different still.) Since probation officers expected to implement orders may not even have been party to the hearings that produced the orders, it is common for probation officers to receive inaccurate orders or not to receive them at all. Yet judges castigate probation officers in open court for failing to execute their orders. Probation officers feel especially humiliated in front of the clients whose respect they need; even probationers, parents, and defense attorneys typically express sympathy for the probation officer after court in these situations by wondering out loud who was supposed to be on trial.

However the tensions that erupt into courtroom displays reflect not merely problems of communication, but deeper frustrations with the limited effectiveness of the court's authority. Although dependent on each other's actions for the consistency toward clients which establishes credibility, the divergent role-strains experienced by judges and probation officers lead each to regard certain of the other's expectations as unrealistic. Probation officers may neglect to enforce judicial orders that seem to them unenforceable, while judges may refuse to impose sanctions for noncompliance that seem to them excessive.

Although judges instruct probation officers to return cases to court for noncompliance with their orders, these judges may show annoyance when confronted with some returning cases—for what are they to do? For lack of motivation, a private psychologist refuses to treat a child the court has ordered into therapy; parents refuse to participate with their child in therapy, even though judicially ordered to do so; a community mental health center refuses to accord priority on the waiting list to a child ordered into treatment. Returning such cases to court just exposes the shallowness of the court's orders. Moreover, a probation officer weighs violations against the behavior pattern of an entire caseload and is aware of circumstances mitigating particular violations. A child resistant to court-ordered counseling may show good progress at home and in school; a child may violate a court order by playing truant, but at a lesser rate than other probationers at the same school. Nonetheless, probation officers leave themselves open to judicial rebuke should children spared from returning to court in such circumstances later face hearings for new trouble.

If probation officers are perhaps more reluctant than judges would like to return less-serious offenders to court for violations, judges are perhaps more reluctant than probation officers would like to revoke suspensions of commitment for probationers with more serious records. Judges, who are properly wary of committing children to state training schools, are especially hesitant to do so without evidence of serious new offenses. Yet probation officers lose leverage over children already under suspended commitment when judges fail to punish their probation violations; paradoxically, the more closely children flirt with commitment, the more infractions they learn they can get away with.

Judicial Inconsistency

Tensions between judges and probation officers are exacerbated by differences among the judges themselves. Judges disagree about matters of legal interpretation and sentencing policy. In a spirit of disputatious collegiality, they in effect agree to disagree about such issues as whether the juvenile court has the authority to preempt administrative reviews of service eligibility, or whether a child who has never been committed to a state training school is eligible to be sentenced "as an adult" to up to a year in jail. Judges attach divergent definitions to the legal emancipation of children from parental control. They establish varying standards of evidence for demonstrating probation violations, just as they disagree over how strict to make probation rules. Some refuse to sign or enforce rules prescribed by others. They also vary in their readiness to revoke suspensions of commitment for new infractions.

These differences among judges are especially troublesome to probation officers because, for reasons of docketing efficiency, cases do not necessarily return to the same judges for subsequent hearings, compounding problems of judicial inconsistency. Probation officers have no way of knowing in advance which judges they will draw for particular hearings; attempts at "judge shopping" through informal appeals to docket clerks are becoming increasingly futile. The judge who finds a child guilty and orders a social investigation may not be the one to decide the disposition based on the report of that investigation. This places the probation officer in a bind, since the various judges make conflicting demands about the specificity with which the concluding recommendations are to be presented in the report and are primarily interested in different aspects of a child's situation—one judge for example focusing on the child's psychological profile, another on the child's school performance. (Switching judges from one hearing to the next also means that judges often issue dispositions without benefit of all the evidence presented at adjudication hearings.)

In general, the random alternation of judges children encounter in successive court appearances conveys to them a sense of inconstant purpose about the court. In each hearing, a judge communicates to the child some schedule of tolerance, indicating consequences of subsequent offenses. Although not part of the official record, the judge typically states a clear warning about the "next time," the effects of which are lost if the child returns to court before a different judge. Indeed to the extent that judges adhere to different tolerance schedules, the message conveyed to the child at each court hearing contradicts the one from the hearing before. This is especially frustrating to probation officers who return children to court for probation violations or for new infractions after sentences of suspended commitment.

The general, well-founded reluctance to commit children to state training schools may lead each judge to give a child just one more chance, regardless of how many "last chances" the child has already received from other judges. The probation officer bears the burden of having to explain the entire history of a case to each judge anew. Despite such an explanation, each judge approaches the case fresh. In one case, for example, a probation officer desperately recommended commitment time after time for a girl who continually ran away to a life of prostitution and drugs. The girl had received every available form of community treatment and had even been "successfully" graduated from the court's residential probation house after a stay of nearly a year. Yet her self-destructive behavior persisted, so that the probation officer feared for her life. But since the only criminal offenses on her record were minor, it was only on the probation officer's fourth try that a judge would finally agree to commitment (which seemed to produce the desired calming effect on the girl).

Conversely, however, judges sometimes commit children despite their probation officers' recommendations against doing so. Probation officers too are reluctant to send children to state training schools. As one probation officer recalls his first commitment, he asked in court for the opportunity to continue working with a notorious family's child who had committed numerous burglaries, a boy he was "so attached to, I couldn't see he was a crook." "Can you give me one reason," inquired the judge, "why I shouldn't commit this boy? . . . By your silence you've answered me." Another probation officer did formally recommend commitment for a boy who had twice refused to admit himself to a residential drug treatment center, even though the boy had in the meantime arranged another entry date, because the probation officer wanted to remain true to his earlier threats to do so. Yet the probation officer couched his recommendation in terms clearly indicating to the judge that he really only wanted the boy ordered into treatment as a condition of suspended commitment. Considering the proposed drug treatment to be a waste of effort, however, the judge deliberately ignored the intent of the probation officer's ploy, choosing to accept the formal recommendation. As the probation officer noted after court, "I lost one."

Judges deviate from recommendations partly to correct for the attachments and frustrations they suspect of influencing probation officers toward undue optimism or pessimism about children's prospects. (Of course judges form sympathies and antipathies of their own toward children, which help form these suspicions.) Just as they sometimes disagree about commitments—and for much the same reasons—judges sometimes disagree with probation officers about judgments at the opposite end of the dispositional scale—about whether to continue children on probation or to close their cases. In certain instances, by extending terms of probation instead, judges emphasize their displeasure with probation officers' requests to close cases early. Judges are upset by inconsistencies among probation officers just as probation officers are upset by those of the judges. The wide variation in the gravity of violations particular probation officers typically report clearly reveals the inconsistencies among them.

To gain judges' assent for their recommendations, probation officers have to demonstrate that their casework plans are workable. A veteran probation officer recalls, "I would always try to have a pretty good plan when I went in [to court], one that offered the judge something . . . and usually if I had a pretty good plan, the judge would go along with it." A probation officer whose career started a decade later similarly found judges very supportive, "if . . . you had a good plan formulated." Confirming the experience of these probation officers, a judge estimates that he accepts 80 percent of recommendations, at least in general outline; according to his own analysis of the decision process, "you have to decide whether the treatment plan has any real possibility of working."

The provision of a seemingly workable plan serves the judge's immediate purpose in the courtroom—to assert authority without exciting the volatile emotions of the various parties involved, by projecting an impression of institutional fairness and competence. As one judge explained at a testimonial dinner for another, "a judge sees daily come into his courtroom people who are angry, emotional, or crazy; the point is to conduct the hearing in such a way as not to add to those feelings, but by rising above them, to reduce them a bit." At a training session for probation officers, another judge observed, "the cosmetic purpose is to make the proceeding look like it knows where it's going so as to inspire confidence and cooperation in children and parents, realizing that the hearing is part of a process." In a different account, the hearing is "an opportunity to let the parents know you know what you're doing, that if they're doing the right thing you're going to support them, if they're not, you're not going to"; the strategy toward parents is to "allow them to have something to say but make it clear that you're going to make the decision." Ostentatiously reviewing the probation officer's work contributes to the air of judicial authority and fairness.

Judges are nonetheless dependent on probation officers for the work of impression management they wish to accomplish in the courtroom. Probation officers can embarrass judges by bringing recommendations significantly different than those judges are prepared to affirm. A glaring divergence of opinion between the probation officer and the judge obviously undermines the presumption of institutional fairness and competence. It is especially awkward for judges to impose harsher punishments than probation officers request, because of the added resentment that provokes. Judges are known to express their displeasure with "unreasonably" lenient recommendations, either in open court or in chambers afterwards. In one case, for example, a probation officer recommended no more than probation and a fine for a purse-snatching by a seventeen-year-old first offender whom the judge sentenced instead to sixty days in jail, prompting the subsequent interrogatory rebuke, "we were way out of line there, don't you think?" Judges note that due to a gradual process of mutual accommodation, the discrepancy between probation officers' recommendations and their dispositions seems to narrow over the course of a judicial career.

The impression management judges seek can be upset by probation officers in another manner—by encouraging clients to appeal questionable judicial decisions to the circuit court, and even by offering to testify on their behalf. Probation officers occasionally resort to this tactic—as often as not successfully—to assert their own treatment recommendations. Not only does this undermine the authority of the juvenile court judges toward defendants, it also calls those judges to the attention of their colleagues on the superior bench in an unfavorable context.

Differences of opinion between judges and probation officers over particular cases also derive from the contrast between casework and legal orientations. Judges take greater account of offense seriousness in their treatment decisions than do probation officers. When departing probation officers describe to their successors the cases they are passing on, they focus on treatment histories and treatment needs to the virtual neglect of offense histories. A judge recalls his astonishment at observing deliberations of the court's diagnostic team as part of an orientation program during his first week on the job. The diagnostic team decided to recommend commitment as the only means of assuring a child a drug-free environment; to the judge's surprise, no one even mentioned the minor nature of the child's offense, possession of marijuana.

Vacillating Support from Parents

Parents are perhaps even more important than judges to probation officers, since they hold the key to relations with both judges and children. To the extent that probation officers can engage parents in support of their casework strategies, not only is it easier to gain judicial support, but it is less necessary to do so. Conversely, to the extent that probation officers alienate parents, their reliance on judges increases even as it becomes more precarious. "If you are opposed in court by parents, judges feel caught in the middle, needing to appease the parents." Similarly, parents exercise an obvious effect on the response probation officers can expect from children. "If you can get any cooperation from parents, you can get through to the kid, no matter how off-the-wall." Without changes in parents' behavior, attempts to change children's behavior may prove futile.

> The parents have the power. You get farther trying to get them to
> see their responsibility and getting them to make changes and

getting them calmed down, and then more often than not the kid
will fall into place. If you get the kid being real functional, and
you haven't really done anything with the parents, the kid won't
be able to sustain it very long because the parents will sabotage it.

Yet relations between probation officers and parents are easily
strained. While infringing on each other's claims to authority, parents
and probation officers each seek to disclaim "ownership" of children's
problems. The probation officer's very first task, to diagnose those problems, inevitably implicates parents in ways they find objectionable. The
majority of parents will not or cannot change their own behavior in ways
probation officers consider necessary. For their part, probation officers
can rarely fulfill the hopeful expectations judges transmit to parents in
initially assigning their children to probation. Parents grow increasingly
antagonistic toward probation officers during the course of cases in
which children's behavior does not improve, as issues arise of apportion-
ing blame for this failure. Parents in such cases gradually discover that
the court cannot deliver the services they want—and conversely, that
they do not want the services the court may order. Some parents, denying their children's troubles, resent the court's interference in their family
lives from the start. Other parents are too overwhelmed by their own
personal problems to concern themselves with their children at all. Still
others, men and women, seek to abdicate parental responsibilities in the
wake of marital dissolution.

Children whose parents are amenable to coaching and prodding constitute the "easy" cases. Simply by getting parents to pay more attention
to their children, define more reasonable expectations, or exercise more
consistent discipline, probation officers can alleviate problems that pro-
voke the most common complaints by parents about their children—
problems of disrespect, hours kept, or chores neglected. A few parents
need nothing more than reassurance from the court.

While preferring to work *with* parents, probation officers often wind
up working *around* and *against* them instead. No less than their adolescent children, parents experience the difficulties of separation. This leads
them to adopt alternating postures—equally troublesome to probation
officers—of rescuing and abandoning their children. At one pole are
parents who fabricate alibis for their children, harbor them as runaways,
or abet their escapes. In one case, just before a hearing for a string of
breaking and entering offenses, wealthy parents sent their son cross-
country to live for a year with relatives, denying any knowledge of his
whereabouts. Upon the boy's return they won dismissal of those charges
with the services of a high-priced attorney, who was able to emphasize

how much time had elapsed since the alleged offenses. (The boy there-
upon resumed his criminal pursuits, eventually serving a lengthy sentence in an adult penitentiary for a series of extremely violent acts,
despite beating charges of abduction and rape.)

At the other pole are parents whose undisguised purpose is to dump
their children on the state. "Do what you want with the child." "Lock
him up—that's fine with me." Adults seize upon children's transgressions to rationalize their abdication of parental responsibilities: a single
mother recoils from the daughter she learns is pregnant; parents expel
their daughter for alcoholism, refusing even to transport her from the
nearby foster home to weekly meetings of an alcohol treatment group; a
divorcee pleads financial distress to obtain public funding for the institutionalization of her "incorrigible" daughter, even while purchasing and
furnishing an expensive house; wealthy adoptive parents refuse to accept home or even help support in any way a son who, on returning
from a residential program for the emotionally disturbed, dares test their
rigid standards of dress and grooming.

Parental efforts to abandon or rescue children express opposite poles
of the same ambivalence. Some parents consistently embrace one posture or the other; others vacillate unpredictably between them. Parents
pressure a probation officer into issuing a detention order against their
child, then show up in court to argue against detention. A father who
has repeatedly excused his son's every theft (on the grounds that "stores
shouldn't place items within such easy reach" or "people shouldn't leave
car doors unlocked") bitterly resents his son's temporary removal to a
court-operated group home, accusing the probation officer of breaking
up his family. Yet not long after, he throws the boy out of his home
himself, and when the boy breaks and enters into his own house, the
father files criminal charges demanding the harshest sentence.

In other cases, the contrasting poles of ambivalence find expression
in the discord between parents, who are then apt to switch positions on
each other. A mother insists on institutionalization of an unruly son,
while the father staunchly obstructs that by denying the boy's disruptive
behavior. A woman steadfastly refuses any involvement with the son her
divorced husband harbors during chronic runaways from a residential
treatment center—until, that is, the child faces imminent commitment,
suddenly prompting the mother to claim custody of the child instead.

The ambivalence that produces the alternation of these postures also
governs the varying mixture of disclosure and concealment in parents'
communications to probation officers about their children; inconsistency of disclosure betrays a shifting ambivalence of purpose. Given the
probation officer's reliance on information as a resource for "hooking"

kids, concealment by parents is a serious hindrance. A mother who immediately notifies the probation officer whenever her daughter fails to clean her room neglects for weeks to report that the daughter has been staying out nights. Parents routinely cover up the gradual deterioration of their child's behavior—until they perceive a "crisis" which prompts urgent retrospective disclosure. By then, despite the parents' exasperation, it is difficult for the probation officer to respond. The particular incident precipitating such disclosure is often in itself relatively minor, while more serious incidents may be too stale to act on. Ironically, according to probation officers, children are more likely to find themselves returned to court for violations their parents attempt to cover up than for ones openly revealed.

Whose Problem?

The support probation officers receive from parents is precarious because parents experience ambivalence toward the court as well as their children. A father who has been perfectly cordial suddenly threatens to kill a probation officer for taking away his son's driver's license, but turns solicitous again just as abruptly when he needs the court's help in extricating the boy from new legal trouble in another state. While many parents resent the court's involvement with their children, others actively seek that involvement, especially for CHINS (or status) offenses. (Parents brought about one-quarter of all nontraffic complaints received by the particular court I observed.) Whatever the manner of parental involvement, however, the probation officer's mandate to define the presenting problem is an immediate source of tension with parents. Judges and probation officers presume that the family situation contributes to a child's behavioral problems, a presumption most parents naturally resist.

This tension is perhaps most pronounced with parents who bring CHINS complaints against their children. In a typical CHINS case, for example, a probation officer explains, "The parents are really angry with me because I've asked them to look at their role in this situation. I've suggested that the family interaction might have some influence on the girl's behavior. They're angry at me because I haven't come down hard in a punitive way against the girl." Probation officers often establish casework goals of guiding children toward autonomy from parents whose influence they consider unhealthy.

The tensions produced in defining underlying problems find expression in the variety of strategies probation officers employ to present the results of their formal social investigations to parents. A probation officer is required to file a copy of the investigation report with the clerk of the court for the parents' (or attorney's) examination three days before the judicial hearing on that report. Some probation officers make a point of reviewing the report with the parents before court; others do not. "The art of writing a social investigation," notes one probation officer, "is how to say things without offending the people who will read it." Another probation officer adds that, to make the parents more receptive to the ensuing analysis of their problems, she always tries to find something positive to say about the family situation in the first part of the report. Inevitably, however, every probation officer encounters an angry challenge to a report from some parents.

Probation officers have mixed success in overcoming parents' denials of their problems. In one case, parents who had sought the court's help and apparently agreed to pay the costs of private residential treatment for their child were so enraged by the probation officer's portrayal of them in court (as a pair of alcoholics who had never legally married) that they withdrew their petition instead, forcing dismissal of the case. In another case, parents wrote letters of complaint to the county executive and the court director about a probation officer's attempt to force their son into an alcohol treatment program. The parents hired a private psychiatrist to testify that, though suffering certain personality disorders, the boy had no alcohol problem. Eventually, however, the mother tearfully confessed to the probation officer the family secret: the boy's father, too, was an alcoholic, who once in a drunken stupor had burned down the family home.

Associated with this struggle to define the underlying problem is a struggle to assign ownership of that problem. While wishing to retain authority over the course of children's treatment, parents and probation officers each seek to disclaim responsibility for children's problems. Judges, probation supervisors, and probation officers offer a stock parody of an attitude they encounter from parents all too frequently: "Here's my child—fix her!" This attitude of entreaty connotes no corresponding willingness to cooperate with the suggested treatment plan.

Probation officers are careful to demarcate the limits of their formal obligation from the very outset of their dealings with parents. In the words of different probation officers: "when I'd get the case I'd start off by saying these are your problems and I'll do what I can to help you with your problems"; "what you'd do a lot is . . . sitting down with a family, getting a sense of what they expect, what problems there are, what their needs are—then telling them what we can and cannot do"; "I'd try to . . . outline at the very beginning what I could and couldn't do . . . get what the parents expected, and get back to the reality of what was or was not going to happen." This message requires continual repetition. Certain parents expect the court to assume the work of parenting in its entirety. It is not uncommon for parents to request probation officers' help in getting their children out of bed or getting them to take out the garbage. A child coming home drunk in the early morning may similarly evoke an urgent call for a home visit. Needless to say, it is important for probation officers not only to spurn such requests but to discourage their recurrence.

Parents tend to resist participation in treatment plans premised however implicitly on possible failings of their own, while probation officers are loath to discipline children of uncooperative parents. Thus parents may pressure the court to adopt the more extreme treatment course of committing their child to a psychiatric institution instead of simply removing the child to a community group home, since by attributing the problem to the child's own mental condition, the former option seems to exonerate the quality of their parenting. Parents who endorse judicial orders for their children to attend counseling typically defy similar orders to attend counseling themselves. The understandable reluctance of judges to punish parents is an unremitting source of frustration to probation officers, who may counter by tolerating children's recalcitrance in turn. Probation officers reject pressures from parents to file violations against their children if the parents themselves have failed to fulfill their shares of the treatment plans. Instead, probation officers may seek judicial approval to terminate court involvement with children whose parents prove uncooperative despite having requested the court's assistance in the first place. In more serious cases, when it proves necessary to commit children partly on account of their parents' irresponsibility, probation officers rue the court's lack of authority to make those parents help defray the costs of maintaining their children in institutional care.

Contention over respective fault aside, parents and probation officers often oppose each other over the best course of treatment for children. Even while delimiting their casework responsibilities, probation officers assert from the start the prerogative to manage cases on their own terms:

> I tell parents I'll be the one to decide about detention, violation of probation, or assignment to some program.
>
> Parents . . . come in assuming that they're in control and they're going to tell me what to do and I have to let them know that they're not in control . . . but I really want them to feel free to tell me what they would like to have happen.
>
> I'm always up front: "Maybe the court has the answers, maybe not, but we share objectives, and if you get in the way of results I think you want, I'll let you know."

157

Such assertions notwithstanding, it is well within parents' power to "sabotage" probation officers' decisions. By abetting misconduct or merely setting a bad example, parents can undermine the effects of any placement program: a mother herself involved in Alcoholics Anonymous keeps sneaking money to her daughter to purchase liquor, in direct violation of the daughter's probation rules. Occasionally, parents force their children into treatments that probation officers consider unnecessary or excessive; yet parents with sufficient means (or sufficiently liberal insurance policies) do not need the court's approval to admit their children to mental hospitals or totalistic drug treatment centers.

Conversely, despite the court's legal authority to assume custody of children, it is difficult to place children in private residential institutions without their parents' consent. Determined parents can discourage institutions from accepting their children, hinder necessary funding arrangements, or devise alternative schemes. Many institutions refuse to accept children whose parents withhold a show of cooperation, so that parents can virtually veto these placements by default, simply by contriving to miss admission interviews or by indicating displeasure with particular programs. As difficult as it is to get the schools to approve special education funding for private residential placement, it is easy for parents to argue that such placement is educationally "too restrictive." Parents also have a way of finding their own dispositional alternatives to placement at the eleventh hour, for example by convincing relatives to accept a child. Although probation officers are wary of such schemes, which commonly prove tenuous, parents can often get judicial approval for them.

Stereotyping the System

Enterprising parents can play on the court's reflexively critical institutional self-consciousness to discredit the positions of probation officers. As individuals, people working for the court are influenced by scholarly and popular criticisms that the court's bureaucratic process dilutes ideals of individualized treatment. Most members of the court staff have direct knowledge about only their own work performance. Court workers, then, are surprisingly open to intimations that their fellows are compromising service ideals. Court officials receive clients' complaints sympathetically.

Thus over a period of several years one woman was able to manipulate the management of her daughter's case according to clearly identifiable interests of her own, despite the contrary judgments of a succession of probation officers, even while she herself was undergoing intermittent periods of alcohol detoxification and mental hospitalization. Despite her apparent mental instability and the suspicion of parental incompetence—she had previously been investigated for abusing and neglecting her daughter, who indeed alleged that the runaway which brought the case into court was provoked by her mother's abuse—the woman was able to divide court staff members against each other by appealing directly to a number of different officials. While seeking relief of her daughter's custody, she desperately wished to prevent her divorced husband from assuming custody in her stead, which to the probation officer involved seemed the most natural course of action. To forestall this she sought her daughter's commitment to a mental hospital.

By dealing directly with a judge in chambers, she was able to schedule a hearing about her daughter's mental commitment before her husband could return to the area. By complaining directly to the court's director of probation services, she was able to schedule a review of the probation officer's performance. By interceding directly with the director of the court's diagnostic team, she was able to gain permission to attend the team's deliberations, from which parents were ordinarily excluded. By consulting directly with the director of the court's less-secure detention home, where her daughter was staying, she was able to involve him as her ally in the decision process. In each case, she was able to play on court workers' suspicions about their colleagues.

While failing to get her daughter committed to a mental hospital, she did manage to prevent her husband from assuming their daughter's custody: the judge transferred custody instead to the Department of Social Services to arrange placement. The woman succeeded in controlling the agenda of the various hearings and deliberations concerning her daughter. Not only did each official agree to speak with her, undermining normal appeal channels, but each responded directly to her requests without even bothering to ascertain the probation officer's side of the story. Only after the fact did the probation officer learn of the various concessions the woman had won. In the hearing to consider mental commitment, it was the probation officer who felt the need to defend her actions—not the woman alleged to be an abusive mother, nor the girl alleged to be a runaway.

The mother similarly managed to stymie the efforts of the veteran probation officer assigned to take over her daughter's case. Between episodes of hospitalization, the mother (who worked as a legal secretary) kept up a steady barrage of notarized messages, drafted in legalese, transmitting instructions about the minutest details of her daughter's treatment. Indeed, she continued calling in instructions to court workers even during periods of hospitalization, foiling one proposed placement alternative after another. As a result, her daughter wound up spending months on end in the court's "temporary" shelter home. Skillfully exploiting court workers' reflexive consciousness of how "the system" works to stereotype clients, she succeeded in accomplishing precisely the opposite, managing to get her way by stereotyping the system.

In most cases, of course, judges do not side as strongly with parents against probation officers. At least in broad outline, judges tend to ratify probation officers' judgments, taking their word about issues of veracity that arise in court. In another case of a mother seeking to relinquish responsibility for her daughter, the woman—whose behavior had been devious from the start—attacked the probation officer in court, adducing a number of "petty lies and accusations" to portray the probation officer as callous, perfunctory, and deceptive. Proclaiming that "my probation staff doesn't have to take this treatment," a judge thwarted the mother's design by simply releasing her daughter from probation. Although the judge's action was by no means extraordinary, the visible relief and gratitude exhibited by the probation officer after court testifies to the fact that probation officers cannot take that sort of support for granted.

Probation officers observe that the types of support and opposition they experience from parents vary with class. Middle-class parents are more likely than lower-class ones to impugn probation officers' competence, challenging their judgment and subverting their case management. Middle-class parents actively seek out the court's involvement in regulating their children's hours, associates, school behavior, and sexual activities, looking to the court for relief from the duties and responsibilities of parenthood. Lower-class parents, less concerned with these aspects of their children's behavior (the grist of CHINS or status complaints), are warier of court involvement. Yet lower-class parents are more willing to acknowledge their children's guilt in adult-style criminal activities, while middle-class parents are more anxious to cover up their children's crimes and to rescue them from punitive consequences of crimes that do become known. In their efforts to get their children off, middle-class parents have the advantage of being able to employ the services of private attorneys.

Legal Counsel: Right or Apparition?

Although the influence of lawyers on the juvenile court is increasing, their presence is still incomplete. And because many of them have not yet adapted their roles to the specialized purposes and operations of the juvenile court, their expanding presence is not entirely constructive. In any particular proceeding, it is possible for a cleverly aggressive defense attorney to defeat the probation officer's intention. Occasionally, a lawyer invokes an evidentiary technicality to force dismissal of alleged probation violations, arguing, for example, that an area school administrator presenting a child's attendance record to the court has only hearsay knowledge of truancy, or that a probation officer needs to produce return receipts for appointment letters in order to prove failure to attend probation meetings. Sometimes a defense attorney can win dismissal of more serious charges on similar technicalities. After a prosecutor had put on several hours of compelling testimony by the arresting officer, the police investigator, the victim, and an accomplice, a defense attorney forced dismissal of a felony charge by successfully challenging the prosecutor to produce official documentation of the defendant's age.

The obstructive effect of such legal devices does not negate the constructive potential of legal reform in the juvenile court. Tales recounted by veteran court workers about the lax informality of the "old days"—before the procedural transformation wrought by *In re Gault* and other U.S. Supreme Court decisions—indicate the dimensions of change already accomplished. Even without new charges, probation officers could admit children to the detention home on their own authority (subject to subsequent judicial review) simply by filling out "green slips" they always carried with them. Children were detained for such evidence of "bad attitude" as wearing their hair too long or failing to wear belts to school.

Court workers credit lawyers with improving communication with clients and increasing clients' sense of fair treatment. A judge observes, "It is much easier to try a case with a lawyer present. If you have to explain a point to a lawyer, you communicate in so doing to the courtroom audience. You can see in their eyes that they know you have a reason." A probation officer discerns similar benefits in her clients' representation by attorney:

> If a kid has an attorney . . . to explain to the kid what can happen, what his options are, that makes my job easier because he's hearing from someone whom he feels is representing him, not just the p.o. whom he thinks is out to get him.
> It makes us better p.o.'s because we have to prepare more. We've got to have all our facts together. We can't just go in there and say, "well, I'm recommending this, judge," and nobody questions it.

Attorneys . . . forced the probation officers as well as the
judges to make sure that what was being communicated was exactly what was intended to be communicated, and that the people
were following up.

Yet the implementation of legal reform in the juvenile court is far
from complete. Legal considerations are secondary to those of social
casework in guiding probation officers' treatment decisions. As a probation officer explains his encouragement of one parent's attempt (unsuccessful, as it turned out) to admit a boy "voluntarily" to a mental hospital
over the other parent's opposition, "Illegal is what you can't get away
with. It may be illegal, but it's not immoral if the kid needs placement,
and you can slide him in without the ceremony of law." The vast majority of probation officers are only partially familiar with the section of
the legal Code pertaining to the juvenile court; even those few who consider themselves to be legally oriented describe children's cases primarily
in terms of their personal, family, and social problems rather than their
legal ones.

Lapses of formal due process are common. The court's legal and social
case files are so disorderly that it is sometimes difficult to discover the
precise charges on which a hearing is being held or the child's supervision status at a particular date. Cases are theoretically set for court
only on the basis of petitions—formal documents that state the precise
allegations; yet some cases somehow find their way into the courtroom
without petitions. Changes to existing orders by judges in the privacy of
their chambers without new hearings often go formally unrecorded.

Courtroom procedures are also abridged. Judges sometimes issue
dispositions in cases before formally determining guilt. Judges can be
observed entering written dispositions before all the witnesses have
completed their testimony. Similarly, to expedite the paperwork generated by the expected outcome, a probation officer may ask a child to sign
probation rules while still waiting for the start of a hearing that is ostensibly to determine whether to order probation at all.

The professional marginality of practicing juvenile law helps retard
the implementation of legal reform in the juvenile court. While com-
mending the standards of professional conduct upheld by some lawyers
before the juvenile court, judges criticize the level of practice by many
others. "There's a self-perpetuating dilemma. Some lawyers feel that
since the juvenile court is the lowest court in the land, it requires the
least preparation. As a result, the quality is lower than it should be."
Judges strain to prevent their evaluations of lawyers' performances from

influencing their findings and decisions. The quality of legal representation is especially problematic for defendants forced to rely on court-
appointed lawyers. Working for a relative pittance on a daily piecework
basis, and tending to be less experienced than their privately retained
counterparts, these lawyers typically confine their preparations to hurried introductions and consultations immediately prior to court.

Many hearings proceed without the presence of lawyers at all. The
right to counsel in the juvenile court established by the Supreme Court's
In re Gault decision extends only to the stage of adjudicating guilt or
innocence. (*Gault* explicitly excludes the disposition stage of juvenile
court proceedings from the right to counsel.) Many children do not
know enough to insist on their right to counsel (although the particular
court I observed required children to have legal representation in cases
where they might lose their long-term liberty). Often, too, many lawyers do not know—or care—enough to be present at the more perfunctory hearings—unscheduled detention hearings or reviews—which
often prove the most fateful for their clients. A lawyer who might, for
example, attend an adjudicatory hearing that assigns a child to intensive
"outreach" supervision, might well miss a hearing called suddenly to
review violations of outreach supervision that carry the presumption of
detention.

The presence of prosecuting attorneys in the juvenile court is even
more limited than that of defense attorneys. The prosecuting attorney's
office also recognizes the marginality of the juvenile court, according
greater priority to covering cases in the adult courts. That office does
not even strive to prosecute more than a fraction of the felonies adjudi-
cated in juvenile court; an unexpected increase in the number of adult
cases on any given day may supersede the prosecution of any juvenile
cases at all. When prosecuting attorneys do show up in juvenile court,
their preparations are confined to on-the-spot consultations with victims, defendants, and defense lawyers—most often to the exclusion of
probation officers, who are therefore unable to participate in plea bargaining or even explain any special circumstances surrounding a case.
Prosecuting attorneys restrict their courtroom presence to the adjudicatory stage of hearings, forfeiting any say in sentencing decisions except
in the most highly publicized juvenile cases.

Prosecutors justify their absence from disposition hearings on the
grounds that the range of sentencing options is much narrower for juveniles than for adults, and that juvenile court judges are in any event
hopelessly lenient (juvenile court judges in the particular state under
study can sentence children to no more than one year in jail). Prosecu-

tors evaluate the significance of cases according to the seriousness of the allegations. But probation officers seek convictions on even minor new offenses to gain leverage for ordering additional services. Probation officers are most vulnerable to the technicalities invoked by defense attorneys in cases involving the least serious allegations; they are perhaps most in need of legal support in allegations of probation violations contended by defense attorneys. Paradoxically, while unopposed defense attorneys are sometimes able to exploit dubious legal technicalities on their clients' behalf, on the whole the absence of prosecuting attorneys from the juvenile court may handicap children's legal defense. Abdication of the proper prosecutorial role transforms the preferred courtroom roles of judges and probation officers, forcing judges to become fact finders and probation officers to become prosecutors. Probation officers particularly resent this role strain, which undermines their claims to benevolent concern for children and compromises the credibility on which their effectiveness with children outside of court depends.

Friends of the Court?

Even when lawyers are present in the juvenile court, their unfamiliarity with the court prevents them—defense and prosecuting attorneys alike—from integrating their efforts to maximum effect with the court's institutional purpose and actual operation. In concentrating their energies on proving or disproving particular instances of guilt, opposing lawyers divert each other from the court's primary focus on formulating appropriate long-term treatment plans. Opposing lawyers seek to "win" in ways that do not take into consideration the child's (or community's) long-term interests. One party seeks the harshest possible punishment, while the other seeks to get the child off, even though either outcome may help confirm the child in a delinquent identity. Difficult children have a way of coming back before the court; a lawyer's "victory" on any given occasion may prove hollow the next time around.

There is no disputing a defense lawyer's obligation to protect clients' constitutional and legal rights, to ensure that all evidence is properly admitted, and to argue for proportionality in sentencing. But recalling dilemmas of professional ethics from their own previous careers in private practice, judges distinguish between the preferences for their children which parents hire lawyers to espouse and more constructive responses to children's needs. Lawyers surrender their credibility with judges by advocating the former rather than the latter. Lawyers can command a respectful audience before the bench by appearing as a "friend of the court," offering to facilitate the determination of the child's best interest rather than attempting to divert the court from its own purpose. As a judge comments, "some of the best work has been done for kids where there's a guilty plea and where the lawyer presents a plan to the court that is workable and has gotten the kid to agree to using outside resources. That's the kind of approach that's very difficult to turn down . . . but there's not that much of it." Another judge commends the approach of "holistic" lawyering, in which lawyers employ outside experts to perform their own comprehensive background investigations.

A lawyer recounts a hearing in which he drew on his own skills as a former probation officer to defeat a new probation officer's recommendation for committing a girl to a state training school. The lawyer earned credibility by forcing the girl to recant dishonest testimony about her drinking habits, getting her to admit a problem. By extensive cross-examination of the girl and her probation officer, the lawyer demonstrated his detailed knowledge of the situation and thorough exploration of available treatment alternatives; he convinced the judge to allow the girl to move back in with her mother. "A good lawyer explores the alternatives before the court, forcing the judge to choose the best among them."

At the other extreme are lawyers who adopt a stance of confrontation toward the juvenile court, a stance some judges describe as "grandstanding." These lawyers employ inflammatory rhetoric and delay hearings with frivolous objections solely to impress their clients. They report probation officer's statements out of context, or misrepresent them entirely, to impugn their motivations or competence. (This is a common enough experience so that probation officers exhibit a general wariness of communicating informally with lawyers.) They subject probation officers to prolonged and hostile cross-examination, gratuitously eliciting disclosure of sensitive information in the emotional public setting of open court. They oppose probation officers' recommendations without proposing alternatives the court would find acceptable. Whether or not their courtroom displays succeed in creating the intended impressions on their clients, they exercise little suasion over judges.

Even lawyers who adopt a narrowly partisan and adversarial conception of their clients' best interests do better consulting probation officers beforehand about possible treatment alternatives that would be at least minimally acceptable to all parties concerned. The most skillful strategy of advocacy is to endorse the court's own highest purposes. A juvenile court judge recalls that in his earlier career in private practice he could always avert commitment for his clients—even those already under suspended commitment charged with serious new offenses—by invoking the rehabilitative ideal and identifying less drastic treatment options that had not yet been exhausted.

Recriminalizing Status Offenders

Just as the tensions between law and social casework impede the full realization of legal reform in the juvenile court, legislative attempts to reform the treatment of status (or noncriminal) offenders remain limited in their effects. Status offenses (such as running away, truancy, and incorrigibility) are behaviors defined as offenses for juveniles, because of their status as minors, but not for adults. In different states, status offenders are variously called CHINS (children in need of supervision) or PINS (persons in need of supervision). Despite the relatively minor nature of their legal infractions, status offenders have always numbered among the most recalcitrant and challenging probationers. Probation officers' relations with the parents of status offenders are similarly among the most easily strained, even though it is frequently the parents who request court involvement in the first place.

By restricting the secure confinement of status offenders as a condition of federal funding—even while leaving the juvenile court with jurisdiction over those offenders—the Juvenile Justice Delinquency Prevention Act of 1974 compounds this intrinsic frustration of working with status offenders. This reform legislation not only curtails the use of formal sanctions against status offenders, it also weakens the informal controls still available to probation officers. Yet the legislation is flawed in a manner that suggests the means of its own negation, since it ignores the latitude of discretion the court derives from the ambiguity of misbehavior. The legislature can proscribe treatments for categories of behaviors, but it cannot fully prescribe how the court will assign behaviors to categories. By curtailing the coercive treatment of status offenders, legislative reform in effect merely constrains probation officers to criminalize them instead.

Probation officers do what they can with status offenders. Some status offenders just need someone to talk to and are amenable to counseling. "They'll describe their problems, abide by the rules, work on their problems, and become fine and upstanding human beings." With these children, the strategy is simply to encourage them to talk. "I guess I acted like their older sister. I tried to talk. I think I was probably warmer and friendlier and a little less therapeutic, maybe, than with the other kids. . . . I always had the kids feel like they could talk about anything but probably a little bit more with CHINS." To other status offenders, probation officers find ways to administer doses of detention, even under the terms of legal restrictions. In the particular state in which this study was conducted, probation officers could still detain status offenders pending the next day's court hearing. Status offenders also stand vulnerable to longer periods of detention in unlocked facilities designed specifically for them. "My greatest success with CHINS is when they've been in less-secure [detention] and learn they can be moved." Although the court can do little to prevent their absconding from an assigned living situation—whether home, less-secure detention, or a longer-term residential institution—it can keep ordering their return.

Both because the court is more limited in its options for treating status offenders and because those children's problems more directly involve relations with their parents, it is even more crucial for probation officers to engage parents constructively in casework with status offenders than with delinquents, and even more difficult. These factors only exacerbate the common tensions between probation officers and parents surrounding the definition of underlying problems and division of responsibilities. Although parents or parent-surrogates are typically the ones who initiate court intervention with status offenders, probation officers almost always attribute to them substantial responsibility for the problems they report with children. A probation supervisor summarizes a series of unit meetings about the frustrations of working with status offenders: "The real issue is not power, but right and wrong: How much do you punish a kid for having crummy parents?" Some probation officers insist on working informally with status complaints before accepting them for formal court processing, making parents demonstrate their willingness to participate in treatment by coming in along with their children for a prescribed series of meetings. Probation officers can offer to negotiate and monitor a family contract explicitly defining mutual rights and responsibilities in behavioral terms. In general, however, probation officers observe that parents of status offenders are even less responsible than parents of delinquents about attending probation meetings, and even more ambivalent toward both their children and the court.

As a result, status offenders tend to pose the toughest frustrations of casework: "20 percent of your cases, 80 percent of your headaches." Judges feel as confused and helpless as probation officers in dealing with status offenders. Some judges order a full battery of investigations and tests before issuing decisions about the treatment of status offenders, while others feel that no amount of evidence can facilitate their decisions. Still others, insisting that status cases do not belong in court, simply throw them out. When a group of probation officers asked a judge what he meant by ordering a status offender onto probation, the judge replied, "It means I don't know what to do."

Judges and probation officers agree that it is senseless to assign the court responsibility for status offenders without the corresponding authority to detain them securely longer than overnight. Even with children who might never be detained, the court's credibility rests on the knowledge that "there is an end to the line." A judge notes that the prohibition against coercive sanctions for truancy makes a mockery of "compulsory education" which the court is supposed to enforce. Probation officers are especially hesitant to return status offenders to court for even serious violations of probation, for fear of merely revealing the court's bluff. Status offenders who realize how little control the court can exercise may go wild. "If . . . they've learned they can do whatever they want and no one can do any different, and they don't believe that court is going to be any different despite what their parents tell them, [and] they test you and they find that court *isn't* any different because they can't get locked up, *then* they have a field day, and you just don't get anywhere with them."

A more modest purpose for wanting to detain status offenders is simply to interrupt their dangerous patterns of behavior, to create the opportunity for working with them at all. "Sometimes they had to be stopped, and that was the only way to stop them. They were like a runaway train . . . and the only way you could get their attention was to stop them. And that detention did sometimes." Even a probation officer who claims that "I don't always disagree with the new laws . . . why should a kid lose his freedom just because he doesn't get along with his parents?" complains, "but the kids who run away, you can't get them to listen to you, you can't hold on to them." A judge echoes this frustration: "They need to change the law, so that once the child has violated probation you can hold on to him or her long enough to do the work that needs to be done. . . . We get chronic runners, who come back into court time after time, and the message they get is that we don't think they're doing anything all that bad."

For difficult status offenders, then, the casework recourse is to "get a criminal charge." "The only thing you can do is hang on, because you know the kid is coming back on a criminal charge." At a Friday night football game of the high school he covered, a probation officer was delighted to be accosted by a policemen who had apprehended a boy attempting to sneak into the stadium without paying. The boy had just been ordered onto probation for truancy; the probation officer found him "the most *hateful* kid you'll ever meet—mention his mother and you get, 'that bitch!' "; leaving court, the probation officer had told the boy, "I don't know you, but I predict I'm going to get a delinquency charge on you," and true to his prediction he did not have long to wait.

Frequently, however, probation officers seek criminal charges against their clients more proactively. Just as they often intercede with police officers or school officials to spare children from further trouble, probation officers are in a position to ask those same authorities to bring formal criminal charges instead of trying to resolve trouble informally. In a reversal of their stereotyped roles, a probation officer complains that "some police officers like to play social worker and run deals with kids"; this practice, she points out to the police, may undercut her own understandings with children. Probation officers may inform parents or school officials who complain about children's behavior that they will only be able to respond effectively if the complainants file criminal charges. Thus when parents of a status offender call to complain that the child took the family car without permission, the probation officer may encourage them to file formal complaints of auto theft.

The "criminalization" of status offenders typically involves less serious offenses. A school troublemaker who hangs around the schoolyard during a suspension day can be charged with "trespassing on school grounds." A child who shoves a parent or throws a piece of furniture during a family fight can be charged with assault or destruction of property. A runaway will invariably shoplift or use a false name in charging a telephone call. In an act of supreme cooperation from a court intake officer, a probation officer was able to charge a school troublemaker with theft for "possession of stolen cookies." When after a number of years the state legislature extended the prohibition against detention to children with offenses less serious than class one misdemeanors, status offenders could still be charged with being drunk in public under a statute of the county code which did not specify classes of misdemeanors. Other children officially become criminals during the course of processing their status charges. A girl who has a violent temper tantrum at the police station after being taken from her home for incorrigibility is charged with destruction of public property. Another incorrigible girl who protests in the courtroom her brother's ten-day jail sentence is detained for "obstruction of justice." A runaway is committed to a state training school on an assault charge for pelting with a wadded-up piece of paper a counselor at a court probation house. Another runaway is convicted of theft for stealing a cigarette from a counselor at the court's less-secure detention home. A probation officer rationalizes the practice of "looking to identify delinquent behaviors" on the grounds that "we see very few pure status offenders." "You know they're out there doing misdemeanors. They all smoke pot with their friends at parties; the police will only charge them if they stumble across them, or if the kids are obnoxious."

9

Disposition by Default

In attempting to phase out the institutionalization of status offenders in secure facilities, the Juvenile Justice Delinquency Prevention Act of 1974 tampers with the core technology of probation work. Removing children from home to residential institutions—short- or long-term—is the court's only real treatment recourse for probationers who prove uncontrollable at home or in the community. Of course, court workers distinguish among *types* of residential placement, in a manner suggesting Emerson's (1981) typology of official responses to trouble: probation officers and judges regard commitment to state training schools as a "last resort," short-term detention as a "first resort," and placement in community treatment homes or private residential institutions as a "normal remedy." Though "normal," institutional placement is a dubious remedy. Residential institutions are markedly uneven in nature and quality, and the process of matching children to placements is governed as much by space availability—itself a function of the probation officer's range of personal contacts—as by children's particular needs. Placement in even the best institutions rarely has any purpose clearer than to "buy time."

Commitment as the Last Resort

Probation officers explain the sense in which commitment to state training schools is a "last resort": "I use commitment when there's nothing else available"; "everything has been tried and there's nothing left"; "there was nothing further you could do for this kid." No one would contend that the state training schools offer any programmatic benefit to children, with the exception of one small training school for girls which, significantly, probation officers still anxiously avoid. However, the court finds it necessary to commit children who defiantly refuse to desist from crime or to stay put in other residential placements. (Children coming to judicial attention for repeated complaints within rapid succession are especially vulnerable to commitment.) As one probation officer expresses it, "You've got to decide where to draw the line."

Nonetheless, the decision to commit a child is always a reluctant one. Children under suspended commitment can return to court time after time without being committed. Judges often order probation officers to find new residential placements for children who have already failed in previous placements, despite reports that no further placements are available. Judges sometimes choose to close "impossible" cases instead of ordering commitment. New probation officers are especially reluctant to recommend commitment, sometimes requiring special prodding by judges or supervisors before being able to bring themselves to do so; veteran probation officers regard their growing "realism" about the inevitability of committing certain children as a sign of career development. Even veteran probation officers, however, especially regret the effects of unfortunate contingencies on commitment decisions. They consider it unfair (though unavoidably so) when the lack of parental sponsorship, of available alternative placements, or of funding for such placements helps lead to a child's commitment. Among dozens of probation officers interviewed, not one regretted a failure to commit any probationers, though in hindsight some did regret giving children who were eventually committed too many chances. (Indeed, some old-time probation officers had received thanks years later from children they had committed, who complained only that they should have been committed sooner.) Probation officers nonetheless criticize judges for occasionally committing children without giving them sufficient chance. The very reluctance of probation officers to commit children accounts for the typical slight spurt of commitment activity by departing probation officers as they "clean up" their caseloads for their successors. Probation officers generally carry a few marginal cases—children they have been tolerating on probation even though they would not expect those replacing them to do the same.

Detention as a First Resort

No such reluctance surrounds the use of the juvenile detention home. The very judge who resists a recommendation for revoking the suspension of a chronic violator's commitment may criticize the failure to request a detention order for a first offender. As a matter of official policy, detention is described as a preadjudicatory holding option, and probation officers are supposed to get their supervisor's approval before requesting the issuance of a detention order. Yet detention is so routine that in usual practice, all but the least experienced probation officers only inform their supervisors about the issuance of those orders after the fact. The code formally restricts detention to children who are seriously dangerous to others or themselves, or who represent a threat to abscond before trial. The formal criteria for detention are stated in vague terms; probation officers informally acknowledge that they are of little moment in influencing detention decisions. "My attitude about detention is not within the code's attitude at all." Rather, detention is used most frequently, according to judges and probation officers alike, "to get a kid's attention" or "to let a kid know we're serious." "I think detention is a good place for kids to cool off when they're not taking probation seriously and think about probation." Probation officers also flaunt the code by using detention for a related purpose—as a form of punishment for an offense not serious enough to warrant more extreme sanctions. "For most kids, the most they have to fear is ten days in detention"; "we need something with teeth in it." Thus, a probationer who poses no serious threat to anyone may well spend some time in detention for being drunk in public past curfew. In especially marginal cases, when the judge at the next court day's detention hearing may release the child, probation officers can assure a stay of at least three nights in detention by arranging for service of a detention order late on a Friday afternoon.

Court workers believe that some children need such a demonstration of the court's authority before they will be amenable to "counseling." Yet this use of detention is self-limiting. Detention can only be used once to get a child's attention, since it is never as fearsome as the first time. Stays longer than a day or two only produce stupefying effects on children, as the initial shock of confinement abates and detainees begin to adjust to the dull institutional regimen. The use of detention is also limited by space constraints. On any given night, a significant number of detention beds have already been reserved for children staying for protracted periods, who tend to be detained for other reasons.

The detention home serves the purpose, not necessarily punitive, of sheltering children who lack the sponsorship of parents the court considers fit. Many children are runaways at the time of their detention. Children wind up in detention because there is no place else for them to go, because their parents refuse to let them come home, or because the court judges their parents to be unfit. A probation officer reports that she was more likely to recommend detention "if I thought there wasn't adequate supervision at home to prevent the kid from getting into further trouble." As a judge expresses his decision rule:

> In a detention hearing you're trying to get some feel for what the relationship between the child and the family is. If it's a good relationship, then it's probably relatively easy to release the kid to his family even if the crime is relatively serious. If the family is falling apart, or the kid's relationship with the parents is falling apart, then he's really a poor risk to put out in the community.

Parents can usually persuade the court to detain their children by aggressively abdicating their parental responsibilities, or by badgering probation officers so relentlessly with complaints about their children that the probation officers agree to detention as a way of stopping the complaints. Conversely, involved parents who impress probation officers and judges favorably can usually persuade the court to let their children return home. It is a sad fact that some children receive the best care of their life in detention. One severely retarded boy, prone to violent outbursts, gained a welcome thirty-five pounds during the several months it took his probation officer to find a special placement for him. Weeping as he left the detention home, he declared, "This is the best place I've ever been."

Children awaiting placement in residential institutions stay the longest in detention, months rather than days or weeks. Besides punishing children who stray out of line, or sheltering children deprived of proper parental support and control, detention serves a purpose even more fundamental to the juvenile court: to facilitate and enforce the long-term placement of children. Some of those awaiting placement during protracted detention stays are wards of the Department of Social Services, too unruly to be kept in the department's own short-term foster and group homes. Others are former status offenders, too unruly for the court's less-secure detention home, eligible for secure detention by virtue of having attracted criminal charges. Ten days is considered an average length of detention; according to policy, detention review hearings should be held every ten days to prevent excessively long stays. But probation officers who foresee difficulty in arranging placement can often get judges to waive the ten-day reviews. Children can languish in detention while their probation officers work on arranging placement; conversely, the immediate urgency of arranging placement diminishes as detention stays expand.

Detention is a way station for children going into longer-term placements as well as children returning from unsuccessful ones. Children have an even harder time adjusting to residential programs if they have never experienced any restraints on their freedom. Probation officers detain children to help coax them into accepting longer-term placement in the first place, as well as to help prepare them for the experience. The probation officer may set a court date far enough in advance for the child to arrange "voluntary" admission to a local inpatient alcohol treatment program, for example, threatening to recommend detention otherwise. Or the probation officer may keep the child in detention until the child starts adopting a more conciliatory attitude during interviews for admission to residential institutions. Even after placement has been arranged, the probation officer remains wary of terminating detention too long before the child's scheduled entry into the new institution, lest the child experience a change of heart. Conversely, those who run away or are expelled from long-term placements most often find themselves back in detention awaiting another round of long-term placement; detention is on the receiving as well as the sending end of institutionalized children.

Inexorable Recourse

Residential placement is the uncertain fail-safe of child welfare and corrections, the normal remedy for children's untenable family and community situations. The same issues of parental sponsorship that influence detention decisions also influence decisions about longer-term placement. Parents who insistently pressure the court to remove their children to residential institutions generally get their way, not so much for their sake as for the sake of the children, since the court considers it necessary to remove children from hopelessly "dysfunctional" families. Of course decisions to place children require stronger justification than decisions merely to detain them. As one probation officer describes the difference, "If a kid *won't* change while staying at home, then I use detention; but if a kid *can't* change, then I use placement." Another probation officer, commenting on his tendency to become overinvolved with frustrating cases, observes that the placement decision marks a deliverance from his own excessive engrossment in a child's situation.

Yet decisions to place children in residential institutions are not taken as hesitantly as commitments to state training schools. Judges encourage probation officers to examine the possible need for placement from the inception of a case, rather than waiting for the predictable failure of more tentative measures. (This judicial prescription contradicts the policy of the state Department of Corrections, which requires that all forms of community treatment be exhausted before it will fund any part of a child's placement.) Coining an analogy between the escalating sequence of court responses and the stops along a subway line, judges declare that certain children belong on the express train rather than the local. Veteran probation officers similarly assert that their experience enables them to recognize which cases call for decisively prompt intervention. Despite the relatively restrictive nature of its criteria for providing placement funds, the state Department of Corrections encourages the use of private residential institutions as an alternative to the expansion of state training schools already filled beyond capacity.

Although probation officers are the key gatekeepers for the network of residential institutions receiving youth in trouble, they tend to underplay the importance of their role, portraying placement decisions as primarily reactive in nature: in the words of one, "The kids make the decisions for me by acting out criminally or acting out crazily." A probation supervisor similarly characterizes these decisions as "residual, when all else fails." As another probation officer expresses it, she starts thinking about placing children in residential institutions when she runs out of fresh ideas for them. This suggests a crucial proactive role probation officers do perform: the generation of fresh ideas, the conception of casework options. Not all probation officers do this equally well.

Probation officers bring varying degrees of skill, talent, and energy to bear on this crucial task of conceiving casework options. Some are more imaginative, flexible, and patient than others. Some are especially effective in exploiting the resources of a child's extended family; some are less reactive to episodes or periods of trouble. A probation supervisor observes that the individual members of his unit specialize in the types of problems they recognize as critical: one tends to characterize probationers as alcoholics, another to characterize them as victims of parental abuse. In a case that illustrates the difference a probation officer can make, a single mother petitioned the court for relief of her son's custody. Residential placement seemed inevitable since the son, who had been fighting bitterly with his mother, also declared an emphatic preference against returning home. The probation officer, however, perceiving a bond between them, interpreted the underlying dynamic as the mother's insecurity about her parenting abilities. While agreeing to arrange residential placement, the probation officer subtly offered reassurance to the mother and encouraged both parties to reconcile, finally persuading them to do so just as the case went into court. Mother and son promptly resumed their "crazy family fights," but in the probation officer's opinion were doing fine.

The obvious lesson of this case is that residential placement is not necessarily as "inevitable" as it appears to be. Nonetheless, as indicated by the range of reasons probation officers give for placing children, they have recourse to placement because they feel they have no better choice, not because they anticipate that placement will provide any clear benefit to children. To one probation officer, residential institutions offer "places for kids to be and grow up, get nine months older, and go back and try to deal with the same damn things because nothing ever got resolved." In the words of another:

> I believe in keeping delinquents moving—run them through as much as we can run them through—tire them out, wear them out, grind them down, to the point where it takes all the piss out of them, and they quit on you.
>
> You've got to take up their time, take up their access to delinquent behavior. The worst thing that a kid can do in a private placement is only run away—and that's no big deal.

The very inability of probation officers to articulate more precisely how placement can contribute to a child's development attests to the "taken-for-granted" nature of placement as a "normal remedy." Probation officers make the case for placement by citing the seriousness of a child's problems and the ineffectiveness of milder forms of intervention, rather than by offering any credible explanation of what placement will accomplish. Thus, preparing remarks for an interagency conference about the case of a hopelessly troubled child, a probation officer's outline spells out a glaring non sequitur—a set of dire disturbances pointing directly to a simple prescription without even a wisp of logical connection:

Issues:
    suicidal
    homicidal
    obsessive
    depressed
    hostile—
        NEEDS PLACEMENT.

"Laying the Seed"

Although the court's decision-logic defaults to residential placement as the normal remedy for difficult cases, implementing the placement decision is by no means automatic. The probation officer needs to obtain enough assent from both parents and child not only to gain the judge's approval for this decision, but also to convince directors of prospective placements of the child's willingness to enter their institutions. The task of matching the child to an available placement is conditioned by the particular probation officer's network of professional contacts, as is the task of arranging the necessary funding.

The process of attempting to persuade parents and children to accept the probation officer's recommendation for placement is a gradual one, commencing with the step sometimes called "laying the seed." Probation officers start conjuring the possibility of placement from their very first meetings with children: "Way early on, I'd say to a kid, 'you have a chance now to change your behavior. If you can do it, we'll give you all the help. If you can't do it, there's no alternative to placement. We'll have a lot of discussion about *which* placement, but it will be a response to your behavior.' So they'd see it coming way down the line."

Probation officers similarly discuss placement with parents from the start. Some parents, of course, are the first ones to suggest placement; other parents' initial reaction is to resist it. As one probation officer presses the subject during a typical phone conversation with a reluctant mother:

> It's my professional opinion, from working with many children, that it just won't work out in the community. We already know what will happen if we keep him home next year. There will be trouble in school. There will be trouble in the family. The boy and his father will be fighting, and there may well be physical injury to one of them. There will be trouble with alcohol. Let's do something positive now.

Probation officers can marshal expert support for their positions by referring children for evaluation by psychologists or the court's diagnostic team. Rarely do such evaluations yield information useful in making casework decisions; rather, probation officers request them to garner support for placement decisions they have already taken. By the wealth of written and spoken information they provide about children's situations in making the referrals, probation officers frame the diagnostic contexts. Although psychologists, for example, are able to derive independent clinical evidence from test batteries, they must respect probation officers' more detailed familiarity with casework circumstances. Psychologists whose findings indicate divergent recommendations often check back with the probation officers to reconcile their differences before issuing their reports. "A lot of times during the evaluation the psychologist will come up with something that doesn't seem to fit and will call and ask certain questions about the case, and then you have the chance to say all the gut feelings that aren't necessarily factual."

By raising the possibility of placement early and often enough, the probation officer can gradually establish a compelling case. The very failure to persuade the parents and child to accept placement on one occasion can increase the pressure on them to accept placement on the next one. Guided by the expectation that the child who requires placement will get back into trouble if left at home, the probation officer may defer an immediate recommendation for placement in exchange for the parent's acknowledgment before a judge that placement would be appropriate in the event of a return to court. Thus, when a boy who had been on probation for a status offense came into court for helping to steal and torch a car, the probation officer wanted to recommend placement. Instead, however, he asked the prosecuting attorney to approve a plea bargain he struck with the boy's lawyer: he would drop the recommendation for the time, if the boy would admit guilt for the criminal charge (making him vulnerable to detention for any violations of probation), and the lawyer would agree to a recommendation for placement for any new offense. The probation officer felt that he had conceded little in the bargain, so certain was he of a new offense.

A necessary aspect of persuading children and parents to go along with placement is to allay their fears about it. Some probation officers explicitly discuss with children the dramatic changes placement would bring to their lives, such as separation from family and friends and adjustment to a new school situation. Probation officers attempt to sell the benefits of the various placements they commend for consideration. They distribute brochures for these placements; some even make use of a slide show to convey a sense of what the various facilities are like. They recount the experiences of other children—some perhaps known to the probationer—attending the various placements. They arrange for parents and children to visit various facilities; parents are typically relieved to find evidence of good hygiene and adequate food.

Perhaps the most general strategy of persuasion is to make the placement decision seem to belong to the parents and child as much as possible. Thus, probation officers insist that the child's behavior ultimately determines the decision. Probation officers also encourage the fullest possible participation of parents and child in selecting the placement. They attempt to provide a list of different placements that would be suitable, inviting the parents and child to investigate all their options before choosing among them, and pledging to honor their choice. Even if there is only one placement available, the probation officer will ask the parents and child to visit it and report back on their impressions, because "if the kid feels like he's participating in the decision making, the chances of success are a little bit better." As probation officers observe, involving parents in the selection process restores to then some sense of parental competence that the decision to remove their child from home implicitly impugns.

Yet while asserting their clients' right to "choose their own paths through the system," probation officers reserve for themselves the authority to establish the parameters of choice, by imposing a sense of "reality." "My philosophy is always to explain the options to children and their families, so that they can make educated choices. . . . My job is to help people see what the reality of the situation is, to help them make educated choices among the options that are realistic." The ways in which probation officers structure their clients' choices often in effect constrain them to a single option. Thus, a child may be induced to reconsider his or her unwillingness for a particular prospective placement by making a subsequent visit to another—clearly less desirable—one. Probation officers often offer children reluctant to accept placement the alternative of commitment to a state training school. One probation officer recounts a technique he ironically terms "ultimatum therapy": he offered a child the choice between commitment or admitting himself for residential drug treatment; "either way, it makes no difference to me— you just tell me which." Another probation officer issued a similar ultimatum to a boy whose parents refused to accept him home, and who had already spent two months in the court's less-secure detention home for possession of marijuana while scuttling a number of placement interviews with displays of defiance: "You've had three chances; you have one more, and then I'm not making any more arrangements, you're going to State. You'd better like this one, and tell them you like it. You have an option." (A few children actually do opt for commitment over private residential placement, to gain a shorter length of stay and freedom from people "messing with your head.") Probation officers may similarly confront parents unwilling to accept particular placements for their child with the choice either to commit the child or to close the court case altogether.

Informal Channels of Referral

Although encouraging as much participation as possible by parents and children in the process of selecting placements, probation officers cannot afford to let them be too choosy, since the supply of residential institutions is limited. Indeed, probation officers rely in part on personal contacts with the directors of those institutions to place children and arrange the necessary funding. It is in the interest of both probation officers and residential directors to maintain informal channels for doing so, given the confused and dilatory nature of the formally institutionalized procedures.

The child's range of choice in selecting a placement depends in part on the extent to which the probation officer has cultivated good personal relations with residential directors. The more frequently a probation officer has used a residential institution in the past, and the better the probation officer's reputation for making "appropriate" referrals, the better the child's chances of gaining admission. The same probation officer notorious for the liberties he took with other community agencies, who confessed that "I'm not liked probably by a lot of different agencies because of the way I abused their processes and went around them," described his relations with residential directors, by contrast, as "good ones—that I never messed around with—they were your bread and butter." This probation officer was among those who became patrons of particular placements by "discovering" them, pioneering their use, and brokering their colleagues' use of them.

Just as veteran probation officers keep in reserve the names of families willing to provide short-term emergency foster care in the neighborhoods they cover, they also develop special relations with directors of long-term placements on whom they can count to accept their cases. Yet such special relations are tenuous. When the director of one placement that had become popular stopped giving preferential treatment to children referred by one-time patrons, word spread among the probation officers to be wary of referring children to that placement.

Probation officers work out financing for residential placements from a fluid mixture of welfare, corrections, special education, mental health, insurance, and private funds. Public funds are subject to periodic sudden interruption, which is disturbing to probation officers and residential directors alike, who share an interest in regularizing the flow of children to placements despite the vagaries of public funding. Probation officers boast of the special cooperation they have received from residential directors in cutting through established procedures to expedite placements. Some placements are willing to accept new residents without charge toward the end of a fiscal year, when the year's appropriation of public funds has been exhausted, in anticipation of the next budget cycle. Indeed, some placements will even reward a probation officer's patronage by waiving payments altogether for some clients.

When the parents' health insurance will pay for the child's placement or when the parents are wealthy enough to pay on their own, probation officers can successfully refer a child for placement without even accepting a complaint for formal court processing.

> I placed kids out of Intake, with a phone call to the dean down there—"Say, these parents have a problem, I think the kid is appropriate for your facility, can they come down this weekend?"—and he'd say yes. I had a stack of applications on file; I'd fill out a referral and give it with an application to the parents, and tell them to take it down with them.

Indeed, probation officers can accomplish placement without even a trace of court involvement. When parents called to complain that after successfully completing a term of probation as a status offender, their daughter had defiantly moved back in with her boyfriend, the probation officer reacted to avert the prospect of having to work with "the little turkey" again. He advised the parents to "kidnap" their daughter from the boy's house—"pick her up by the scruff of the neck and throw her in the back seat"—and take her to a placement, without informing her of their plans to leave her there. The probation officer called the residential director, who agreed to admit the girl. When the girl finally realized what was happening to her, she threatened to run away from the placement; but the parents convinced her to stay by threatening resolutely to keep bringing her back, as the probation officer had prompted them to do.

Uncertain Fail-Safe

Although placement in residential institutions is the court's "normal remedy" for difficult cases, it is a dubious one. The assignment of children to placements tends to be indiscriminate. Because the removal of children to residential institutions is often decided by default, the fit between children and placements is elastic, governed to an unfortunate degree by situational pressures. Probation officers tend to confine their referrals to the same few institutions they know from personal experience. They make little use, for example, of one residential institution because of the delays imposed by its thorough compliance with the formal procedures of the state Department of Corrections, even though the institution is reputed to be excellent and well enough endowed to offer scholarships to needy children. Despite variations in the needs of particular children, probation officers treat different institutions as essentially interchangeable. When the community mental health board temporarily closed a therapeutic group home, probation officers had little trouble reclassifying four displaced residents as children with drug problems so they could transfer them to the drug treatment facility down the road.

The matching of children to residential placements is not effectively supervised within the court. The court created a specialized position for a probation officer to expedite the processing of placement applications by serving as a liaison with residential directors and state correctional officials, and to visit children in placements; the successive probation officers who assumed this role regretted their lack of authority to veto prospective placements, since they considered many of them inappropriate. Probation supervisors similarly complain that probation officers inevitably prevail over them in disputes about the appropriateness of placements, since probation officers communicate with judges directly.

Judges are in no position to question the selection of placements, since as one judge states, "I don't know anything about the placements. We don't have time to visit them. So I have to rely on the probation officers' knowledge of them." Another judge attended an informational meeting probation officers had arranged for themselves with the staff of a commonly used therapeutic community group home so that she could learn more about it, since as she explained, "Often judges do not know what the program components of placements are." The first judge asserts that in deciding case outcomes, she cannot afford to be concerned with issues about the quality of care: "I just make a decision on the basis of what is best among the available placements. Then I look at funding." She observes that she is forced to commit more children to state training schools when correctional funding for private residential placements is suspended.

Nor do the state correctional authorities who disburse funds for the placement of children in private residential institutions effectively screen the selection of placements. The court's placement coordinator notes— with disappointment—that the state review committee approves virtually all requests for placement funds, assuming they still have money available, as long as probation officers can demonstrate the failure of community treatment and the amount of money requested falls within guidelines. "Any probation officer with a shred of manipulative ability can fill out the form successfully."

Although the court uses residential placement as a normal remedy, the quality of the various residential institutions is unevaluated. The court had to discontinue its own operation of community group homes when it could not recruit suitable replacements for several houseparents dismissed because of abusive or neglectful behavior. Some private institutions reputed to be among the best routinely employ corporal punishment. One child successfully sued a residential drug treatment program for kidnapping and keeping him against his will; this program was commonly used by the court. A number of court-involved children managed to run away from that program, terrified by the prospect of ever returning. Children occasionally experience abuse or neglect in other institutions as well. An interagency committee of state officials responsible for investigating and certifying residential institutions is extremely reluctant to close any down, preferring instead to "rehabilitate" even those found abusive or neglectful, because placements are in such short supply.

On the community level, the overlapping involvement of different agencies makes it difficult to attribute to any one of them the responsibility for particular placement decisions. Despite spending over a million dollars on the creation and maintenance of a "comprehensive" computerized management information system—a system attracting national attention—the court did not even have reliable computerized information about the children in residential institutions under its own operation, much less about the children it helped place in other institutions.

Residential institutions vary widely in expense and quality. Some small treatment centers have long waiting lists, while certain wilderness programs "will take anybody and keep them three or four years." Private psychiatric hospitals are unaffordable except for the very wealthy or those with high-option insurance; for some, the state mental hospital is the sole option, "the best placement available for the money." Yet even the most expensive institutions are not necessarily good. Certain private psychiatric hospitals mulct insurance companies shamelessly, tailoring clinical diagnoses to indicate treatment needs lasting precisely as long as periods of coverage. Probation officers observe sarcastically how invariably these hospitals find children of means to be in need of treatment, and how precipitously their conditions are found to improve as insurance coverage nears expiration. In one case, the director of a psychiatric hospital berated a court intake officer for having refused to issue a mental commitment order for a girl covered under a generous insurance policy, whom no member of the hospital staff had ever even seen. On the other hand, probation officers complain that in the absence of financial incentives, small community-based public residential facilities tend to refuse difficult cases and release children prematurely.

Even in community-based institutions, placement disrupts children's home and community ties. The ostensible purpose of placement is to prepare the child for a successful return home, but the effect is to separate the child from family, friends, and school. It is unclear how even good adjustment to institutional life alters the underlying personal and family problems which led to the child's removal from home; few parents involve themselves in the course of their children's treatment while they are away from home. Although some parents formerly unwilling to keep their children may nonetheless be willing to accept them home after periods of institutional placement, the court could work harder at convincing them to keep their children in the first place. Other children returning from residential placement have no suitable homes awaiting them; in the absence of programs helping them establish the independent living arrangements many of them need, probation officers or social workers wind up scrounging to find them foster care. Many children fail to adjust satisfactorily to residential institutions. For them, the court's primary recourse is placement in different institutions.

Placement separates children not only from family, friends, and school, but from probation officers as well. Probation officers complain that residential institutions do not keep them informed about the progress of the children they refer, failing to tell them about children's problems or runaways, and even going so far as to release the children without warning the probation officers. Yet some probation officers do not visit the children they refer to residential institutions and most ignore the parents of those children. Even though they are supposed to meet with those parents regularly to help prepare them for the children's return, probation officers relegate those meetings to the lowest task priority. Thus placement allows probation officers to distance themselves from their most trying cases.

Probation officers experience the constraints of normal casework in a context of evasion, as the responsibilities for child welfare and supervision contentiously evaded by parents and by public agencies devolve upon them. Parents abdicate these responsibilities to public authorities, who seek to disclaim them in turn. Lawmakers, administrators, oversight officials, judges, and lawyers collaborate in this chain of evasion. Lawmakers evade the difficult issues of public choice by enacting vague and contradictory child welfare legislation, legislation honoring process over substance, establishing only frameworks for ad hoc bargaining instead of authoritative guides to conduct. This type of legislative confusion only magnifies political conflict by displacing it away from the center of government to child welfare agencies in the community, which stake out the grounds of contentious evasion by defining their competencies and responsibilities in narrowly specialized ways. In seeking to enforce responsibility for serving children's diffuse needs, probation officers receive little support from juvenile court administrators, whose preoccupation with ceremonial demands of oversight bodies and opportunistic strategies of organizational growth leads them to neglect issues of interagency coordination. Nor do probation officers receive support from juvenile court judges, who refuse to bind themselves to clear and consistent judicial policy. Nor does the incomplete presence of lawyers in the juvenile court focus issues of public accountability. Probation officers can however find public and private funds for removing children to residential institutions.

Those responsibilities probation officers cannot discharge through normal casework within the context of public evasion, they can themselves evade through the normal remedy of residential placement.

10

Limits of Instrumental Rationality in Casework

robation officers experience the disorganization of juvenile justice as a combination of constraint and laxity. They are constrained by the scarcity of resources and the scarcity of political and administrative coordination. The very federal statutes that establish children's services as rights of citizenship also sanction the evasive practices of local officials who control the distribution of those services. Although the task environment in which probation officers operate spans different political jurisdictions and levels of government, there are no effective institutional arrangements to compel cooperation across those boundaries. Treatment options are limited. Caseload pressures strain the ultimate resources of time, hope, and energy.

To deal with this systemic disorganization, probation officers are left largely on their own. Just as they receive little support from organizational and political superiors, neither are they subject to effective supervision. (Neither for that matter are their superiors: the court as an agency is itself subject to only ceremonial oversight.) Casework supervisors can deny—for the moment—the filing of violations or detention orders. However, in cases of continuing disagreement with supervisors, probation officers almost always prevail. They strongly influence judicial decisions, since they determine for the most part when cases return to court, and represent the most reliable source of information for judges. Probation officers, then, are "forced to be free" in their choice of casework strategies, especially in the early stages of supervision.

Research Problem

In examining juvenile justice in the United States, it is necessary to ask what kinds of case outcomes eventuate from such a system. Taking the measure of juvenile justice requires statistical tools rather than quali-

187

tative ones. This chapter, then, switches from ethnographic description to hard numbers, in exploring a series of evaluative questions: How effective are court treatments? How equitable? How much do they vary by decision agent and by type of client? At which stage is court intervention most productive?

How indeed are outcomes even most usefully conceived? Traditionally, outcomes have been conceived in terms of recidivism, the commission of new offenses. This variable lends itself to a range of operational definitions, corresponding to different conceptions of the relation between unofficial and official criminal activity. Should recidivism be measured by self-reported rule infractions, police contacts, arrests, arrests leading to prosecution, convictions, or other indicators? Should offenses or alleged offenses be treated equally, differentiated by offense type, or weighted by seriousness? Does the choice of operational definition alter the substantive findings of delinquency or correctional research?

Before considering such definitional issues about recidivism, however, it is necessary to identify another outcome variable, equally important though usually ignored. In the wake of the receding rehabilitative ideal, the objective of the juvenile justice system should be stated not merely as the reduction of recidivism but, more precisely, as *the reduction of recidivism through the least coercive means possible.* The aim is not just to minimize new delinquency, but to do so with a minimum of court intervention, substituting whenever possible less formal means of control for more formal ones. The full articulation of this system goal suggests the incompleteness of research focusing on either outcome variable alone. Reducing recidivism and imposing coercive sanctions are best evaluated against each other.

Coercive sanctions have typically been operationally defined as incarceration or involuntary commitment to traditional secure institutions. This is an archaic choice of definition since, as Paul Lerman (1982) has demonstrated, over the past decades placement in nontraditional residential institutions has become much more frequent than incarceration. Although complete and accurate data about all types of out-of-home placement are difficult to obtain while data about incarceration are readily available (an example of cultural lag in organizational record-keeping practices), the former constitute a more valid indicator of coercive sanctions. Out-of-home placement—whether nominally voluntary or involuntary, in settings secure or nonsecure—is the core technology of probation supervision, the common dispositional recourse for children beyond control in the community. Although placement in nontraditional institutions may be less coercive than commitment to traditional secure institutions, ignoring such placement severely understates the court's recourse to drastic formal sanctions. In the jurisdiction under study, for example, approximately 40 percent of all probationers eventually found themselves in residential institutions, while fewer than 5 percent were committed to state training schools or sentenced to the local jail. (Among other considerations, using the broader indicator of coercion is statistically advantageous, since marginal distributions for placement in general are much less skewed than for commitment or incarceration.)

In any event, both recidivism and out-of-home placement are *dynamic* aspects of delinquent careers. Both imply rates (frequencies per unit of time) rather than dichotomies (yes-no condition states). Nor do they imply constant rates. In both recidivism and placement, the element of timing is significant: exactly when do the new offenses or removals from home occur? Risks of such occurrences in any given time interval are a posteriori probabilities, conditional on the outcomes of prior intervals. Simple rates, then, cannot capture the complexity of these phenomena; adequate models require a more sophisticated statistical tool.

The Suitability of Survival Analysis

Survival analysis provides such a tool. This technique cumulates sequential transition probabilities of events over time, producing graphic images of dynamic career paths. Compensating for the presence of censored and truncated observations, it calculates the proportion of an original sample still "surviving" after successive time intervals. Also known as failure-rate analysis, reliability analysis, and life-table analysis, survival analysis was originally developed to evaluate medical treatments and to test the reliability of electrical equipment. In a prominent sociological application, Heinz and Laumann (1982) use it to plot stayers and movers among Chicago lawyers. Although since the early seventies criminologists have made use of such discrete-time stochastic models as Markov chains to study recidivism, it is only recently that they have begun to make similar use of survival analysis (Maltz 1984; Schmidt and Witte 1984); Greenberg's (1979) comprehensive text *Mathematical Criminology*, for example, makes no mention of it.

Survival analysis is a statistically efficient technique for studying recidivism and removal-from-home because it preserves the full measure of variability of the phenomena themselves. Statistical efficiency is especially important in criminal justice research, where findings often prove to be nonfindings (Martinson 1974). It is hard enough, given the nature of things, to discern significant differences in rates of recidivism or removal-from-home, without dampening their natural variability through time by treating them merely as dichotomies (skewed dichotomies at that) or even as steady rates.

By partitioning the original sample into subgroups according to client characteristic, organizational server, or organizational treatment, survival analysis can yield instructive comparisons of recidivism risk, treatment bias, and treatment effectiveness. Beyond preserving full measures of statistical variation, survival analysis also preserves valuable information about the timing of recidivism and removal-from-home. Changes in survival rates over different time intervals are significant; for a treatment group, an unusually sharp decline in the remainder still recidivating in a given time interval might, for example, reveal a treatment effect. Time itself can act as a suppressor variable; an effect during one time interval might be reversed in the next, so that a static measure would indicate the absence of any effect instead of the coincidence of two opposing ones.

In compensating for censored or truncated observations, survival analysis also makes full use of inevitably incomplete data. Logistical constraints on the research process, definitional constructs of the juvenile justice system, and inherent ambiguities all generate incomplete data about recidivism and removal-from-home. Follow-up periods for tracking delinquent careers are finite; cases "surviving" at the end of the period are "censored" since their possible subsequent failures would go unobserved. Children who graduate from the juvenile justice system because they turn eighteen prior to the end of the follow-up period represent "truncated" cases, as do probationers whose supervision terminates when their families move away from the area, as many do. Survival analysis compensates statistically for necessarily imperfect data about cases whose exposure to the possibility of failure is either shorter or longer than a standard follow-up period.

Data Sources

The cases of 629 children provide the data to be analyzed. These cases, selected at random from the daily logs of the court's intake department, represent approximately 18 percent of all delinquency intakes in the particular locality under study during calendar year 1975; these logs were the only complete listing maintained during that period. In selecting a cohort of delinquents who shared the common experience of court intake during this time, I found it unfeasible to include only first offenders or to stratify the sample in any way. The resulting simple random sample of intake subjects contains disproportionate shares of children having multiple intakes during the selection period (although no single child is included more than once). It is statistically advantageous for analyzing the advanced stages of delinquents' careers to capture greater numbers of cases "surviving" that long. While limiting the validity of point estimates, this selection procedure does not invalidate observed relations among variables.

Complete offense and treatment histories through the summer of 1978 were gathered for these cases from the court's official social and legal files. Thus each case was tracked retrospectively for a minimum of two and a half years; those cases originating before 1975 were tracked for longer periods ranging up to eight years. Although some of these case histories are extensive, most are short: of the 629 children in the cohort, only 395 ever had even a single judicial hearing, only 237 were ever subject to a social investigation by probation officers, and only 202 were ever placed under any form of probation supervision. Only 79 were ever placed out-of-home in a residential institution, either traditional or nontraditional.*

* For this and other reasons, the statistical analyses reported in the pages to follow are based on samples of different sizes. Most graphs in this chapter, charting survival probabilities from the start of supervision, refer to nonmissing cases among the sample of 202 probationers. Some graphs, however, refer to particular subsamples of that group. Figure 10.1 refers to nonmissing cases among the 66 children removed from home by direct judicial action. Figures 10.23 and 10.24 refer to nonmissing cases among the 180 probationers who were white; figures 10.25 and 10.26 refer to nonmissing cases among the 70 probationers whose fathers had neither professional nor managerial jobs; figures 10.27 through 10.28 refer to nonmissing cases among the 104 probationers whose mothers never attended college.

Plots of survival probabilities from other processing points are based on different samples. Figures 10.38 and 10.41 refer to nonmissing cases among the 237 youths subject to social investigation. Figures 10.3, 10.37, and 10.40, which measure survival probabilities from the time of first intake, refer to nonmissing cases among a subsample of 370 first offenders in 1975, selected from the entire set of 629 cases according to a weighting procedure designed to correct for the disproportionate inclusion in that larger sample of children with multiple intakes in that year. (Since this subsample therefore represents a random sample of first offenders rather than of intakes, the point-estimates displayed in those graphs are valid.)

An entire range of reasons accounts for the cases missing, in varying number, from the statistical analysis depicted in each graph. Sloppy record-keeping practices of court staff and the incomplete transfer of information from other courts result in the loss of considerable data. Such unusual case circumstances as referral for social investigation only after (rather than before) assignment to supervision cause other cases to be treated as missing. Still other cases are excluded from a particular analysis because they fall into a category whose frequency is too low for inclusion: the 7 children removed from home by various substitute judges are treated as missing cases in figure 10.1, just as the 17 children whose

Court files are deservedly notorious for their disorganization. In addition to the "good organizational reasons for bad organizational records" that Garfinkel (1967) describes, court staff are often too busy with more pressing matters to do justice to their paperwork. Records are incomplete and inconsistent. The process of gathering data on these 629 cases involved cross-validating the separate legal and clinical files about each child, interviewing court staff when necessary to fill in obvious gaps or reconcile evident contradictions.

In an improvement over usual techniques of gathering data from court files, the coding instrument was specifically designed to reflect the recursive nature of the case flow. Disposition of a single complaint often requires multiple hearings, and additional hearings may always be convened for reviews or violations; yet any number of separate complaints originating at different times may receive partial or total disposition in a single hearing. Court proceedings become especially entangled when new complaints against the same individual arrive in such rapid succession that processes overlap. Juvenile court dispositions involve not only judgments of guilt or innocence and orders of treatment or punishment, but also repeated determinations of short- and long-term custody. The coding instrument was designed to capture the processing and disposition of each complaint in its full complexity.

Even though coded on a complaint-by-complaint basis, the records were then reorganized though a process of data manipulation to treat the individual offender as the unit of analysis. Unfortunately this sort of data manipulation is lacking in many studies of court decision-making. There is good reason to *code* data on a complaint-by-complaint basis, mirroring the organization of court files. Court files are primarily designed to organize the flow of legal and organizational documents, which tend to be keyed to complaints. Yet judges and other court officials make their decisions about people. The dispositions of complaints are not statistically independent of one another, since the disposition of any particular complaint is directly affected by previous dispositions involving the same person—as well as by any subsequent dispositions already in the works. Although it is all too common in studies such as this to analyze the outcomes of discrete complaints, the appropriate focus of analysis is instead the career paths of individual offenders.

---

probation was supervised by court workers outside the three major probation units are treated as missing in figure 10.2.

The very concept of sample size is ambiguous in survival analysis, since that procedure explicitly recognizes the gradual attrition of every sample through censorship and truncation as well as termination of cases. The *n* indicated for each category on the graphs to follow identifies the number of nonmissing cases entering the initial time interval.

Strategy of Analysis and Choice of Variables

The essential strategy for analyzing these career paths is to contrast, for selected groups of children on probation, the risk of recidivism with that of removal-from-home. These risks are not simple ratios, but rather series of conditional transitional probabilities. Survival analysis provides the tool for contrasting these types of risk.

Recidivism is defined as the receipt of new complaints by court intake. The problematic relation of official to unofficial delinquency statistics need not be of concern, even aside from findings (e.g. Hindelang, Hirschi, and Weis 1981) of impressive congruence between such data sources. Since new complaints provide the best information available to court officials, this definition is the most valid for the research problem at hand: recidivism as a factor in court decision-making. Complaints brought by probation officers themselves, such as those alleging probation violations or requests for review, are excluded because they vary according to the discretion of probation officers as well as the behavior of their probationers. The chosen definition focuses on complaints rather than adjudications of guilt because decisions to divert or dismiss complaints are made primarily for informal or organizational reasons rather than substantive evidentiary ones.

To measure recidivism over time requires a number of operational definitions, since no single one captures the different dimensions of variation. Recidivism careers extend over time, suggesting time as one obvious measure. Yet in a given time span, complaints may arrive with varying frequency, so counting complaints is also necessary. Since these complaints may vary in seriousness,* recidivism should also be measured as a cumulation of seriousness-scores. In combination, this complement of operational definitions—time, frequency, and seriousness—covers the significant dimensions of recidivism.

Conceptualizing *survival* in different ways facilitates the contrast of offense and treatment histories for selected subgroups of probationers. One type of survival consists in continuing delinquent activity; another consists in continuing permission to remain in the community. In the first conceptualization, survival functions plot recidivism risks *directly*; in the second, risks of removal-from-home are plotted *inversely*. Thus, when "recidivism" survival functions for distinct subgroups are superimposed in plots of *offense* histories, the highest line on the graph

---

*Offense seriousness is scaled as the product of two factors—offense type (against persons = 3; against property = 2; other = 1) and legal classification (felony = 3; class-one misdemeanor = 2; other = 1). To prevent attrition of the sample size, the average of a child's known seriousness scores is used in place of each missing score.

Table 10.1 Complementary Dependent Variables

Metric	Type of Survival	Variable Name
Time	Recidivism	Time actively recidivating during supervision
	Freedom from removal-from-home	Time during supervision until placement
Complaint count	Recidivism	New complaints during supervision
	Freedom from removal-from-home	New complaints during supervision prior to placement
Cumulative se- riousness score	Recidivism	Sum of seriousness scores of new complaints dur- ing supervision
	Freedom from removal-from-home	Sum of seriousness scores of new complaints dur- ing supervision prior to placement

represents the *greatest* risk of recidivism; but when "freedom-from-placement" survival functions for distinct subgroups are superimposed in plots of *treatment* histories, the highest line on the graph represents the *least* risk of removal-from-home.

Time, complaint count, and cumulative seriousness-score provide the metrics for both types of survival, yielding the six complementary dependent variables listed in table 10.1.

Partitioning the sample makes it possible to compare the contrasting types of survival rates among the resulting subgroups. This approach suggests the essential strategy of the analysis to follow. For given categories of children under supervision, do the relative risks of removal-from-home correspond to the relative risks of recidivism? If not, can this be explained by the choice of metric? If, for example, lower proportions of a particular subgroup are permitted to remain in the community at each complaint transition, though no more likely to recidivate, is that because they tend to commit more serious offenses? Do the same effects persist when cumulative seriousness-scores rather than complaint counts chart the transition intervals?

The sets of categories which form the bases of intersubgroup comparison describe a set of independent variables. These variables range from court decision-agents to client demographics, family backgrounds, institutional statuses, and living situations. Table 10.2 lists these variables, with their category values and marginal distributions among children under probation supervision.

The set of all hypothetical combinations of recidivism risk with removal-from-home risk defines a typology of treatment modes associated with these independent variables as potential effects. Comparisons among subgroups may reveal insignificant* differences in either type of risk, indicating the apparent absence of any effect (although it is necessary to remember that such weak zero-order effects may conceal suppressed higher-order effects). Alternatively, intersubgroup comparisons may reveal significant differences in both types of risk. If these differences are in the same direction—that is, if the subgroup at greater recidivism risk is also at greater removal-from-home risk—this indicates "firm but fair" treatment; if the differences are in opposite directions, this indicates "blatantly unfair" treatment. Finally, these comparisons may reveal significant differences in only one type of risk: a subgroup at greater risk of removal-from-home but not at correspondingly greater risk of recidivism may be said to receive "unfair" treatment; conversely, a subgroup at greater risk of recidivism but not at correspondingly greater risk of removal-from-home may be said to receive "the benefit of the doubt."

Negligible Effects

Longstanding concern with problems of "discretionary justice" (Davis 1969) has assumed renewed urgency with recent emphases on sentencing disparity among judges and the power of "street-level bureaucrats" (Lipsky 1980). This concern warrants inquiry into the variation of treatments administered by different judges and probation officers. There are too many probation officers to treat them individually as distinct decision-agents, but there is strong rationale for treating the three probation units separately. Previous research (Jacobs 1978) indicates that the various decentralized probation units of this court, ecologically segregated from one another, exhibit subcultural differences which affect the processing of cases. (One unit, for example, expressed its distrust of judicial

---

*Throughout this study, a confidence level of .10 is used as the criterion of statistical significance.

Table 10.2 Independent Variables and Their Category Values

	Category Values	No. of Cases
Decision agents		
Judge ordering placement	A	15
	B	19
	C	17
	D	7
Probation unit	North	46
	Central	59
	South	47
Demographics		
Area	High delinquency	33
	Low delinquency	175
Race	Black	21
	White	180
Sex	Male	158
	Female	42
Age	12 or younger	14
	13–14	46
	15–16	112
	17 or older	30
SES		
Father's occupation	Professional and managerial	81
	Other	70
Mother's education	Some college	39
	No college	104
Institutional factors		
History of crime in family	Yes	45
	No	88
School enrollment	Yes	172
	No	18
Child's employment	Yes	33
	No	116
Age at first offense	12 or younger	32
	13–14	75
	15–16	80
	17 or older	14

Table 10.2 (*continued*)

	Category Values	No. of Cases
Offender classification at first intake	CHINS	92
	Delinquent	103
Situational factors		
Parents' marital status	Both natural parents	103
	Other	98
Child's living situation	Both parents	102
	One parent	78
	Neither parent	17
Runaway	Yes	31
	No	167

discretion by delaying the return of social investigations to court significantly longer than the others, despite a relatively light workload.)

Yet figures 10.1 and 10.2 indicate no significant difference in the rates of removal-from-home among cases handled by different judges or different probation units. These figures superimpose survival functions for separate caseloads. At each interval along the horizontal axis, the vertical coordinate indicates the proportion of the original caseload not yet removed from home. In each figure, the separate survival functions essentially plot a single line. (Because the children's cases as they return to court are routinely reassigned to different judges, figure 10.1 attributes a case to the judge who first ordered long-term removal from home. Consequently the survival functions in this figure all ultimately decline to zero, since they track only those children eventually removed from home. By contrast, since children generally retain the same probation unit throughout the course of this supervision, figure 10.2 plots the treatment careers of all children assigned to supervision, including those never removed from home.) Despite the concern over treatment disparities resulting from official discretion, no such treatment effects appear to exist.

The effects of other variables are negligible as well, some surprisingly so. As suggested by delinquency research deriving from the classic studies of Shaw and McKay ([1942] 1969), first offenders at intake who come from "delinquency areas" are significantly more likely to recidivate than those not from such areas. Figure 10.3 depicts this observation. Delinquency areas are defined as those subcensus tracts producing the great-

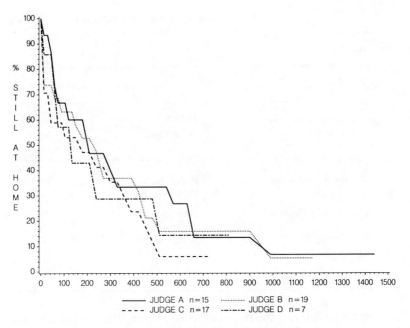

Fig. 10.1. Removal-from-home risk, by judge (as measured against time in days).

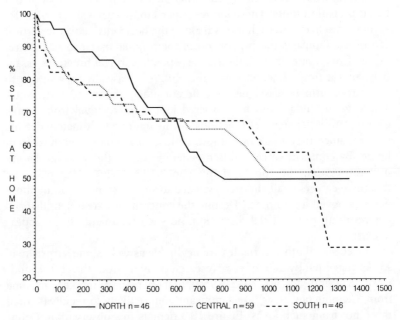

Fig. 10.2. Removal-from-home risk during supervision, by probation unit (as measured against time in days).

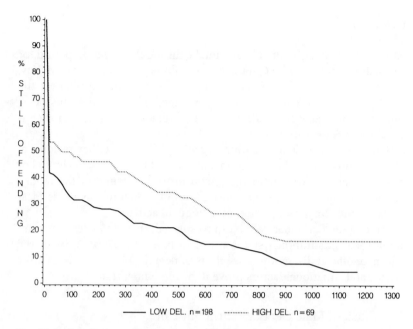

Fig. 10.3. Recidivism risk after first intake, by area (as measured against time in days).

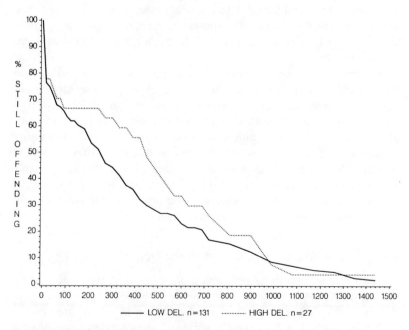

Fig. 10.4. Recidivism risk during supervision, by area (as measured against time in days).

est number of alleged offenders at intake during the selection period for the sample under study. Contrary to the findings of Shaw and McKay, however, these same delinquency areas do not significantly affect the recidivism risks of children under probation, as figure 10.4 illustrates; nor do delinquency areas affect the risk of removal-from-home for children under court supervision.

Other variables demonstrating negligible effects on either recidivism risk or removal-from-home risk include type of first offense (criminal or noncriminal), child's employment, and history of crime in the family. School enrollment affects recidivism, but only when recidivism is measured by the temporal duration of delinquent activity.

Among the particular variables investigated, then, the effects of community and institutional status prove to be negligible along with the effects of official discretion. The effects of demographic variables, family status, and situational factors prove to be more important.

The Effect of Male Gender: "Firm but Fair"

After each given number of complaints during the course of supervision, lower proportions of boys than of girls have escaped out-of-home placement. This trend (as fig. 10.5 shows) is especially pronounced after four complaints. Yet (as fig. 10.6 shows) boys are not significantly more likely than girls to remain active in delinquency after successive numbers of complaints.

Although this comparison of contrasting survival rates would seem to imply that boys receive unfair treatment, plotting these same rates against a different metric reverses this impression. Figures 10.7 and 10.8 chart survival against cumulative offense-seriousness rather than complaint count. Boys are significantly greater recidivism risks than girls according to this metric (as fig. 10.7 demonstrates), so they are not at significantly greater risks of removal-from-home (as plotted in fig. 10.8). The apparent unfairness suggested by figures 10.5 and 10.6 is simply explained by the tendency of boys to commit more serious offenses than do girls; the treatment accorded boys is "firm but fair."

The Effect of Young Age: "Benefit of the Doubt"

Few variables occupy as venerable a place in the literature about predicting delinquency as age at first offense (Reiss 1951; Mannheim and Wilkins 1955; Glaser 1964; West and Farrington 1973). Whatever metric is used—whether, for example, survival is measured in terms of time (as in fig. 10.9) or cumulative seriousness-score (as in fig. 10.10)—the

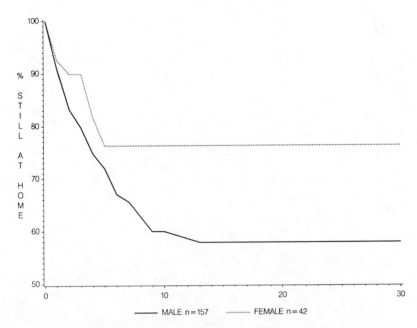

Fig. 10.5. Removal-from-home risk during supervision, by sex (as measured against complaint count).

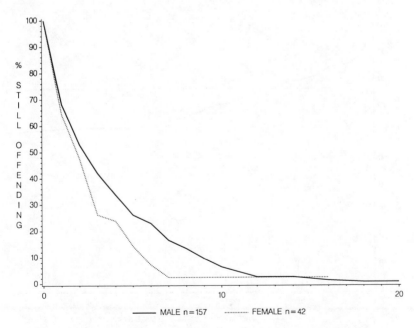

Fig. 10.6. Recidivism risk during supervision, by sex (as measured against complaint count).

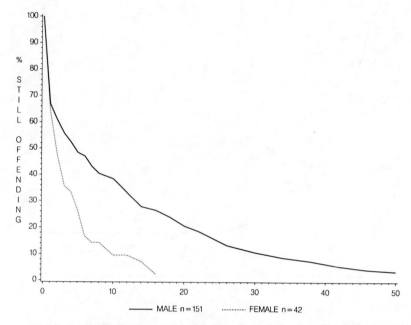

Fig. 10.7. Recidivism risk during supervision, by sex (as measured against cumulative seriousness-score).

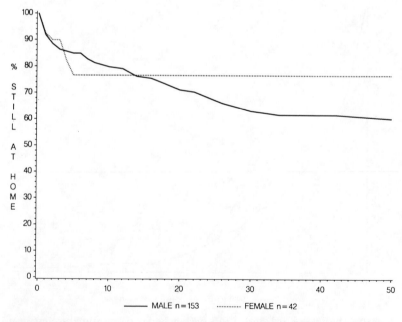

Fig. 10.8. Removal-from-home risk during supervision, by sex (as measured against cumulative seriousness-score).

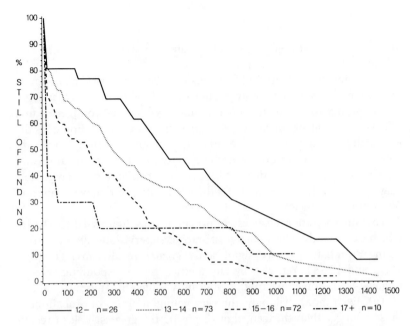

Fig. 10.9. Recidivism risk during supervision, by age at first intake (as measured against time in days).

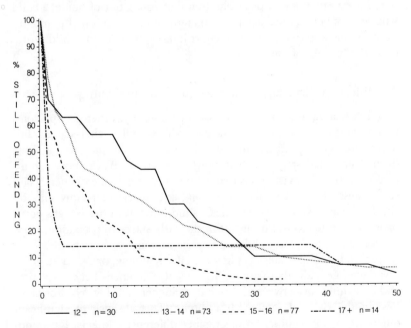

Fig. 10.10. Recidivism risk during supervision, by age at first intake (as measured against cumulative seriousness-score).

younger the age at first offense, the greater the rate of recidivism. This relation is statistically significant.

According to the metric of seriousness-score, the risk of removal-from-home is correspondingly greater as well (as fig.10.11 illustrates). Yet according to the metric of time, those who were younger at first offense are not at significantly greater risk of removal-from-home (as the essentially overlapping separate survival rates graphed in fig. 10.12 indicate). Court officials do not hesitate to remove from home at greater rates those who were younger at first offense than others at comparable stages of their offense histories. Yet they do hesitate to remove them from home at too young an age.

This interpretation receives confirmation from figures 10.13–10.16, which examine the effects of age at start of supervision. By any metric, younger probationers are significantly greater recidivism risks (figs. 10.13 and 10.14). Yet, also by any metric, the corresponding risks of removal-from-home are not significantly different (figs. 10.15 and 10.16). Even more strikingly, the very youngest group of probationers, those younger than thirteen, though posing the greatest risk of recidivism, are least likely to face removal from home. Whether because placements for children under thirteen are relatively scarce or because court officials are unwilling to place children that young out-of-home, a child who has not yet attained age thirteen enjoys a presumption of immunity from the most extreme forms of court intervention. Young children receive the "benefit of the doubt."

The Effects of Race and Family Status: "Parental Dump"

While young age confers this sort of immunity, other groups commonly presumed to be advantaged—whites and higher-status children—are actually at heightened risk of removal-from-home, at least during the initial stages of their court supervision. Blacks pose significantly greater recidivism risks than whites, judging by the frequency and seriousness of new complaints; so—by any metric of recidivism—do children from lower-status families, as indicated by either father's occupation or mother's education. Yet in the early stages of probation, more whites and higher-status children experience removal from home.

Survival analysis makes explicit the effects of time, or career stage, as a variable. Overall, there are no significant differences between whites and nonwhites, or between children from higher- and lower-status families, in the risks of removal-from-home. This absence of significant differences is misleading, however, since differences do exist but in opposite directions during the early and late stages of probation supervi-

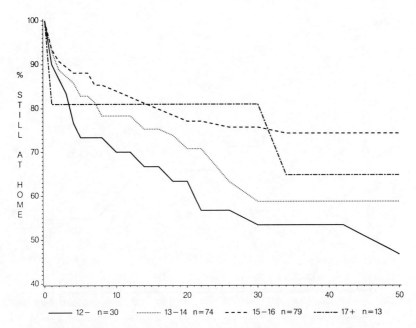

Fig. 10.11. Removal-from-home risk during supervision, by age at first intake (as measured against cumulative seriousness-score).

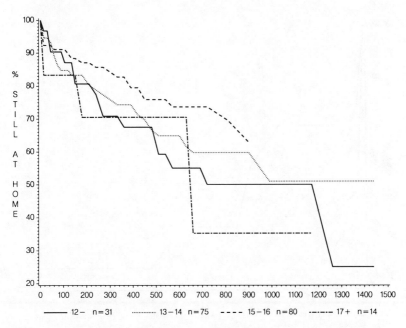

Fig. 10.12. Removal-from-home risk during supervision, by age at first intake (as measured against time in days).

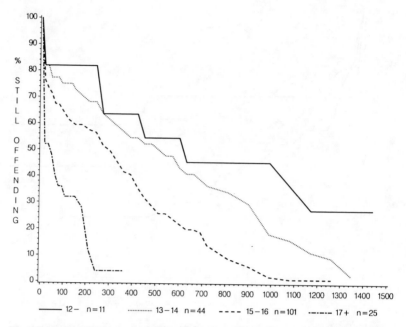

Fig. 10.13. Recidivism risk, by age at supervision (as measured against time in days).

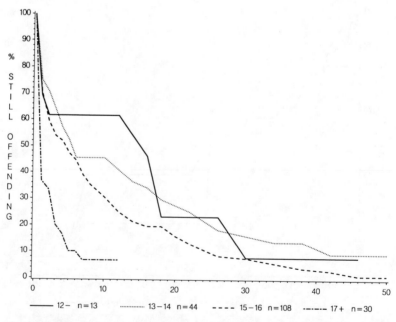

Fig. 10.14. Recidivism risk, by age at supervision (as measured against cumulative seriousness-score).

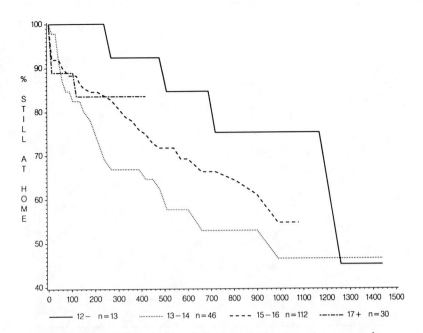

Fig. 10.15. Removal-from-home risk, by age at supervision (as measured against time in days).

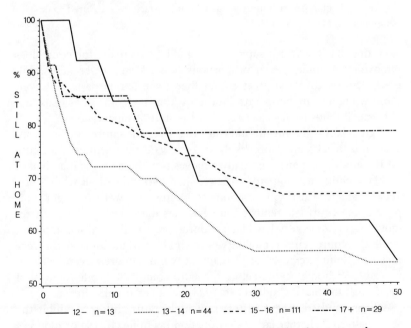

Fig. 10.16. Removal-from-home risk, by age at supervision (as measured against cumulative seriousness-score).

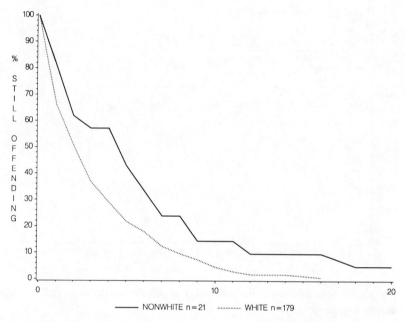

Fig. 10.17. Recidivism risk during supervision, by race (as measured against complaint count).

sion; time itself acts as a suppressor variable. Eventually the court does remove from home greater proportions of black and lower-status children, who recidivate at greater rates than their counterparts; however, those white and higher-status children whom the court does place out of home, it tends to place sooner after the start of supervision.

Figure 10.17 graphically indicates that over the entire course of supervision, blacks are more likely to recidivate than whites. As figure 10.18 shows, the court eventually removes from home more than half of all black children, compared to fewer than two-fifths of all white ones. Yet as that figure also shows, among children with fewer than eight complaints, the court has removed more whites than blacks. The court removes from home very few black children prior to their fifth complaint, while the court starts removing white children from home at the very first complaint. Removal of virtually all white children eventually removed from home occurs before the sixth complaint, while removal of nearly half the black children eventually removed occurs after it.

Offense and treatment histories of high-status children exhibit the same pattern. Whether father's occupation (as in fig. 10.19) or mother's education (as in fig. 10.20) serves as the indicator of family status,

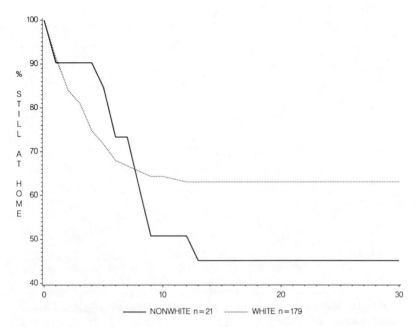

Fig. 10.18. Removal-from-home risk during supervision, by race (as measured against complaint count).

lower-status children pose consistently and significantly greater risks of recidivism.

Relative risks of removal-from-home, however, are quite different in the first year and a half of court supervision than in the period that follows. Figure 10.21 reveals that children whose fathers work as professionals or managers are at greater risk for the initial period than children whose fathers occupy lower occupational statuses, while according to figure 10.22 it is only in the later period that children whose mothers did not attend college are at greater risk of placement than children of college-educated mothers.

These findings seem paradoxical. Why are white and higher-status children, whose parents are relatively powerful, at more immediate risk of removal-from-home than others less privileged? The statement of this paradox suggests the most plausible solution: the treatments accorded these "privileged" children must be the ones sought by their parents. Even black and lower-status parents can delay the court's placement of their children out-of-home by resisting that placement. White and higher-status parents, with greater resources at their command, can be even more successful at resisting the court's removal of their children;

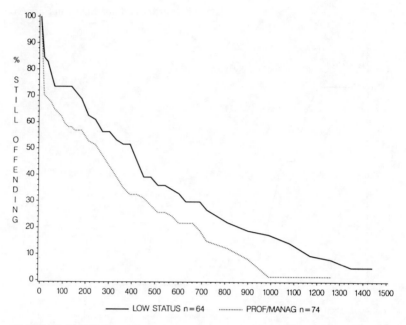

Fig. 10.19. Recidivism risk during supervision, by father's occupation (as measured against time in days).

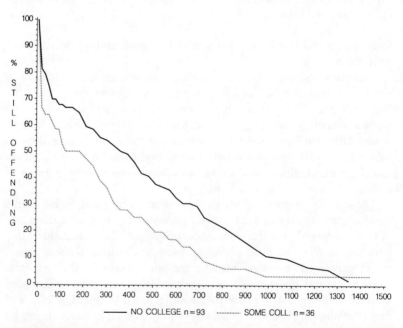

Fig. 10.20. Recidivism risk during supervision, by mother's education (as measured against time in days).

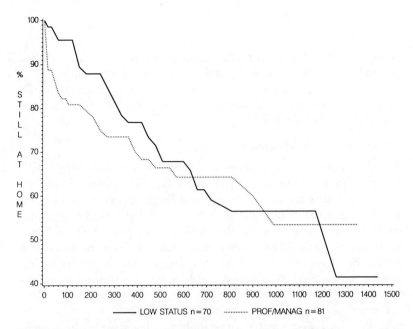

Fig. 10.21. Removal-from-home risk during supervision, by father's occupation (as measured against time in days).

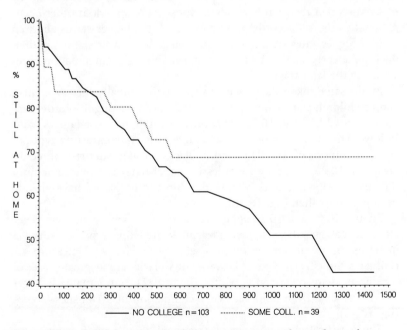

Fig. 10.22. Removal-from-home risk during supervision, by mother's education (as measured against time in days).

on the other hand, those same parents can often use the court for their own ends if they choose to seek relief from parental responsibilities. The statistical evidence that placement comes quickly when it comes for white and higher-status children may well reflect a practice familiar to court staff as the "parental dump."

Testing Statistical Independence

In the particular sample of cases at hand, it so happens that virtually no black children come from higher-status families. This would make it easy to confound the effects of race and family status, suggesting the need for further statistical analysis: what are the effects of race among children from lower-status families, and what are the effects of family status among whites? (Since the sample includes almost no black children from higher-status families, it is not possible to investigate the possible interaction of race and family status any more thoroughly than this.)

Figures 10.23 and 10.24 suggest that family status exercises essentially the same effect among whites only as among the entire sample. White children whose fathers work as professionals or managers exhibit lower recidivism rates (measured, as in fig. 10.23, by cumulative seriousness-scores) than white children whose fathers work at other occupational levels. Yet according to figure 10.24, the higher-status children exhibit higher rates of removal-from-home than lower-status children during the early stages of supervision, even though that situation is reversed in the later stages.

By the same token, race seems to exercise essentially the same effect among children from lower-status families only as among the entire sample. Figures 10.25 and 10.26 apply only to children whose fathers work in lower-status occupations; these figures measure contrasting types of survival in terms of complaint count. Blacks are at greater risk of recidivism (fig. 10.25); yet they are at lesser risk of removal-from-home until the sixth complaint, since almost all whites to be placed have already been placed by then (fig. 10.26).

Figures 10.27 and 10.28 apply only to children whose mothers never attended college; these figures measure contrasting types of survival in terms of cumulative seriousness-score. This choice of measure accentuates the effects of race. Lower-status blacks are at greater risk of recidivism than lower-status whites (fig. 10.27), but actually at lesser risk of removal-from-home at every cumulation of seriousness-scores (fig. 10.28).

The statistical effects of race on treatment, then, remain strong even while controlling for family status, even as the effects of status remain

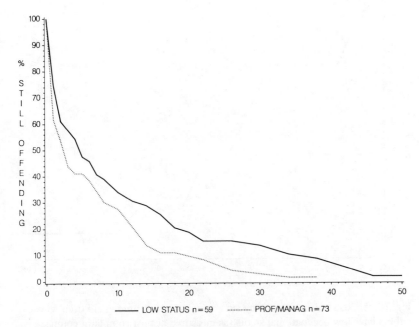

Fig. 10.23. Recidivism risk during supervision, by father's occupation, among whites (as measured against cumulative seriousness-score).

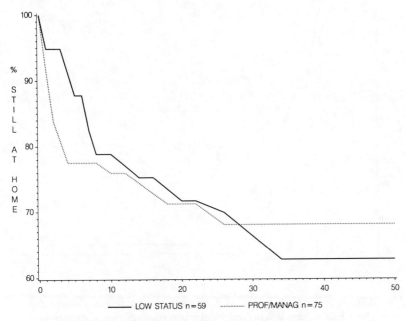

Fig. 10.24. Removal-from-home risk during supervision, by father's occupation, among whites (as measured against cumulative seriousness-score).

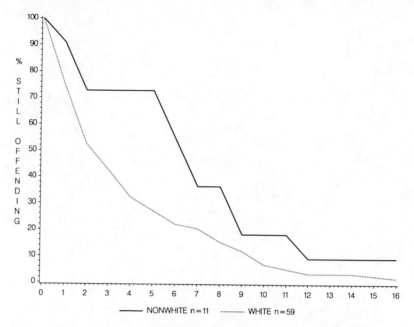

Fig. 10.25. Recidivism risk during supervision, by race, among children whose fathers have low occupational status (as measured against complaint count).

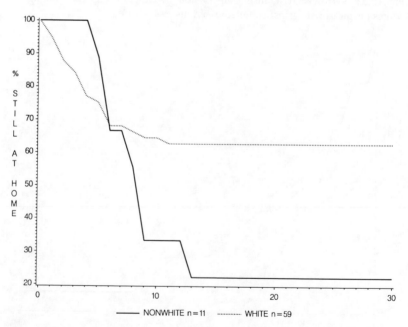

Fig. 10.26. Removal-from-home risk during supervision, by race, among children whose fathers have low occupational status (as measured against complaint count).

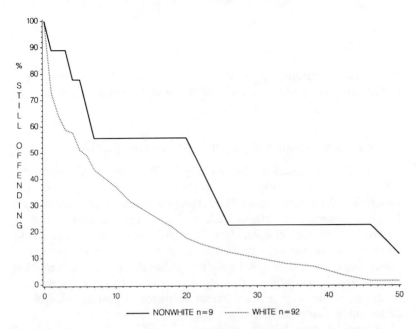

Fig. 10.27. Recidivism risk during supervision, by race, among children whose mothers never attended college (as measured against cumulative seriousness-score).

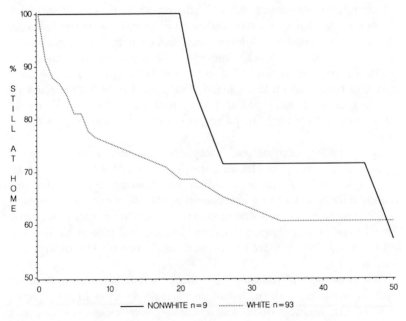

Fig. 10.28. Removal-from-home risk during supervision, by race, among children whose mothers never attended college (as measured against cumulative seriousness-score).

strong while controlling for race. These effects are in large degree statistically independent; both whites and upper-status children appear vulnerable to the "parental dump."

The Effects of Situational Factors: "Unfair Treatment"

The effects of situational factors suggest even more emphatically the influence parents exercise over the court's decision making. The related variables of the parents' marital status and the child's living situation are largely unrelated to recidivism risk but significantly related to risk of removal-from-home: children from broken homes and children living apart from their parents experience out-of-home placement at significantly higher rates than other children, although their recidivism rates are no greater than others'. It is more complicated to characterize the treatment of runaways, since different measures suggest different interpretations of that treatment.

Figures 10.29 and 10.30, comparing the effects of parents' marital status on recidivism and removal-from-home, respectively, plot those risks against a metric of elapsed time; figures 10.31 and 10.32, comparing the same effects of child's living situation, plot risk against a metric of cumulative seriousness-score. With respect to these two variables, however, the choice of metric makes no difference. By any measure, as these figures illustrate, children from broken homes are significantly more likely to experience removal-from-home than children whose natural parents are still married, even though the children are no more likely to recidivate; children already living apart from both parents are similarly at significantly greater risk of out-of-home placement than children living with at least one parent, although their recidivism risk is no greater.

These findings can be readily explained by the powers of "parental sponsorship" (in David Matza's phrase) to dissuade the court from removing a child from home. Children from nontraditional families and children living apart from their parents are at risk of out-of-home placement entirely out of proportion to the risk of recidivism they pose. There may be compelling organizational and institutional reasons for this sort of treatment, but they are not correctional in nature. The treatment is "unfair."

The treatment of runaways, fair in one sense, is unfair in another. Judged according to the metric of time remaining active in delinquency (fig. 10.33), runaways do pose significantly greater recidivism risks than nonrunaways, justifying their greater risk of removal-from-home (figure 10.34).

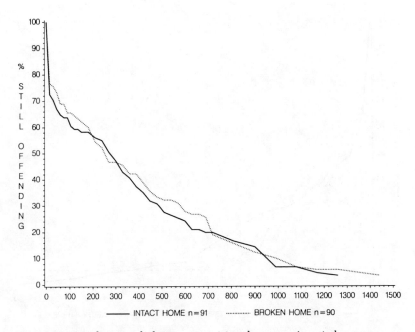

Fig. 10.29. Recidivism risk during supervision, by parents' marital status (as measured against time in days).

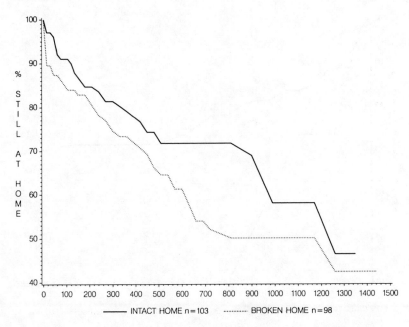

Fig. 10.30. Removal-from-home risk during supervision, by parents' marital status (as measured against time in days).

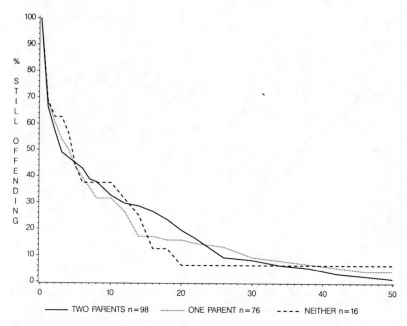

Fig. 10.31. Recidivism risk during supervision, by child's living situation (as measured against cumulative seriousness-score).

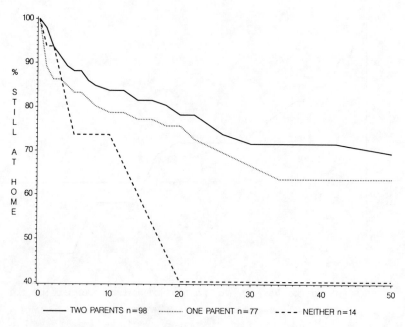

Fig. 10.32. Removal-from-home risk during supervision, by child's living situation (as measured against cumulative seriousness-score).

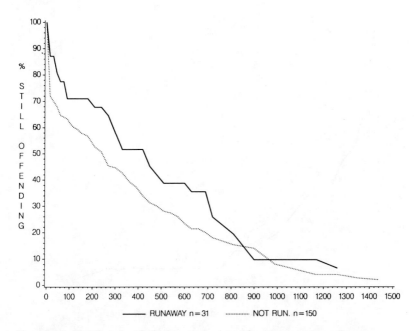

Fig. 10.33. Recidivism risk during supervision, by runaway status (as measured against time in days).

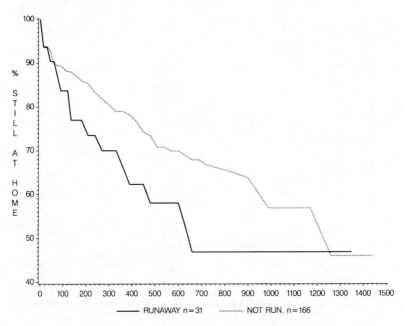

Fig. 10.34. Removal-from-home risk during supervision, by runaway status (as measured against time in days).

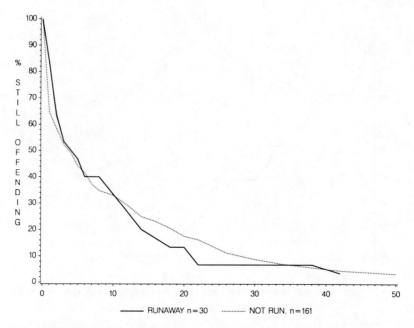

Fig. 10.35. Recidivism risk during supervision, by runaway status (as measured against cumulative seriousness-score).

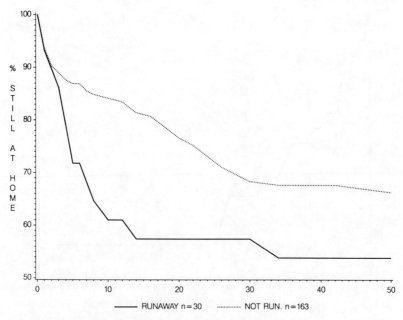

Fig. 10.36. Removal-from-home risk during supervision, by runaway status (as measured against cumulative seriousness-score).

Runaways tend to have longer delinquent careers than nonrunaways, but their offenses tend to be less frequent and even less serious. Judged according to the metric of cumulative seriousness-score, runaways are no more likely to recidivate than nonrunaways (fig. 10.35), yet are more likely to experience removal-from-home (fig. 10.36). (The differences in removal-from-home risk charted by figs. 10.34 and 10.36 are not quite statistically significant at the .10 level.)

Despite this ambiguity in interpreting the effects of runaway status, such other situational factors as the parents' marital status and the child's living situation clearly produce "unfair" treatment.

Table 10.3 summarizes all the treatment effects (or noneffects) revealed so far. This table reports the significance levels of differences in both recidivism risk and removal-from-home risk (using several metrics) among the categories of probationers defined by each independent variable. To the degree that for any given group these two types of risk are incommensurate, the court's treatment is inequitable. The statistical comparisons summarized in table 10.3, then, measure one important dimension of the court's performance—that of fairness. Another such dimension is that of effectiveness.

The Effects of Intervention at Different Career Stages

How great an effect overall does court supervision exercise? In the absence of a true experimental situation, with "experimentals" and "controls" randomly assigned to supervision or not, it is impossible to answer this question definitively. Yet it remains instructive to make certain statistical comparisons. Before deciding whether to assign children to supervision, it was customary (at least during the period of time covered by this study) for judges to order investigations into the children's backgrounds and circumstances. Most children were assigned to court supervision directly upon completion of those investigations; others were not assigned to formal supervision, at least for the while. Among children under court investigation for the first time, how do recidivism rates of those assigned directly to supervision differ from the rates of those not directly assigned?

This comparison can be replicated to explore the effects of court intervention at other career stages, both prior and subsequent to the investigation stage. Among children subject to their first complaint before the court's intake department, how do recidivism rates of those sent on to formal judicial hearings differ from the rates of those diverted from

Table 10.3 Observed Treatment Effects: Significance Levels of Comparisons among Subgroups of Probationers for Different Types and Metrics of Survival

Independent Variables	Dependent Variables						Treatment Mode
	Time Recidivating during Supv.	Time until Plcmt.	Complaints during Supv.	Complaints until Plcmt.	Seriousness Score during Supv.	Seriousness Score until Plcmt.	
Decision agents							
Judge	.33	.72	.69	.53	.69	.42	Negligible effect
Probation unit	.65	.86	.68	.91	.32	.96	Negligible effect
Demographics							
Area	.80	.96	.30	.60	.92	.66	Negligible effect
Race	.12	.76	.05**	.60	.01**	.50	Parental dump
Sex	.51	.12	.15	.09*	.03**	.20	Firm but fair
Age	.00**	.16	.00**	.37	.00**	.34	Benefit of the doubt

SES							
Father's occ.	.06*	.27	.06*	.57	.00**	.83	Parental dump
Mother's occ.	.04**	.77	.02**	.80	.01**	.41	Parental dump
Institutional factors							
History of crime in family	.23	.30	.51	.41	.13	.36	Negligible effect
School enrollment	.02**	.86	.11	.50	.19	.56	Negligible effect
Child's employment	.38	.79	.35	.83	.36	.96	Negligible effect
Age at first offense	.00**	.47	.00**	.10*	.00**	.09*	Firm but fair
Offender classification	.90	.70	.94	.96	.87	.50	Negligible effect
Situational factors							
Parents' marital status	.60	.08*	.67	.05**	.85	.02**	Unfair
Child's living situation	.27	.07*	.59	.05**	.76	.02**	Unfair
Runaway	.02**	.11	.10	.24	.56	.13	(Ambiguous)

NOTE: The significance levels are based on the Lee-Desu statistic.

* .10 level.

** .05 level.

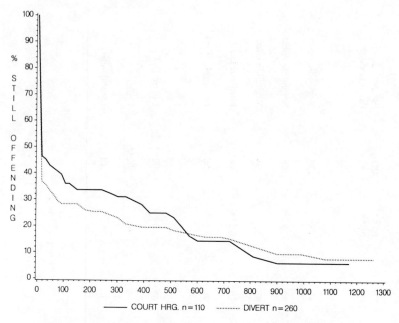

Fig. 10.37. Recidivism risk after first intake, by disposition of first intake (as measured against time in days).

formal processing? Among children under court supervision, how do recidivism rates of those placed out-of-home in residential institutions differ from the rates of those not placed?

As indicated by figure 10.37, formal court intervention seems successful at the time of first intake. Intake counselors exercise sensible discrimination in issuing the petitions that initiate formal judicial processing, since children receiving petitions represent greater recidivism risks—at least for the first year and a half following the intake—than those diverted from formal processing. Formal court processing also seems to produce the desired result, since the slope of the cumulative survival function graphing recidivism rates declines more rapidly for those subjected to judicial processing than for those diverted from such processing, so that the recidivism rate of the former group eventually drops below that of the latter. Thus selection for formal court processing is not only appropriately discriminating but also effective.

By contrast, selection for supervision among those under court investigation for the first time seems neither effective nor appropriately discriminating. As figure 10.38 reveals, the group of children assigned to

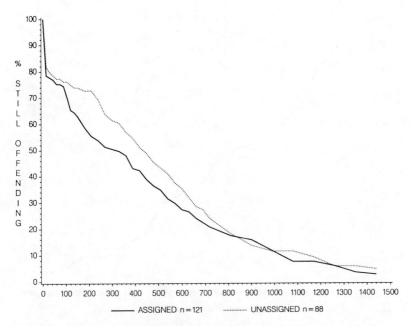

Fig. 10.38. Recidivism risk after start of investigation, by immediate decision about assignment to supervision (as measured against time in days).

supervision at the time of first investigation exhibits essentially the same recidivism rate as the group unassigned at that time; the survival functions plotting recidivism for these two groups overlap at all points. It is worth emphasizing again that since these groups are not matched, the comparison is not conclusive. The observations presented in figure 10.38 lend themselves to other possible interpretations. It could be argued, for example, that the children assigned directly to supervision do pose a greater recidivism risk, but that the effectiveness of probation reduces that risk to the same level as the others'. Assuming however that probation supervision requires some time to produce its effects, this argument cannot explain why the two groups' levels of recidivism risk are so equal *at all time intervals*. If figure 10.37 seems to indicate that the issuance of a petition at first intake is both properly discriminating and effective, figure 10.38 seems to indicate that selection for supervision is neither.

Among children under court supervision, further court intervention takes the form of removal from home to long-term residential institutions. As figure 10.39 demonstrates, out-of-home placement seems ap-

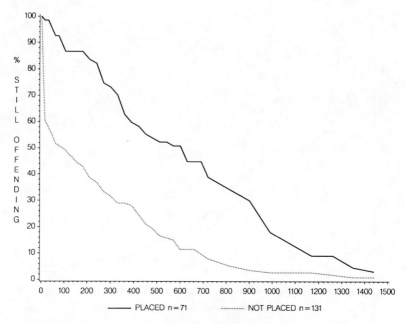

Fig. 10.39. Recidivism risk during supervision, by decision to remove from home (as measured against time in days).

propriately discriminating but ineffective: the group of probationers selected for placement exhibits a steadily higher recidivism rate than the group allowed to remain in the community.

Comparing the effects of court intervention at various career stages on recidivism rates, then, it appears that only at the time of first intake is the court capable of truly discriminating and effective intervention. The social psychology of adolescence and delinquency helps explain the heightened susceptibility of children at first intake to the effects of formal court intervention. In Erikson's (1968) theory, experimentation with a negative identity is a normal adolescent process; in Matza's (1964) term, the early stages of a delinquent career are most likely to be characterized by "drift." At later career stages, successively greater proportions of offenders are committed to delinquency, confirmed in negative identities. These social psychological theories receive empirical support from the increase in the probability of recidivism at each intake transition among the shrinking number of those still criminally active, as illustrated by figure 10.40.

These same social psychological processes help explain why formal

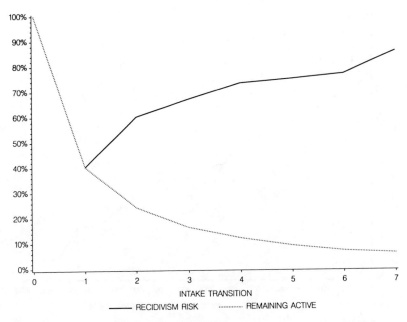

Fig. 10.40. Increasing risk of recidivism among diminishing portion of children still criminally active at successive intake transitions.

court intervention is ineffective at later career stages, and why it is difficult even to achieve appropriate discrimination in selecting children for supervision. Juveniles at first intake comprise the richest mix of tentative and confirmed delinquents, a group whose prospective careers exhibit the greatest measure of statistical variation. These juveniles present court decision-agents with the broadest band of risk within which to exercise their judgment. By contrast, juveniles under consideration for removal-from-home are near the end of their careers; they have in effect had the opportunity to demonstrate whether or not they require placement as a "last resort."

Risk assessment, then, is relatively easy at either end of a delinquent career. But children under court investigation for the first time are neither just starting to experiment with delinquency nor yet fully confirmed in delinquent identities. They confront decision makers with a relatively narrow range of risk within which to base discriminating judgments, and the degree to which each requires further intervention is ambiguous.

Nor is the ineffectiveness of court supervision surprising, since those selected for supervision represent a group of children more uniformly

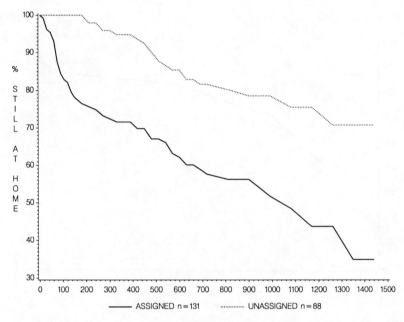

Fig. 10.41. Removal-from-home risk by immediate decision about assignment to supervision (as measured against time in days).

committed to delinquency than those selected for judicial hearings at first intake. Court supervision does not seem to reduce recidivism. Yet as figure 10.41 shows, children first under court investigation are placed at higher risk of removal-from-home by assignment to supervision. This indicates that the very selection for supervision is a form of "unfair" treatment, since the heightened risk of removal-from-home apparently does not correspond to any higher risk of recidivism.

Conclusion: Constraints on Instrumental Rationality

The major conclusions that emerge from the findings presented in this chapter, then, indicate significant limitations in the practice of juvenile justice. The court exercises less influence over its environment than its environment exercises over it. With few exceptions, client characteristics and situational factors produce statistically more significant effects than do variations in court treatment. Neither different probation units nor different judges vary significantly in their patterns of casework decision-making. Neither supervision nor removal-from-home has any discernible effect on recidivism.

The severity of the treatments the court administers to various groups of children does not necessarily correspond to the magnitude of the recidivism risks those groups pose. Indeed supervision is on the whole an "unfair" form of treatment in this sense. Of course, the court assigns treatments to individuals rather than groups, based on clinical judgment rather than actuarial calculation. It is nonetheless valid to infer from the disparity between aggregate recidivism risks and aggregate risks of removal-from-home, that the court's casework decision-making is limited in its instrumental rationality.

Structural and situational pressures exerted on the court by its environment obviously limit the court's instrumental rationality to a large extent. The court is susceptible to the designs of resourceful parents determined to "dump" their "privileged" children. At the same time, because of its growing fiduciary role, the court is ultimately responsible for the placement of children with neither homes nor resources—those at the other end of the socioeconomic spectrum. Considerations of recidivism risk have little effect on placement decisions in these cases, even though they are processed as "criminal" cases.

Such structural pressures at once reflect and create cultural strain, which also limits instrumental rationality. The store of social-scientific knowledge available to agents of juvenile justice is too vague in relation to the fateful casework decisions which confront them daily, and in any case the knowledge is too costly to apply, to offer more than general guidance. Mark Breuer's (1979) review of "the intellectual development in parole prediction" demonstrates the difficulty of both achieving relevant scientific understanding and applying it to the rational assignment of delinquency treatments. Despite over a half century of substantial improvement in statistics and research methodology, repeated efforts have failed to provide a prediction instrument appreciably more efficient in validation samples than the crude device originated in 1928 by Ernest Burgess (Farrington and Tarling 1985). Perhaps more to the point, never in fifty years has such an instrument been usefully integrated into the actual work of practicing decision-agents.

Not merely in response to the absence of useful scientific knowledge and of administrative guides to conduct, clinical judgment is largely *expressive* in content. The terms of practical reason, as Marshall Sahlins (1976) notes, are always *symbolically* constituted. That childhood and family arrangements, for example, are symbolic constructs undoubtedly contributes to the "benefit of the doubt" accorded young children and the unfair treatment accorded children from broken homes. Practical constraints on casework decision-making do little to curtail the expressive freedom of clinical judgment. In a setting like the juvenile court, where casework decision-making is only loosely guided by scientific knowledge or by administrative arrangements, expressive culture is especially disembodied from social organization. The next chapter explores the expressive rationality of juvenile justice.

11

Probation Officers' Tragic Narratives

The sociology of delinquency itself creates a serious ethical dilemma for the society it studies and informs. This sociology does not absolve delinquents of legal and moral responsibility for their delicts, since as David Matza (1964) has argued, individual will is causally necessary for the commission of delinquent acts. But at the same time, this sociology does establish that societal arrangements exercise a "soft determinism" over delinquency. If certain communities produce much higher delinquency rates than others, isn't the responsibility for delinquency partly collective? Isn't it then unjust to punish none but the delinquent? Delinquency is in part the result of *institutional* failure, the breakdown of social controls as well as personal ones. Yet there is no authoritative system of collective beliefs to guide the public response to delinquency, nor even to provide persuasive common understanding of it.

Originally, the rehabilitative ideal did provide such a system of beliefs. In Francis Allen's definition, "the rehabilitative ideal is the notion that a primary purpose of penal treatment is to effect changes in the characters, attitudes, and the behavior of convicted offenders, so as to strengthen the social defense against unwanted behavior, but also to contribute to the welfare and satisfaction of offenders" (1981: 2). As Allen's definition makes clear, this ideal embodies the assumption that society's interests are congruent with those of the delinquent, so that it is possible to serve both sets of interests at once. Conceiving penal treatment as a contribution to the delinquent's welfare eliminates ethical concerns about punishment. As long as it remained credible, the rehabilitative ideal provided a satisfying ideological foundation for juvenile justice.

The prominent reformers of the Progressive Era wedded a spirit of evangelical mission to respect for "scientific" principles of philanthropy in seeking to ameliorate social conditions through public policy. By introducing techniques of modern administration, leaders of the charity organization movement sought to improve the efficiency and effectiveness of the "friendly visitors" they sent out as Christian missionaries to the homes of the urban poor. They also sought to apply the laws of biology and economics to problems of individual, family, and social disorganization (Lubove 1965). Progressive reformers were confident that with scientific enlightenment and God's help, the public will would prevail.

Today practitioners of juvenile justice enjoy no such confidence of success. Those who work at juvenile justice are all too aware of the ambiguity of their mission, the scarcity of resources—cultural as well as organizational—they command, the intractability of the problems they face, and the institutional gaps and cross-purposes that impede their efforts. The rehabilitative ideal has lost credibility, creating a profound cultural void which leaves unanswered fundamental questions of meaning. In an age of skepticism—of declining religious faith, declining faith in public authority, and declining faith in the ability of science to solve human problems—what provides meaning and motivation to those who work at juvenile justice, if those were the very faiths that inspired the birth of the juvenile court movement in the last century? In particular, what justifies punishing individuals for behavior in which the entire society is implicated as well?

Merely to recognize the import of these questions is to challenge those currently influential theories of social control in general and of juvenile court process in particular which implicitly postulate that these questions do not arise. Stanford Lyman and Marvin Scott's theory of "accounts" (1968) suggests, for example, that social order inheres primarily at the surface of appearances; accounts repair breaches of social order at that surface. Aaron Cicourel (1968) and Robert Emerson (1969), among others, have similarly emphasized the negotiated character and plasticity of juvenile court judgments, their ready adaptability to situational contingencies. These theories are consistent with social histories of juvenile justice (e.g., Schlossman 1977; Rothman 1980), which trace the inevitable perversion of periodic reforms in juvenile institutions, condemning officials to sacrifice their humane intentions to compromised forms of organizational practice. These theories are supported too by models of public administration (e.g., Lipsky 1980) which emphasize the compulsion of contemporary "street-level bureaucrats" to abridge unrealistic service ideals by adopting callous workaday routines to ration and restrict services and manipulate clients.

Yet despite these scholarly characterizations, evidence abounds that judges and probation officers resist the temptations of organizational expedience in the conduct of their official duties, demonstrating instead genuine commitment to their casework. Consider the heroic efforts devoted to the "special cases" described in part 1, or the remarkable ingenuity for brokering services displayed even in the course of "normal" casework. Probation officers are often visibly disconcerted when their efforts to help children fail. What could inspire this commitment in the current religious, intellectual, and political climate?

Reports that probation officers make about their casework are revealing on this issue. Offered as accounts of casework decisions proposed or already taken, these reports take such official form as written social investigations, statements made in court, and regular case conferences with probation supervisors. Especially informative are the reports departing probation officers bequeath to their successors as they prepare to leave the job. Probation officers attempt to achieve resolution to their own careers as well as those of their probationers. Upon leaving, they "clean up" their caseloads, reducing them to "manageable" size and making them "presentable" to their successors. They "prune" their caseloads of especially trouble-free or especially troublesome probationers, either closing the cases or placing them out-of-home earlier than they might have otherwise; they provide their successors with a descriptive "handle" for each of the cases remaining to be passed on. Typically, they assure their successors that everything is under control, even though the new worker soon learns otherwise. As a probation supervisor notes, "Workers have a tremendous tendency to want to leave things in order, to gloss over problems when they leave . . . all cases resolved, no loose ends."

Casework reports also take such unofficial form as "shop talk" bantered during lunches, happy hours, and parties. Even as banter, these reports are most "serious" (in Durkheim's sense), not only reflecting judgments about delinquents by probation officers, but also providing the bases of judgments by peers and superiors about the probation officers themselves. Probation officers can learn to abide all sorts of casework frustrations, but they cannot abide challenges to their cultural authority. Probation officers' infrequent displays of open anger or frustration are usually occasioned by judges, lawyers, psychologists, or other professionals who impugn their underlying interpretation of a case. Whatever the success of their case outcomes, probation officers are expected to achieve *understanding* of children's biographies and prospects.

These reports are serious too because they address the moral issues not only of individual transgression but also of societal injustice. Whether or not parents are considered "deserving," it is a tenet of the civil religion that all children are entitled to at least equal opportunity for attaining respectable social standing. In constructing biographies for

233

contemporary delinquents, probation officers inevitably discover unfair handicaps these children have had to suffer, many attesting to what Bellah (1975) calls "the broken covenant." This evidence continues to obligate probation officers to make every effort to help children, despite their awareness of how formidable are the difficulties involved.

Reports of delinquents' pasts and prospects, then, not only express but also help constitute the meaning and motivation of probation work. These reports articulate and provide catharsis for deep social and emotional tensions; to borrow Kenneth Burke's phrase ([1961] 1970), they employ the "rhetoric of religion." No longer, however, do they embody confidence in the rehabilitative ideal—belief in the ability of government to enlist social science and Christian charity for preserving the public safety by improving delinquents' private welfare. To explore how that ideal has been transformed and which beliefs have taken its place, this chapter examines the poetics and dramaturgy of casework narratives.

The Spirit of Modern Tragedy in Probation Work

As expressed in probation officers' narratives, it is the spirit of modern tragedy which fills the cultural void created by the decline of the rehabilitative ideal. Employing the classic themes of tragic flaw, fate, reversal, recognition, and suffering, these narratives dramatize delinquents' adventures as moral struggles illustrating the interaction of character and destiny. They interpret the delinquent act as a combined product of fate and hubris, creating the possibility for redemptive rebirth through recognition (evidenced through adherence to a prescribed form of treatment) and heroic commitment to the painful quest for self-knowledge.

Probation officers generally empathize with the children they work with. One probation officer explains that the most attractive children are "the ones who are going through the same things you went through," but probation officers train themselves to find the good in children. A comment from a set of informal case notes a probation officer drew up for her successor exemplifies this attitude: "likeable kid—a loser who may make it." There are children whom court workers do find unredeemable. A judge profiles "life-style" (as opposed to "episodic") offenders as children without remorse, sensitive to their own pain but insensitive to that of others, living only for the moment. But as a probation officer claims, "When I start working with kids I can see where they have qualities, that they could, in fact, change their lives. I'd say a majority of the kids I've worked with are that way." Reinforcing this expectation are unexpected discoveries about even the least appealing types.

> This kid verbally intimidated a night watchman into surrendering his money and the keys to his car. He claims he didn't use any force, but when I met him I was totally repulsed by him—I didn't see anything in him redeeming or vulnerable. . . . The teacher at the detention home is getting kids to put their feelings down on paper, and it's showing me things I didn't know about my kids before. This kid writes that his grandmother tells him each day how to act in detention. He has a picture of his grandmother holding him when he was a baby, and he thinks she is the only person who ever loved him.

The empathy court workers feel for most children derives in large part from the cruel role they attribute to fate in helping to cause delinquency. In the most frustrating cases, according to one probation officer, "You feel that if you were in the child's shoes you wouldn't make it either." Another probation officer expresses similar sentiments about a boy in serious trouble. "Having that knowledge of what the background was like—was there any way possible for him to be successful in life, with those surroundings?" Probation officers commonly distinguish children who commit offenses "just because they like to . . . for personal gain or whatever," from those who commit offenses "because of all the crap going on in their lives and all their family problems." Similarly, probation officers feel that "the ones who are real disturbed, you can't hold them accountable." Challenging the description of a child as an arsonist, a probation officer argued, "It would be one thing if he had drunk wine, taken drugs, and gone out and burned down a building. But it's not his fault that he's missing something upstairs. He's like an underdog. . . . You have to give a kid like that a chance."

The probation officer's empathy may accord the child a chance, but only to seek the painful recognition considered a prerequisite for developing the motivation necessary to reshape his or her own fate.

> Easiest to help are the bright ones who are really desperately saying, "I want some help. I don't like the way I am. I don't like what I'm doing to my family; I don't like what my family is doing to me. I don't know what to do, but I want things different." And then I tell them, "It means you change too." And most of them say, "okay." Especially if they're bright enough to look in and see the part they play, really there's a lot you can do there.

Or, in the words of another probation officer, "I would always want these kids to try to understand, the assumption was that they had done something wrong or something was going on." Still another probation officer stresses the therapeutic benefits of "confession" as a first step toward recognition: "I wonder what the recidivism is for kids who plead guilty in court as opposed to those who plead innocent. It would be good feedback for members of the Bar Association. I think it's a good experience for a kid to come in and make a confession, confessing that he did something wrong and accepting society's consequences." This probation officer conditioned an offer to recommend private residential placement for a child instead of commitment to a state training school on the child's recognition of the need for placement: "If you can't admit you're a crook, you're not ready for residential [placement]."

Recognition is seen as the first step in choosing to be responsible for oneself. In one probation officer's description, her aim is to inspire "the moment of decision" when a young person resolves to adopt a standard of mature conduct. Recounting a boy's triumph over alcoholism and family turmoil, a probation officer suggests, "It was lucky that early in the case he had the automobile accident which was clearly caused by his drinking, got scared that he almost died, and got scared enough to reverse how things were going." That recognition motivated the boy "to become an adult . . . being able to set goals for himself and figure out how to meet those goals, how to solve problems, how to see in what kinds of circumstances he created problems for himself." Probation officers learn that though they do not have the power to impose change on children, they can sometimes influence children to change themselves, by demonstrating to them how it is in their own interest to do so. Judges, who command greater power to impose change, seek in the words of one "to hold children accountable for choice." A different judge even discerns some benefit in committing children to state training schools, if that prods children to recognition.

> I think with kids you have somehow or other to get across to
> them that they are the architects of their own destiny, that it isn't
> somebody else who's constantly getting into trouble, it isn't some-
> body else who's doing this. Often I say to them, "You can improve
> yourself. We'll help you but it has to be your decision. When you
> come before me and I have to send you to a learning center, it's a
> choice you've made, not me," and I'd say a very high proportion
> of the kids will say, "well, you told me." That's the first step I
> think to understanding . . . getting them to see that they have an
> individual responsibility. . . . At least they're going to the learning

center with the thought that . . . as easily as they went downhill
they can go uphill, and a lot of them do.

Since the probation officer helps prescribe the terms of a child's
recognition, the child's acts of heroic will are hardly as autonomous as
the probation officer pretends. However by agreeing to those terms, the
child gains not only the opportunity to expiate past sins but also a certain degree of immunity from punishment for future ones. Subsequent
troubles only serve to confirm the court's own analysis of the child's
unpropitious situation, and the court must recognize the especially formidable difficulty of reconstructing an ignoble protagonist's tragic fate.
Like any agency of social control, the court is reluctant to invoke "last
resorts" (Emerson 1981) without having exhausted all other alternatives.
The child can renew entitlement to the court's understanding tolerance
through regular displays of commitment to the tragic scenario legiti-
mated by the court. By convincing demonstrations of constructive resolve, the child can earn official respites from new troubles. At a weekly
staff meeting, the members of a probation unit agree that probationers
qualify for counseling, as opposed to mere surveillance, by presenting
definable problems which they are motivated to work on. Members of
other probation units echo this view. One probation officer describes the
satisfaction of learning that an alcoholic is finally starting to take medication to counter the physical craving of addiction. "There's a glimmer
of hope. It will be really hard, and he'll probably fail, but at least he's
trying." Comments made independently by various other probation officers indicate that they share similar personal criteria for extending tolerance to probationers. "I expect kids to try. That's all I expect from
them. If not, they need sanctions." "I take kids back to court on violations when I'm working harder than they are to keep them out of
trouble." "While working with kids, when you see their potential you
develop expectations. The only thing I really expect is to give an honest
effort for themselves, to be interested in what happens to them. When a
kid sits in front of me and says, 'I don't care,' I go crazy. Those are the
ones you give up on. You wind up locking them up."

Court workers' casework narratives conform to the rhythm of tragedy. A judge observes that some children can only begin to pull their
lives together "after hitting rock bottom, like alcoholics or drug addicts."
This judge tailors his courtroom dramaturgy and dispositional strategies
to the different phases of the tragic cycle.

You see cases at various stages. There are kids who are on their
way down to the bottom, there are kids who are making progress,

falling back from time to time but it's generally an upward trend. I think you have to make that evaluation first. Looking at this kid overall, there are some successes that he's beginning to have. If there are, you try and support those and at the same time try and do something about the bad things that he's doing. If things have now gone sour, experiencing difficulty at home, at school, or jobs, you don't let him now wait until he hits flat bottom. Then it's time to be very assertive and take action. It may be early in the case, but if you see those indicators it's time to pull him out of the home and get him out of the tailspin and have him do something else. There are cases you don't know, don't have enough information at this point, and what you're trying to do is maintain the status quo and put off the final decision because inevitably those other stages will come up—he'll either start to do better or start to do worse.

A probation officer, just returned from devoting his summer vacation to conducting a church youth group on the theme of "death and resurrection," notes that he tells his probationers, "probation is a time of loss—but it can also be a time of growth." Another probation officer describes the decision to place a child out-of-home as the culmination of a progression of events triggered by further trouble and the child's failure to make any progress at home. Similarly, she sees some benefit in the fact that commitment "is the following through of a process."

Toward a Poetics of Casework Narratives

It is the genre of tragedy which animates and shapes casework narratives, providing both their thematics and rhythms. A poetics of tragedy, then, at once informs and explicates these narratives. Aristotle's classic statement remains most authoritative and useful. Aristotle discovered the themes of character flaw, reversal, recognition, and suffering, noting that the most terrible or pitiful situations occur "when . . . suffering is inflicted upon each other by people whose relationship implies affection," such as family members (1958, chap. 14). The ideal course of probation casework follows the plot identified as "best" in chapter 14 of the *Poetics*: the protagonist recognizes the terrible nature of a contemplated deed just in time to refrain from committing it. Plot is more important to the construction of tragedy than character development (chap. 6): "Tragedy is an imitation, not of men but of action and life, of happiness and misfortune. . . . The purpose of action on the stage is not to imitate character, but character is a by-product of the action."

Plots must be "whole" (chap. 7), having a beginning, a middle, and an end. They must have "unity" (chap. 8), meaning "the various incidents must be so constructed that, if any part is displaced or deleted, the whole plot is disturbed and dislocated." Tragedy is more sharply focused than history, since "the historian relates what happened, the poet what might happen" (chap. 9); it is because tragedy accords "with probability and necessity," exploiting artistic license to neglect contingencies which may complicate actual history, that poetry "is a better thing than history." (This is not to say that the tragedian "is any less a poet if he happens to tell a true story, for nothing prevents some actual events from being probable or possible.")

Modern philosophers and critics elaborate this poetics of tragedy. Suzanne Langer identifies guilt and expiation as "the tragic theme" (1953: 326), just as Kenneth Burke proclaims:

> Tragedy is a complex kind of trial by jury in which the author symbolically charges himself or his characters with transgressions not necessarily considered transgressions in law, and metes out condemnation and penance by tests far deeper than any that could be codified in law. . . . Tragedy is essentially concerned with the processes of guilt and justification. . . . Tragedy reveals most clearly the workings of the criminal and expiatory processes implicit in human relationships. ([1935] 1984: 195)

The "tragic rhythm" culminates in a form of redemption. For Burke, that rhythm plots a progression from sin to guilt to expiation to redemption. "This is the process embodied in tragedy, where the agent's action involves a corresponding passion, and from the sufferance of the passion there arises an understanding of the act, an understanding that transcends the act" ([1945] 1969: 38). Suzanne Langer (citing Francis Fergusson, who was in turn highly influenced by Burke) describes "the tragic rhythm of action" as the growth of reason "through inner struggles against passional obstacles, from an original spark to full enlightenment" (1953: 337–38). Nietzsche too conceives redemption as an achievement of vision, though for him the redemptive vision must transcend reason: "There is need for a whole world of torment in order for the individual to produce the redemptive vision and to sit quietly in his rocking rowboat in mid-sea, absorbed in contemplation. . . . the esthetic necessity of beauty is accompanied by the imperatives, 'Know thyself,' and 'Nothing too much'" (1956: 33–34).

The "inner passional" obstacles confronting the tragic hero correspond to external challenges programmed into the hero's fated destiny. Langer asserts that "the action itself must reveal the limit of the pro-

tagonist's powers and mark the end of his self-realization" (1953: 358).
In Northrop Frye's independent formulation of the same observation,
"tragedy seems to lead up to an epiphany of law, of that which is and
must be" ([1957] 1968: 208).

> Tragedy presents the . . . theme of narrowing a comparatively free
> life into a process of causation. . . . The discovery or *anagnorisis*
> which comes at the end of the tragic plot is not simply the knowl-
> edge by the hero of what has happened to him . . . but the recog-
> nition of the determined shape of the life he has created for
> himself, with an implicit comparison with the uncreated potential
> life he has created. (212)

Character and destiny help form each other. Yet Langer cautions
against reducing tragedy to the unity of character and fate: "Tragedy . . .
is expected to illustrate the workings of Fate. But that is not necessary;
it may just as well illustrate the workings of villainy, neurosis, faith,
social justice, or anything else the poet finds usable to motivate a large,
integral action" (1953: 360).

Although expressed through the dramatic involvements of particular
individuals, tragedy crystallizes *social* conflicts and contradictions. He-
gel interprets the action of tragedy as a dialectic of ethical substance,
the triumph of eternal justice over competing particularistic ethical
claims; the Marxist critic Raymond Williams conceives tragedy as "the
dramatization of a particular and grievous disorder and its resolution"
(1966: 53). Burke conceives tragedy similarly, as the perfect imitation
of a tension. As Burke's expositor William Rueckert explicates this
notion, Burke "usually uses tension in combination with a number of
other terms, all of which seem to be synonyms: the most important of
these are psychosis, pollution, civic disorders, civic pollutions, disorders
within the polis, civic guilt, class conflicts, temporal tensions, and mys-
teries" (1982: 210). To invoke another Burkean phrase, tragedy inevitably dramatizes the "hierarchic psychosis," the "uneasiness stemming
from the social order."

Social-Historical Conditions of Tragedy

Every age may be said to have its own form of tragedy, but great
tragedy is the product of "cultural moments" associated with characteristic sets of social-historical conditions. As Gilbert Murray describes
the Hellenistic stage of Greek religion which produced the birth of tragedy, it "was the time when the Greek mind, still in its full creative
vigor, made its first response to the twofold failure of the world in which
it had put its faith, the open bankruptcy of the Olympian religion and

the collapse of the city-state. Both had failed, and each tried vainly to supply the place of the other" (1951: 3). Raymond Williams locates the conditions for tragedy at the same phase in the cycle of history, when received arrangements and beliefs are no longer compelling enough to provide meaning and motivation, yet still vital enough to impede the newly emerging order. "Its condition is the real tension between old and new: between received beliefs, embodied in institutions and responses, and newly and vividly experienced contradictions and possibilities" (1966: 54).

It is tempting to speculate whether the spirit of tragedy may come to exercise a more permanent influence as the periodicity of social change accelerates and a climate of "tension between old and new" becomes more chronic than episodic. At any rate, contemporary America fits the profile of social-historical conditions conducive to this spirit. The faiths in religion, science, and public institutions which once inspired general hopes for ameliorating social conditions of the urban masses in the United States have receded, generating "newly and vividly experienced contradictions and possibilities." These problems of meaning are as inescapable for contemporary agents of juvenile justice as they were for the tragedians of ancient Greece.

Tragedy and Modernity

Despite the eternal nature of the questions tragedy addresses, the distinctive traits of modernity naturally condition the spirit of tragedy in the present time. The collapse of confidence in the very possibility of constructing rational justifications for either morality or religious faith provides one distinctive basis for characterizing modernity and, in particular, modern tragedy. Spanning the divide of theistic belief, both Kierkegaard and Nietzsche are among the antiprophets of this moral and spiritual uncertainty in the modern age. Alasdair MacIntyre laments the "unharmonious melange of ill-assorted fragments" (1981: 10) in contemporary moral discourse: "The distinctively modern standpoint . . . envisages moral debate in terms of confrontation between incompatible and incommensurable moral premises and moral commitment as the expression of a criterionless choice between such premises, a type of choice for which no rational justification can be given" (38). He explains this predicament as the result of both the success of Enlightenment philosophers in discrediting traditional sources of moral, religious, and political authority, and the failure of "the Enlightenment project" to provide a rational secular grounding for moral allegiances in their stead.

Eliminating the assumption of moral intelligibility introduces elements of ambiguity and incoherence into tragic narratives, which focus on the moral consequences of action in exploring the relations of character to destiny. Modern tragedy contains no popular chorus, narrator's voice, or even inherently comprehensible plot-line to guide the audience in making sense of the action, so that interpretation becomes purely individualistic and subjective. Nietzsche notes the significance of the Greek chorus as the object of the audience's identification: "the audience of Attic tragedy discovered *itself* in the chorus of the orchestra. . . . All was one grand chorus" (1956: 54). By contrast, T. S. Eliot recounts his inability to find convincing staging for the chorus in *The Family Reunion*, a play he consciously patterned on a theme of Aeschylus. As Eliot reports his own retrospective criticism of that play, "the deepest flaw of all was in a failure of adjustment between the Greek story and the modern situation. . . . we are left in a divided frame of mind, not knowing whether to consider the play the tragedy of the mother or the salvation of the son" (1951: 38–39).

These distinctively modern aspects of tragedy are evident in casework narratives. The "scientific casework" movement of the early twentieth century, led by such figures as Mary Richmond and William Healy, embodied precisely "the great optimist-rationalist-utilitarian victory" derided by Nietzsche; contemporary casework narratives, reflecting the disappointing experience with that movement, tend to embody more the spirit of "strong pessimism" which Nietzsche championed instead. In constructing such a narrative, the probation officer confronts much the same ambiguity and incoherence as the reader of a modern novel or audience at a modern play: the details of a child's life history are typically inconsistent and confused, unframed by any authoritative guide to their interpretation.

The Deterioration of the Hero

There is another respect as well in which these narratives exemplify the spirit of *modern* tragedy: the "heroes," ignoble in status and occupying roles of social isolation, should more accurately be designated "antiheroes." Northrop Frye traces the gradual decline of the hero's "power of action" in European fiction, marking the "descent" from the "high mimetic" tragedy of the Renaissance to the "low mimetic" tragedy of the seventeenth century to the "tragic irony" of today. In tragic irony, the hero's actions lose even some of their moral significance. This erosion occurs as tragedy takes on the qualities of irony. "Tragedy is intelligible because its catastrophe is plausibly related to its situation. Irony isolates from the tragic situation the sense of arbitrariness, of the victim's having been unlucky, selected at random or by lot, and no more deserving of what happens to him than anyone else would be" ([1957] 1968: 41).

Tragic irony provides the mode of expression for sociological theories of delinquency which inform casework narratives. Frye's description of a hero "inferior in power to ourselves, so we have the sense of looking down on a scene of . . . frustration" (34) precisely defines the situation described by Robert Merton (1968), of a young person driven to delinquency by the social-psychological "strain" produced by inequality and anomie. The pervasiveness of anomie in American culture which Merton documents would lead the observer to feel, in Frye's words, that "he is or might be in the same situation" as the delinquent. Merton's theory has retained tremendous influence among sociologists despite a preponderance of empirical disconfirmation (Kornhauser 1978). That delinquents themselves may not actually evince strain does not disturb the tragic mood; pathos, as Frye remarks, "is increased by the inarticulateness of the victim" ([1957] 1968: 38–39).

Richard Sewell also notes the natural tendency of tragedy to deteriorate into irony. "Few artists have for long been able to sustain, and few audiences endure, the tensions of tragedy. The necessary involvement is demanding, costly. The dark problem must be decided either way and transcended" (1980: 81–82). Sewall argues that literature itself assumes the style of casework narrative; this deterioration into irony "is the way toward reportage, naturalism, clinical detail, and case history" (82). The social psychologist Orrin Klapp similarly finds evidence of "the deterioration of the hero" in American culture, not only in literature but also in the survey data he interprets. In addition to supporting and elaborating Merton's theme, he also documents the "*heroization of deviant behavior* by sub-groups in conflict with square values" (1962: 137); thus he echoes the "cultural conflict" image of American delinquency exemplified by Becker's *Outsiders* (1963). Klapp emphasizes alienative and anomic elements of American culture in speculating about reasons for the deterioration of the hero.

Of course what Klapp characterizes as the "deterioration of the hero" can be characterized from an alternative perspective as part of a larger social trend: the extension of citizenship rights and entitlements to the masses (Marshall 1964), the diffusion of charisma from the center to the periphery of mass society (Shils [1961] 1975). Reflecting on how processes of social change affect the conception of a tragic hero's proper status, Frye notes that the two greatest expressions of tragedy, in fifth-century Athens and seventeenth-century Europe, "both belong to a period of social history in which an aristocracy is fast losing its effective power but still retains a good deal of ideological prestige" ([1957] 1968: 37). The modern American tragic hero, no longer representing an elite whose claim to status has outlasted its warrant, represents instead the

243

everyman whose claim to status still awaits full realization. The leveling of status distinctions involves the elevation of subordinate strata as well as the relative devaluation of superior ones. Because of the extension of entitlements which characterizes mass society, even the delinquent is eligible to become a modern American hero. Murray Krieger observes that tragedy "frequently dwells on the exceptional man; and when it does choose a normal man it does so only to convert him, by way of the extremity he lives through, into the exceptional man" ([1960] 1966: 20).

This, then, is the poetics of probation officers' casework narratives. Inspired by the spirit of modern tragedy, these narratives relate the moral struggles of delinquents as the interaction of personal character and destiny in a context of social conflict and contradiction, during an age when collectively received arrangements and beliefs are no longer compelling. Building on the classical themes of character flaw, reversal, recognition, and suffering, these narratives are distinctively modern in their attempts to transcend both science and religion, and in their tolerance of moral ambiguity and incoherence. Their protagonists are not noble but ignoble, not heroic but antiheroic, reflecting the leveling effects of the diffusion of charisma from the center to the periphery of mass society. The deterioration of narrative mode from "high mimetic" to "low mimetic"—tending toward the ironic—parallels the "deterioration of the hero" in modern American culture. By contrast with the "child-savers" of the past century, modern probation officers have moderated their aims a bit, forsaking hopes of salvation for their clients. Yet probation officers' narratives remain dramas of guilt and expiation, asserting the tragic rhythm of redemption. The explicitly religious impulse which helped inspire the founding of the juvenile court has not disappeared, but has been desacralized and routinized by bureaucratic process.

The Dramaturgic Significance of Casework Narratives

It is important to explicate the poetics of casework narratives because the narratives play such a vital part in the dramaturgy of probation casework. These narratives help define and redefine not only official attitudes toward delinquents but delinquents' own self-images. In the terminology of analytic philosophy (Austin 1962), these narratives are "performative utterances" (that is, not simply descriptive statements, but rather statements that in and of themselves accomplish certain actions), establishing the terms of decisions by agents of juvenile justice about possible intervention into the lives of children. In particular, the narratives frame the most fateful treatment decisions—those concerning the removal of children from home to residential institutions. Delinquents can claim a considerable measure of tolerance for legal infractions from court workers by adhering to the roles cast according to these narratives; conversely, they invite intolerance by deviating from these roles even if they formally abide the law. In this way, the mimetic qualities of casework narratives tend to be self-validating.

Tragic casework narratives, then, are akin to the "sad tales" of the mental patients studied by Erving Goffman, although tragic narratives help govern an earlier stage of their subjects' "moral careers." Goffman observes that in response to the degrading social situation of a total institution, "a milieu of personal failure in which one's fall from grace is continually pressed home," "the inmate tends to develop a story, a line, a sad tale—a kind of lamentation and apologia—which he constantly tells to his fellows as a means of accounting for his present low estate" (1961: 67). As an inmate's attempt to preserve a remnant of self-esteem against the institution's totalistic assault on individual dignity, the sad tale emphasizes the inmate's lack of responsibility for obvious personal misfortune. "Just as any normal member of his outside subculture would do, the patient often responds to this situation by attempting to assert a sad tale proving that he is not 'sick,' that the 'little trouble' he did get into was really somebody else's fault, that his past life course had some honor and rectitude, and that the hospital is therefore unjust in forcing the status of mental patient on him" (152). Goffman describes the struggle between the inmate and the staff over the credibility of this sad tale, in which staff members collude to marshal and disseminate evidence damaging to the inmate's claims in order to further their own purposes of custodial control. The sad tale thus becomes a strategic focus of staff-inmate contention concerning not only the particular details of the inmate's account but indeed the very poetics of the narrative form:

> Although there is a psychiatric view of mental disorder and an environmental view of crime and counterrevolutionary activity, both freeing the offender from moral responsibility for his offense, total institutions can little afford this particular form of determinism. Inmates must be caused to self-direct themselves in a manageable way, and, for this to be promoted, both desired and undesired conduct must be defined as springing from the personal will and character of the inmate himself, and defined as something he can himself do something about. In short, each institutional perspective contains a personal morality, and in each total institution we can see something akin to a functionalist ver-

sion of moral life. The translation of inmate behavior into moral-
istic terms suited to the institution's avowed perspective will
necessarily contain some broad presuppositions as to the character of human beings. (86–87)

Conflict over the sad tale expresses the purely adversarial nature of
inmate-staff relations in the types of custodial settings Goffman describes. To delinquents who find themselves committed to such institutions, probation officers appear retrospectively as partners in the
"alienative coalitions" or "betrayal funnels" (to use Goffman's terms)
which got them there. Yet during the "prepatient stage" of a delinquent's
moral career, relations are only partly adversarial with the probation
officer, who holds out the realistic prospect of potential support in circumstances of present or future trouble. The probation officer's tragic
narrative is analogous to the inmate's sad tale in expressing and governing the dramaturgic relations with social control agents at particular
stages of a deviant career; Emerson and Messinger's focus on "the natural
history of trouble" usefully complements Goffman's in calling attention
to the antithesis between prospective and retrospective views of dramaturgic relations.

Many such approaches [as Goffman's] cut into the production of
deviants at late stages. Frequently, those who have suffered some
major, perhaps irrevocable sanction, such as institutional placement, are identified as the subject population. Such sanctioning
or placement provides an "end point" . . . for treating an actor as a
particular sort of deviant, and past activities and events are ordered as leading to this "end point." These sorts of deviant career
notions, however, often organize events in ways foreign to per-
ceptions prevailing earlier, when outcomes were in doubt and
definitions ambiguous. In addition, these approaches focus on
cases that have made it to an eventual deviant designation, neglecting those that have failed to do so. . . . The idea of "trouble"
keeps open the possibility that many troubles with deviant possibilities "come to nothing" or come to something devoid of imputations of deviance. (1977: 131)

More children on probation escape institutionalization than experience
it. Issues of biographical reconstruction are subject to a freer play of
negotiation in the casework narrative than in the sad tale because ultimate case outcomes are so much more in doubt.

While the contested versions of the sad tale at once reflect and sustain the adversarial relations between inmate and staff, the delinquent's

assent to the probation officer's tragic narrative (as negotiated between them) at once reflects and sustains the probation officer's credibility as "helper." The poetics of the tragic narrative represents a compromise between the competing poetics of the inmate's and staff's sad tales, attributing the delinquent's fall to a combination of determinism, character flaw, and personal irresponsibility. This compromise serves and expresses the ambiguous prospects of probation casework. The recognition of deterministic influences commands sympathetic understanding, warranting suspension of such "last resort" remedies as commitment to a state training school. At the same time, recognition of character flaw and personal irresponsibility demands some sort of remedial intervention, since as Emerson and Messinger argue, the identification of troubles must be validated by remedial outcomes. The probation officer's tragic narrative, then, typically culminates in a recommendation for some type of "normal remedy," which Emerson defines as a "routinely considered, conventionally applied response to the 'normal cases' or normal troubles . . . regularly encountered in and processed by a particular control institution" (1981: 5). To the degree that it is likely to fail, the application of a normal remedy increases the prospects for the eventual imposition of a "last resort" remedy. On the other hand, to the extent that the remedial outcome confirms the terms of the tragic narrative (as, within limits, most of them do), the tragic narrative provides the medium through which "many troubles with deviant possibilities 'come to nothing.'"

Expressive Satisfactions of Casework Narratives

As a strategic focus of dramaturgic relations the probation officer's tragic narrative is multivocal, incorporating expressive preferences—aesthetic, psychological, and moral—of the delinquent, the probation officer, and the public at large. Casework narratives provide a sense of form to casework process, turning ordinary experience into *an* experience for all parties involved. These narratives cast both probation officers and delinquents in heroic roles. They assert moral boundaries and transform moral identities, while regulating the distribution of obligations and entitlements in a complex system of moral reckoning. They address moral dilemmas on a societal level as well as on an interpersonal one, offering catharsis for deep tensions not only emotional but social.

According to John Dewey's philosophy of art, not only is all artistic activity intrinsically practical in nature, but all practical activity is potentially aesthetic. Arising out of the practical concerns of casework, the probation officer's tragic narrative reconstructs a delinquent's biography in such a way as to discover—and prescribe—a nondelinquent identity. For Dewey, it is this imputation of identity which—if successful—lends an aesthetic quality to casework.

> Only when an organism shares in the ordered relations of its environment does it secure the stability essential to living. And when the participation comes after a phase of disruption and conflict, it bears within itself the germs of a consummation akin to the esthetic. . . .
> Only when the past ceases to trouble and anticipations of the future are not perturbing is a being wholly united with his environment and therefore fully alive. Art celebrates with peculiar intensity the moments in which the past reinforces the present and in which the future is a quickening of what now is. ([1934] 1980: 15, 18)

The condition that for Dewey constitutes the aesthetic quality of experience is the very one that for Erik Erikson constitutes a person's psychosocial identity: "The young person, in order to experience wholeness, must feel a progressive continuity between that which he has come to be during the long years of childhood and that which he promises to become in the anticipated future; between that which he conceives himself to be and that which he perceives others to see in him and to expect of him" (1968: 87).

The achievement of such an identity represents for Erikson an ideal of perfection, requiring successful resolution of an entire series of "epigenetic crises," a feat of ego development never fully realized. The process of ego development is social as well as psychological, involving the provision of institutional support as well as personality growth at each stage of the life cycle. The absence of identity creates a condition Erikson terms "identity diffusion."

Erikson provides a dimension of social-psychological explanation to "social control" theories of delinquency causation, theories that ascribe delinquency to the absence of institutional and personal controls. One prominent exponent of control theory is David Matza, who describes the absence of such controls as a state of "drift."

> Drift stands midway between freedom and control. Its basis is an area of the social structure in which control has been loosened. . . . Freedom is not only the loosening of controls. It is a sense of command over one's destiny, a capacity to formulate programs or projects, a feeling of being an agent in one's own behalf. Freedom is self-control. If so, the delinquent has clearly not

achieved that state. . . . Those who have been granted the potentiality for freedom through the loosening of social controls but
who lack the position, capacity, or inclination to become agents
in their own behalf, I call drifters, and it is in this category that I
place the juvenile delinquent. Drift is motion guided gently by
underlying influences. (1964: 28–29)

What Erikson calls identity diffusion is the social-psychological compo-
nent of the structural condition Matza calls drift, which he describes as
the necessary precondition for most types of delinquency.

Dewey anticipates Matza's description of drift as well as Erikson's description of identity. Just as people ordinarily fail to attain full realization
of their own personal identities, ordinary experience, Dewey notes, often
fails to realize its aesthetic potential. Drift for Dewey is the antithesis of
aesthetic experience.

In much of our experience we are not concerned with the connection of one incident with what went before and what comes
after. There is no interest that controls attentive rejection or selection of what shall be organized into the developing experience.
Things happen, but they are neither definitely included nor decisively excluded; we drift. We yield according to external pressure,
or evade and compromise. There are beginnings and cessations,
but no genuine initiations and conclusions. One thing replaces
another, but does not absorb it and carry it on. There is experience, but so slack and discursive that it is not an experience.
Needless to say, such experiences are anesthetic. ([1934] 1980: 40)

In claiming that "tragedy dramatizes human life as potentiality and
fulfillment" (1953: 352), Suzanne Langer finds in tragedy precisely
the aesthetic realization of the experience it reconstructs. Langer, who
acknowledges Dewey's influence, characterizes the "artistic purpose" of
tragedy (405) as "the envisagement of individual existence as a whole";
she believes that "tragedy is a source of deep satisfaction" due to "the joy
of revelation, the vision of a world wholly significant." The casework
narrative performs this artistic purpose by emphasizing how the reborn
delinquent's newly emergent identity promises to redeem the unfortunate consequences of past drift.

Casework narratives transform not only the delinquent, but also the
probation officer and the public at large. As Dewey explains, the production of any art object involves a process of symbolic interaction which
re-creates and redefines not only the material shaped into art, but also
the artist and audience as well. The transformative effects are perhaps

most obvious upon the raw materials reworked by the artist. "Until the artist is satisfied in perception with what he is doing, he continues shaping and reshaping" ([1934] 1980: 49). Yet the act of artistic production is transformative for the artist as well. "Expression of the self in and through a medium, constituting the work of art, is itself a prolonged interaction of something issuing from the self with objective conditions, a process in which both of them acquire a form and order they did not at first possess" (65). The transformative effects experienced by the artist are shaped not only by the nature of the materials at hand, but also by the artist's need to take into account the attitude of the audience toward the art object.

> The doing or making is artistic when the perceived result is of such a nature that its qualities as perceived have controlled the question of production. The act of production that is directed by intent to produce something that is enjoyed in the immediate experience of perceiving has qualities that a spontaneous or uncontrolled activity does not have. The artist embodies in himself the attitude of the perceiver while he works. (48)

Finally, the appreciation or consumption of an art work is transformative for the audience in much the same way as for the artist.

> To perceive, a beholder must create his own experience. And his creation must include relations comparable to those which the original producer underwent. . . . With the perceiver, as with the artist, there must be an ordering of the elements of the whole that is in form, although not in details, the same as the process of organization the creator of the work consciously experienced. Without an act of re-creation the object is not perceived as a work of art. The artist selected, simplified, clarified, abridged, and condensed according to his interest. The beholder must go through these operations according to his point of view and his interest. . . . There is work done on the part of the percipient as there is on the part of the artist. (54)

The production of tragic casework narratives, then, is as transformative of the probation officers who compose them and the public who perceive them, as of the delinquents who supply the biographical raw materials for them. These narratives are aesthetic not only insofar as they construct nondelinquent identities for children who have experienced delinquent drift, but also insofar as they construct creditable professional identities for probation officers who experience repeated casework frustration, and insofar too as they construct an honorable moral identity for a public at large remorseful for the societal conditions that help cause delinquency. For delinquents are not the only ones in American society to experience drift. Rather, drift in Dewey's sense—incomplete realization of the aesthetic potential in practical activity—is endemic not only in the casework efforts of probation officers, but more generally in all efforts to achieve greater justice and efficiency in public life.

Reflexively Attributing Character Ambiguity

In a work of art, however prosaic, the artist gives objective expression to a subjective sense of self. The tragic casework narrative, then, is as much about the probation officer as the delinquent. Through such a narrative, the probation officer manages the public impression not only of the delinquent but also of the probation officer's own competency. By casting ignoble delinquents as modern tragic heroes, probation officers reflexively make heroes of themselves as well. Indeed, since a single probation officer manages dozens of cases at a time, each probation officer takes on the appearance of being a hero many times over. Despite the demoralizing practical frustrations of casework, this self-cast role of superhero affords the probation officer considerable expressive satisfaction.

Tragedy has the power to transform discreditable personal identities into heroic ones. Dewey explains that this property of tragedy derives from the emergent nature of symbolic interaction.

> The conception that objects have fixed and unalterable values is precisely the prejudice from which art emancipates us. . . . That to which the word "ugly" is applied is the object in its customary associations, those which have come to appear as an inherent part of some object. It does not apply to what is present in the picture or drama. There is transformation because of emergence in an object having its own expressiveness. . . . Something which was ugly under other conditions, the usual ones, is extracted from the conditions in which it was repulsive and is transfigured in quality as it becomes part of an expressive whole. In its new setting, the very contrast with the former ugliness adds piquancy, animation, and, in serious matters, increases depth of meaning in an almost incredible way.
>
> The peculiar power of tragedy to leave us at the end with a sense of reconciliation rather than with one of horror forms the theme of one of the oldest discussions in literary art. . . . A particular subject matter in being removed from its practical content has entered into a new whole as an integral part of it. In its new

251

relationships, it acquires a new expression. It becomes a qualitative part of a new qualitative design. ([1934] 1980: 95–96)

Jack Katz similarly emphasizes the emergent nature of symbolic interaction and the reflexive nature of identity construction in explaining the inherent ambivalence of moral "essences." Katz conceives deviance as the imputation of diminished social responsibility and competency, the antithesis of charisma. Since deviance and charisma are imputations of relative competency, defined in contradistinction to each other, attributing one of these statuses to another person is tantamount to asserting the opposite status for oneself. But since such a change in status itself alters the context of judgment, a person's moral status is always subject to reinterpretation and redefinition, so that the attribution of relative status is always subject to reversal. Katz's analysis of this paradoxical emergent process explains how the delinquent can turn into a hero.

> By limiting the possibilities of cooperative activity in recognition of another's incompetence, a person indicates the limits of his own power. . . . Once a person has defined another as deviant and realized his own resulting deviance, he has established conditions for his recognition of the other's charisma. If the deviant is unable to control himself, and if the labeler is rendered impotent by a consequent inability to control the deviant, then if the deviant escapes his status he indicates that his ability is superior to the labeler's. (1975: 1385–86)

This analysis also explains why it is in the probation officer's interest, while constructing casework narratives, to acknowledge character strengths that enable delinquents of sufficient resolve to attain redemption. By imputing to delinquents latent moral promise from the start, probation officers in effect hedge the risk of reversing status with delinquents who may improve their lot, while establishing a rationale for casework involvement in the first place. At the same time, it is also important to insist on the essential deviance of delinquents, if the wider public is to credit probation officers with charisma for any casework success they may experience.

Reconstructing Moral Identities

Casework narratives serve not only the self-presentational strategies of probation officers, but the communal rituals of justice as well. As Katz explains, moral identities are "essences" which cannot directly be inferred from observed acts. "When a person imputes an essence rather than an act by making his identification in terms of the present rather than the past, by using nouns instead of verbs, and by referring to inherent qualities and not expressed activities, he does not directly observe or experience but assumes his knowledge of the designated identity" (1975: 1374). Yet, as Harold Rosenberg (1960) observes, the very nature of the legal process contradicts this principle of attributing moral essences, by characterizing the identities of defendants solely according to their acts.

> The law pronounces, or should pronounce, its judgments and penalties with regard only to the acts of individuals and without recognition of the individuals as persons; its judgments are applied at the end of a series of acts. Thus the law creates a definite fiction, an individual who is identified by the coherence of his acts with a fact in which they have terminated (a crime . . . for example) and by nothing else. . . . This assertion that the individual is what we may call an identity in contrast with a personality, that is, one defined solely by the coherence of his action with an adjudged fact and not by the continuity of his being, is entirely contradictory to the . . . concept which visualizes action as serving for a clue to the existence and endurance of a thing *in esse* whose real definition can only be attained by an intuition. (57)

What renders the law unjust for Rosenberg is "the discrepancy between action and being, the failure of the individual to conform in every respect to his role" (58). Probation officers' casework narratives serve in part to create precisely that dramatic "fiction" which the law requires to appear just.

> Characters may change in a drama not through moral or psychological modification but by means of a change of identity. . . . A special process causes the central fact which identifies the character to give place to another of a different type and value, and the fact to which the character's action was previously attached becomes powerless to motivate or explain him. . . . It is especially in the substitution of one identity for another . . . that the type of coherence which marks the identity is clarified, since the change of identity takes place . . . all at once, in a leap, and is not, as in personality, the result of a continual flow. (61–62)

Like Burke and other literary critics, Rosenberg notes that tragedy embodies a rhetoric of religious rebirth: "The fact that the phenomenon of religious conversion is the only one 'in life' which effects a change of identity, in which, through the touch of death, a course of action and valuation is completely annulled and another substituted without breaching the duration of the individual, relates religion and drama in a special way" (63). Tragic casework narratives, then, are dramaturgic devices for endowing the formal processes of law with the necessary semblance of substantive justice. "Dramatic and religious thought . . . retrace the steps which social legality overleaps; they reconstruct the entire individual to fit him into their schemes of justice" (70).

Casework narratives define moral boundaries, regulating the complex counterbalancing of obligations and entitlements among delinquents, the public at large, and the probation officers who mediate between them. As Katz suggests, in strengthening its own collective identity by designating as deviants and excluding from full community participation persons considered unable to discharge normal social responsibilities, the public incurs a fiduciary obligation toward those persons, which it delegates to such special agents as probation officers. "The labeler of deviance shifts between an exclusionary morality which announces the unworthiness of the deviant and an inclusionary morality which finds him worthy of ameliorative attention" (1975: 1383). The public assigns its agents to rehabilitate those designated as deviant even while enforcing their segregation from the community. These agents assume liability for the misdeeds of those entrusted to their care, over whom they are granted correspondingly broad license. This assignment of liability helps explain the common complaint that judges (transmitting public pressure) treat probation officers in court as if they rather than their probationers were on trial.

As reports of activities for which delinquents and probation officers alike are accountable, casework narratives serve this ambivalent mixture of exclusionary and inclusionary public purposes. Indeed, perhaps their most important function is to address the fundamental paradox of the public philosophy underlying juvenile justice, articulated by David Matza: How could a society that perceives its own collective responsibility for delinquency causation punish a delinquent for acts that are thus not entirely the product of individual will? Matza notes that an attitude of empathy is antithetical to one of judgment: "Those who judge can never completely understand, for if they could they would in that measure no longer be able to render routine judgment" (1964: 159). Yet casework narratives embody both attitudes at once.

The narrative as literary device, as Alasdair MacIntyre argues, shapes the recounting of events into a form intelligible enough to assign personal accountability, despite the general tendency of the age toward morally unintelligible discourse.

Narrative history of a certain kind turns out to be the basic and essential genre for the characterization of human actions. . . . To identify an occurrence as an action is . . . to identify it under a type of description which enables us to see the occurrence as flowing intelligibly from a human agent's intentions, motives, passions and purposes. It is therefore to understand an action as something for which someone is accountable, about which it is always appropriate to ask for an intelligible account. (1981: 194–95)

The casework narrative attributes delinquent acts to lapses of individual will and responsibility; the delinquent's confession is an act of repentance. The community demands repentance partly because of its own guilt for wanting to exclude the delinquent. As Kai Erikson explains,

Repentance is a public ceremony of admission as well as a private act of contrition. To repent is to agree that the moral standards of the community are right and that the sentence of the court is just. To repent is to say . . . that one has 'sinned against his own conscience' and entirely understands why the community has to punish . . . him. . . . The people of the community, vaguely aware of the contradictions of their own doctrine, . . . [are] somehow anxious for the condemned man to forgive them. (1966: 195)

Yet at the same time, the casework narrative betrays deep empathy for the situation of the delinquent, the forces of "soft determinism" that skew susceptibility to delinquency involvement unfairly. As Dewey asserts, "Craftsmanship to be artistic in the final sense must be 'loving'; it must care deeply for the subject matter upon which skill is exercised" ([1934] 1980: 48–49). Tragedy, as Kenneth Burke remarks, "deals *sympathetically* with crime. Even though the criminal is finally sentenced to be punished, we are made to feel that his offence is our offence, and at the same time the offence is dignified by the nobility of style" (1984: 39n). Wayne Booth observes that the narrative technique of recounting a novel through the eyes of the protagonist invariably elicits sympathy for the protagonist. "The sustained inside view leads the reader to hope for good fortune for the character with whom he travels, quite independently of the qualities revealed" (1961; 246, quoted in Scheff 1979: 157).

James Bennett (1981) in effect traces the operation of this principle in the rhetorical uses to which criminologists have put delinquents' oral histories. The oral history communicates across class lines the social problems that help breed delinquency. In the words of Ernest Burgess (quoted in Bennett 1981: 24), "It admits the reader into the inner experience of other men, men apparently widely different from himself. . . . As he lives, for the time being, their careers and participates in their memories and mistakes, aspirations and failures he comes to realize the basic likenesses of all human beings." In Bennett's own view, "the aim of the delinquent's oral history is to move readers toward a sociological, environmental, or community-based perception of the causes of delinquency" (8). As Henry Mayhew, whose epic study *London Labour and London Poor* introduced the use of this rhetorical device, declared his purpose (quoted by Bennett, 29), referring to the squalid conditions of the urban masses, "I am anxious to make others feel, as I do myself, that *we* are the culpable parties in these matters"; "it is *our* fault to allow them to be as they are and not theirs to remain so." Mayhew recognized that not all misfortunes befalling the poor were "beyond their control," that some were indeed "brought about by their own imprudence or sluggishness" (quoted by Bennett, 30). Yet Mayhew's epic is tragic in outlook. Although the casework narrative is less elaborate in its statement than the oral history, it too creates an attitude of sympathetic identification with the delinquent by providing a sustained inside view. Thus it combines in a single statement the potentially antithetical attitudes of judgment and understanding.

The casework narrative, then, expresses the mutually ambivalent attitudes of all parties to a complex network of moral transactions, while honoring each party's own moral pretensions. The public at large remains at once understanding and judgmental toward both the probation officer and the delinquent. The delinquent offers repentance reassuring to the public, but at the same time claims entitlement to tolerance and redress for social injustice. By imputing to the delinquent a paradoxical mixture of social disability and personal heroism, the probation officer reflexively claims those same attributes for him- or herself. The narratives are precisely as ambiguous as the stage of the bureaucratic process they fit, when the prospects for remission or escalation of official troubles hang in the balance.

Catharsis All Around

The tragic casework narrative provides still another type of expressive satisfaction to each of the parties involved—the experience of catharsis. "Through pity and fear," according to Aristotle's classic statement of the defining characteristic of tragedy (chap. 6), "it achieves the purgation (catharsis) of such emotions." Tragedy, the imitation of a serious action, arouses such profound feelings of sorrow and terror as to exorcise its audience's sense of their own troubles. By dramatizing the mortification and societal estrangement of the delinquent, the casework narrative helps satisfy the public's exclusionary impulse. At the same time, through the psychological mechanism of identification, the dramatic resolution of the tensions centering around the delinquent as tragic hero helps purge the public's own emotional conflicts. As Burke explicates "the principle implicit in Aristotle's view of tragedy," "We are cleansed of emotional tensions by kinds of art deliberately designed to affect us with those tensions under controlled conditions" ([1952] 1968: xii).

Thomas Scheff, who similarly studies "catharsis in healing, ritual, and drama," argues that "the playwright uses the structure of awareness as a device independent of the story line, to ensure the proper amount of identification between the audience and the various characters, thus providing the conditions which lead to balance of attention and the possibility of discharge of distressful emotions" (1979: 170). Scheff claims that "the occluded emotions of the audience . . . are touched if the audience identifies with the characters neither too little nor too much, if they are able to act as both participants and observers simultaneously" (179). The ambivalent mixture of inclusionary and exclusionary attitudes the public experiences toward the delinquent creates just such a "balance of attention."

Of course the intended audience for casework narrative includes the delinquent as well as the public. The objectification of the delinquent's story in the form of a publicly recognized narrative creates a certain "balance of attention" for the delinquent in reviewing his or her own biography, with therapeutic effects. Scheff hypothesizes that "catharsis is a necessary condition for therapeutic change" (13), the resolution of painful experiences in a person's past. Composing the narrative similarly provides cathartic expression for the dramatist—the probation officer—too.

The cathartic properties of casework narratives provide not only therapeutic but also ritual benefits, resolving collective tensions as well as personal ones. As Rueckert (1982: 211) quotes from Burke's unpublished *Poetics*, tragedies "are designed to ritually cleanse" "civic 'pollutions' " "intrinsic to the nature of the state." Through analogical imagery, the symbolism of tragedy radiates out to encompass ever-broadening social circles. "To be complete, catharsis must involve the entire realm of privacy, along with personal and social relationships (*Poetics*, 76, quoted in Rueckert 1982: 219–20). As Burke illustrates this principle with reference to *Coriolanus*, the catharsis gives "form to the complexities of family, class, and national motives as they come to focus on the self-conflicts of an individual" (1966: 94). Burke notes that as a matter of literary technique, societal tensions are evoked most effectively when translated into personal terms. His "final formula for tragic catharsis" could serve as a guide for the probation officer's casework narrative:

> Take some pervasive unresolved tension typical of a given social order (or of life in general). While maintaining the "thought" of it in its overall importance, reduce it to terms of personal conflict (conflict between friends, or members of the same family). Feature some prominent figure who, in keeping with his character, though possessing admirable qualities, carries this conflict to excess. Put him in a situation that points up the conflict. Surround him with a cluster of characters whose relations to him and to one another help motivate and accentuate his excesses. So arrange the plot that, after a logically motivated turn, his excesses lead necessarily to his downfall. Finally, suggest that his misfortune will be followed by a promise of general peace. (1966: 94)

As if produced according to this formula, the casework narrative offers catharsis not only to the delinquent, the probation officer, and members of the public individually, but to society as a whole.

Impeding Instrumental Rationality

Yet these emotional, psychological, aesthetic, and moral satisfactions of casework narratives involve considerable cost. The very qualities of dramatization which make casework narratives so expressively satisfying impede the instrumental rationality of probation casework. The unity imposed by dramatic form is, as Suzanne Langer emphasizes, after all an "illusion." Probation officers' narratives tend to portray the genuine drama of children's lives in melodramatic terms, overdramatizing events and situations with undesirable effects for all parties concerned.

Overdramatizing the casework narrative promotes the probation officer's overinvolvement with clients, inevitably leading to internalization of blame for the failures of persons over whom, realistically, the probation officer exercises little control. As one probation officer comments, "We all think we're going to make the difference." Another reports, "I try to remember that I don't fail, others do—but I can't accept that." Ironically, the harder the probation officer tries to "save" a child from unavoidable commitment to a state training school, the more guilt—and heartbreak—the ultimate commitment usually causes the probation officer to experience.

Overdramatizing the casework narrative also leads the probation officer to reify aesthetically satisfying constructs as inflexible and unreasonable standards for the probationer's behavior. Harold Rosenberg suggests that it is misleadingly easy for the dramatist to synthesize the multiple incidents of a character's life into a coherent identity, since the dramatist—unlike the real-life judge—has the luxury of creating a character out of whole cloth. Suzanne Langer also notes this dramatic convention: "We can view each smallest act in its context, as a symptom of character and condition. . . . A character stands before us as a coherent whole" (1953: 310). Life imitates art as this element of the "dramatic illusion" shapes the narrative reconstruction of delinquents' moral identities. Katz observes that supporting publics grant probation officers and other formal agents of social control the license "to moralize otherwise inconsequential conduct when performed by the deviant" (1975: 1379). Thus does the overdramatization of the casework narrative create new orders of prohibitions for the probationer.

Overdramatization leads court workers to enforce their narratives rather than the law. Even while demonstrating close familiarity with the clinical details of casework, probation officers often cannot recall children's offense histories. In selecting among alternative treatment options for a particular case, the probation officer weighs compliance with the prescription for redemptive treatment more heavily than the frequency and seriousness of any legal infractions. Children who defy the court's authority to establish the basic terms of their narratives in effect seal their own commitment to a state training school, regardless of their offenses. A probation officer who had arranged for private residential placement of a girl already expelled from the court's own probation house reported to a judge the girl's threat to run away from the new placement; this resulted in the girl's commitment instead. As the probation officer expressed her regrets about the case, "The kid was making it happen—I hated to play out her scenarios for her." In another typical case, a girl before the court indicated her dissatisfaction with a number of different treatment options, leading the judge to ask her what plans she had instead. According to her probation officer's account, "Her plans were so pie-in-the sky, you could see the judge start writing out the commitment order as soon as she started talking." Judges are forced to temper this commitment response when the legal charges are truly insignificant. By refusing in court to participate in a drug-treatment program, a boy provoked the following judicial reaction: "Fine. Probation terminated. I'll place you under suspended commitment and review your case in a year. But the next time you come into court, bring a toothbrush."

More commonly, children resist the terms of their narratives in a more passive manner, although with the same risk of sanction. A probation officer had interceded to have assault charges reduced against a cooperative probationer whom he felt had been processed unfairly, obtaining for the probationer a relatively lenient sentence of 250 hours community service plus reimbursing his mother for his own legal expenses. However the probation officer became incensed when the boy planned to go away over a holiday weekend.

> With all the time he owes, and all the money he owes, I've just learned he's arranged to take for himself a three-day weekend. Can you imagine that! He's court-ordered to attend drug treatment on a previous charge, and he's missed the last few sessions, claiming his work schedule isn't flexible enough for him to attend. But suddenly, he has time for a three-day weekend! I've told him, if he doesn't get back here, I'm going to lock him up. I'm going to schedule a violation of probation hearing with the one judge who ordered drug treatment, and give him ten days in jail. Then I'll schedule another violation hearing for two weeks later with the other judge, and he'll get right out of jail to go before a judge again.

Confidential notes another probation officer left her successor about each child on the caseload indicated that the ones heading for trouble, though not especially serious offenders, were demonstrating insufficient commitment to their own redemption. "Total washout on probation. . . . He's like a lump here [in the office, during probation appointments] and at home. He's doing nothing about his life, so he's getting into consistent trouble, but no charges." "This boy will soon be committed to state. We've tried lots of stuff with him, and he recently split from residential placement. He doesn't have a huge criminal record but has a poor attitude, is an alcoholic in my book, and has not made it through any efforts."

Once the tragic rhythm has run its course, closure is attributed to the process of redemption. Significantly, the tolerance which the court routinely extends to children who display the will for redemption despite new infractions does not extend to children who have completed a cycle of moral struggle; the closure they are supposed to have attained in that cycle disqualifies their claims to further tolerance. Paradoxically then, children are more vulnerable to punitive sanctions after protracted periods of trouble-free behavior than before. A probation officer explains feeling compelled to seek residential placement for a child because the unity of his casework narrative has suddenly collapsed: "You know, I worked my butt off for him, and he was doing great, great in school, and then—everything fell apart for no rational reason." Probation officers express regret but not compunction over the commitment of such "back-sliders." A child who runs away from a residential placement after a long period of apparently good adjustment is more likely as a result to be committed to a state training school than a child who has run repeatedly during an initial period of predictable resistance.

Overdramatizing the casework narrative penalizes the public at large, which suffers the effects of inefficient decision-making by the juvenile court. Overdramatization produces the two familiar types of judgment error—excessively severe treatment of delinquents who pose relatively little risk to the community, and excessively lenient treatment of those who pose relatively high risk. Children placed residentially for noncompliance with prescribed treatment plans represent errors of the first type; errors of the second type are also readily apparent. Even fellow probation officers commonly recognize children who "sucker" their colleagues into giving them too many chances. Children who seem especially heroic may be forgiven repeated offenses. It was eminently rational to recommend restitution and continuation for dismissal on the first grand larceny complaint against a high school football hero described as an ideal student and ideal child, who planned to major in math in college. It was less rational to repeat the same recommendation, on different occasions in the following months, for that boy's next three offenses of exactly the same nature. The "exemplary" boy who received such lenient treatment from the court went on to commit dozens of subsequent offenses as a juvenile.

Not only does the probation officer's tragic narrative diminish the efficiency of court decision-making, it is not necessarily even the most efficient literary form for capturing the events of a delinquent's life story. If, as David Matza suggests, delinquency is primarily the result of drift, it would be more appropriate to portray the delinquent's destiny as a product of fortune rather than of fate. Among the various character-types in Orrin Klapp's typology, it would be more credible to cast the delinquent as a fool or villain rather than a hero. In purely literary terms, romance might prove a more suitable genre than tragedy for the probation officer's narrative materials.

Yet the genre of modern tragedy does effectively capture the marginal character of probation work. The juvenile court, which mediates between the system of criminal justice on the one hand and the system of child welfare on the other, is in practice peripheral to them both. Adolescence is a particularly marginal age grade, and probationers are disproportionately drawn from marginal statuses within the stratification system. Probation work is a marginal profession (or semiprofession). The dependence of probation officers and their clients on the remote and unresponsive system of welfare and corrections is in fact tragic. The tragic casework narrative is an effective rhetorical response to this situation of marginality. Tragic themes are central enough in modern society to attract attention to narrator and subject alike, despite their peripheral statuses; in this sense, the casework narrative is like the delinquent's oral history to which it is related and which, in James Bennett's phrase, "works at the margins of what is professionally possible" (1981: 245).

The cultural significance of the casework narrative lies in the serious moral and dramaturgical interests it expresses, not only for the delinquent whose fate hangs in the balance, but also for the probation officer and public at large. The narrative appropriates the spirit of modern tragedy to make coherent a delinquent's inherently confused and ambiguous biography, creating the possibility for purposeful action by indicating how a prescribed course of treatment can lead to redemptive rebirth. Because the process of symbolic interaction is *reflexive*, the promise of redemptive rebirth for the delinquent affords similar promise to the probation officer and public as well. Thus the casework narrative is no mere "account," repairing a breach on the surface of social order. Rather its function is much more profound: to affirm meaning and motivation essential to social control on a number of different levels. It represents a public admission of societal injustice implicated in delinquency causation. Yet it also commits the delinquent to recognize character flaws and summon the will to redress those flaws. In asserting the delinquent's allegiance and entitlement to central societal values and institutions even while enforcing accountability for the delinquent's actions, the casework narrative offers symbolic resolution to the structural contradiction of probation casework.

Unfortunately however, the resolution is only symbolic, and dysfunctional in its practical consequences. While empowering the probation officer and delinquent in certain respects, at the same time it creates new orders of prohibitions. It overdramatizes events and situations, tending to reify aesthetically satisfying constructs as inflexible and unreasonable standards of behavior. Probation officers tend to enforce their narratives rather than the law; they remove children from home not only for new offenses but also for deviations from their cast roles. By fostering "the dramatic illusion," the casework narrative impedes the exercise of instrumental rationality, contributing to errors of judgment. It is expressively satisfying for probation officers to reconstruct the experience of delinquents—and their experience with delinquents—according to the religious themes of modern tragedy. Unlike their predecessors, the "friendly visitors" of the last century, no longer do probation officers work with children in the name of God; in effect, however, modern-day probation officers play God with children in the name of work. Ironically—indeed, tragically—in striving to reconstruct delinquents' identities according to tragic narratives, probation officers ultimately only compound the social disorganization of juvenile justice.

12

Conclusion: The No-Fault Society

W ho is responsible for government's failure to deliver services to which citizens are entitled by right? Who is responsible for the commission of delinquent acts? As the findings of this study indicate, it is altogether too easy for Americans—public officials and delinquents alike—to evade responsibility for their actions. At least with regard to child welfare and juvenile delinquency, the United States lacks not only the authoritative capacity for achieving valued social goals, but even a civic philosophy capable of appointing individual or institutional responsibility. To borrow a phrase coined by Gerald Suttles, this condition describes a "no-fault society."

Society's capacity to achieve collective goals—its level of social control, in Morris Janowitz's (1978) use of that term—derives from a strong mixture of authority and integration. Since authority rests on respect for its legitimacy, it can only be exercised over people integrated into a social order; integration in turn rests on a reciprocity of obligation and entitlement whose basis must be authoritative. A no-fault society is weak in both integration and authority, and hence in social control. Whatever the case regarding other segments of the population, American society has not successfully integrated those segments at greatest risk of delinquency; nor can it successfully exercise authority over them. This weakness of social control poses the intractable problems of juvenile justice.

The practice and ideology of juvenile justice are conditioned by such general problems of social control as an overly individualistic conception of social life, the inability to distinguish between public and private spheres of action, and laxity in the rule of law. The combined effect of these related conditions is to erode the very bases of individual and institutional accountability, the defining characteristic of the no-fault society. The rhetoric of modern tragedy serves the interpersonal strategies

265

of artifice and special pleading that are imposed on both delinquents and probation officers partly because they cannot rely on law to enforce mutual obligations in an openly authoritative manner. This same rhetoric however helps both parties evade their own responsibilities in turn. The disorganization of juvenile justice at once expresses and contributes to these deficiencies in authority, integration, and civic philosophy of the no-fault society.

Constrictive Individualism

Recall how confusing it was for the agents of juvenile justice even to comprehend the problems of children whose cases were described in part 1 of this book. Was Rose, for example, brain-damaged with low intelligence (as a court psychologist found), emotionally disturbed (as a neurologist found), or socially maladjusted as the result of family dysfunction (as a school psychologist found)?

It is revealing that in Rose's case—as in so many others—each expert diagnosed a condition that one of the other experts was ostensibly more qualified to discover but did not. In effect, each expert presumed to render a diagnosis outside her own specialty in order to shift responsibility for the case to somebody else. Although the interest of each expert's own organization may be to disclaim responsibility, such arcane clinical disputation is counterproductive to their common interests since it diverts attention from the institutional deficiencies that frame delinquents' problems. An inauthentic rhetoric of therapeutic individualism inevitably frustrates the attempts of court workers to comprehend the problems of delinquents.

In addition to the failure of personal control, delinquency represents in large part a failure of community—inadequate socialization stemming from institutional discontinuities among the family, school, and workplace. Adolescents stand the best chance of developing healthy selves within communal contexts in which family, civic, and political institutions all nourish each other. Yet whatever social structural causes contribute to delinquency, probation officers can prescribe only personal treatments. This accounts for their recourse to a therapeutic discourse that is exclusively individualistic, devoid of civic consciousness.

William Sullivan explains why civic discourse is a necessary complement to therapeutic discourse. "The civic tradition is important to us because it articulates an understanding that the interdependency of the members of society is a moral and political relationship" (1986: 184). Not only does an exclusively individualistic discourse confuse attempts to comprehend the nature of children's problems, it constricts the grounds of character judgment which unavoidably inform casework decisions. Were the children described in part 1 helpless or dangerous? Victims or victimizers? Did Mary for example have "the appeal of a poor, hopeless little girl" (as her first probation officer believed), or was she simply "extremely manipulative" (as her next one claimed)? How could Henry become transformed so unambiguously in just a few years from an "insecure" and "vulnerable" victim of early childhood traumata (as the first psychologists to examine him found) to a remorselessly impulsive aggressor (as later psychologists found)? Ignoring the civic dimension of moral character assigns too much weight in such judgments to situational vagaries, leaving those judgments especially labile.

Blurring Public and Private

Constrictive individualism prevents agents of juvenile justice from marking a boundary crucial to civic discourse—that between the public and private realms. They transgress that boundary obliviously in their ad hoc dealings both with children and parents and with other agencies and service providers, treating certain inherently public matters as private ones and vice versa. In this indiscriminate mixing of the two realms, they exacerbate a larger social trend.

The confusion of these realms is characteristic of modern society. In the Greek *polis*, according to Hannah Arendt, "the distinction between a private and a public sphere of life corresponds to the household and political realms, which have existed as distinct, separate entities at least since the rise of the ancient city-state" (1958: 28). The emergence of society as a hybrid realm associated with the modern nation-state blurs this distinction.

> In our understanding, the dividing line is entirely blurred, because we see the body of peoples and political communities in the image of a family whose everyday affairs have to be taken care of by a gigantic, nation-wide administration of housekeeping. . . . With the rise of society, that is, the rise of the "household" (*oika*) or of economic activities to the public realm, housekeeping and all matters pertaining formerly to the private sphere of the family have become a "collective" affair. (28, 33)

In Daniel Bell's (1976) parallel formulation, the "public household" expands in modern society to encompass a limitless range of private wants.

The public and private realms have always existed in symbiotic relation. The public realm depends on private households for the upbringing of its citizens and the production of sufficient surplus for the provision

267

of collective goods. Private households depend on the public realm to regulate and coordinate their relations, supporting their child rearing by providing those collective goods. Yet despite the fluid terms of this symbiosis in modern society, it is important to respect the essential distinction between the realms—keeping the private realm closed off from scrutiny and coercion as a field of autonomous choice in personal matters, while keeping the public realm open as a forum of interaction over matters of common concern.

As a judicial agency authorized to intervene in households in the interests of public safety and child welfare, the juvenile court straddles this confused and neglected boundary between the public and private realms. The vague, ambiguous, and conflicting nature of the court's child welfare and public safety goals attests to this confusion and neglect. Probation officers in particular, answerable to judges on the one hand and parents on the other, are especially subject to conflicting pulls.

Publicizing Private Matters

How deeply or shallowly does the probation officer's purview penetrate into domestic affairs? Persistent enough delving into any family situation will likely expose to public notice an entire Pandora's box of health, education, and welfare problems. Can or should the probation officer attend to the whole range of these troubles, in their full profundity? What criteria exist for either involvement or noninvolvement? Conversely, adolescence is in part defined by family tensions surrounding such matters as curfews, wake-up times, chores, homework, drugs, and alcohol—tensions inherent in the liminality of passage from youth to adulthood. Since parents press probation officers most insistently for support in such ordinary household matters, probation officers typically do what they can, even though the amenability of these matters to formal public control is far from evident.

How much information, of what kinds, can or should probation officers gather about the private lives of delinquents and their families? Probation officers acting as helpers entice delinquents to reveal information about themselves in the process of "hooking" them into casework; yet those same revelations serve enforcement purposes, if the probation role turns adversarial. According to law, all casework information probation officers gather is confidential, since the juvenile court is a court not of record. In practice, however, military recruiters and law enforcement officers can gain formal access to court records under certain circumstances. And the very existence of formal barriers to the exchange of client information among different agencies and jurisdictions fosters informal exchange among probation officers, social workers, mental health workers, educators, police officers, and others, which also compromises confidentiality.

How much information, of what kinds, can or should the probation officer disseminate, not only as barter for information or services, but also in the interests of fostering casework cooperation? Was it proper for a probation officer to inform the community mental health therapist of Joseph's sexual relations with his mother? Was it proper to inform the vocational rehabilitation worker as well? Or to take another example, was Larry's probation officer in effect "dumping" on Boys' Town, as the counselor there contended, in attempting to break the cycle of stigmatization by emphasizing to them the appealing and helpless side of Larry's character?

Without principled grounds for determining either the court's need to know and divulge or its obligation to respect privacy, the extent and nature of information that influences particular casework decisions are determined—arbitrarily—not only by the probation officer's personal powers of persuasion and cultivation of informal exchange networks, but also by the probation officer's tacit (and partly idiosyncratic) frames of relevance. In an extreme example, a probation officer's recommendation to remove a child from home hinged on her observation that a wealthy mother appeared for an early morning interview with a run in her stocking so large that it must have existed when the woman dressed for the interview; the probation officer took this "evidence" of personal disorganization as indication of parental incompetence.

Privatizing Public Issues

The juvenile court's oblivious transgressions of the boundary between the public and private realms cut both ways. In penetrating the domestic lives of delinquents' families, the court publicizes certain private matters. Conversely, however, due to its limited capacity for promoting social change, the court is forced to treat intractable public problems which establish the context for delinquents' troubles as matters of only private concern. The prevention and treatment of delinquency are quintessentially *public* matters, as William Sullivan's observation implies: "The whole classical notion of a common *paideia*, or moral-civic cultivation, rested on the assertion that growth and transformation of the self toward responsible mutual concern is the realistic concern of public life" (1986: 168). Yet lacking the means to attack delinquency at its root—by strengthening the social ecology binding the family to community, workplace, and nation—probation officers can do no more than construe those weak ecological bonds as private pathologies of families and individuals.

Recall once more "the lack of any precise diagnosis of Rose's problem," which Rose's probation officer justifiably complained was "part of the difficulty in this case." A breakdown of social ecology contributed strongly to the disruptive behavior at home and school that led to Rose's court involvement. Rose's parents were divorced, and her mother lived hand to mouth. Whatever Rose's personal problems, her family life did not equip her to perform adequately in school, and school offered no realistic prospect of eventual integration into the workplace. Rose's "problem" thus inhered at least in significant part in the *relation* among family, school, and workplace. Because none of the parties involved could recognize the ecological dimension of this problem, each could only isolate one of the others as a target of blame. Thus, Rose's mother blamed Rose's "uncontrollable" nature; the court psychologist blamed Rose's neurological deficiency (an "organic" condition); the neurologist blamed Rose's "emotional disturbance" (something the schools were responsible for and presumably competent to overcome); while the schools blamed Rose's "social maladjustment" (the "fault" of Rose and her mother, something outside their responsibility and competence). Unable to recognize the problem as ecological, the various parties were constrained to conceive it as some form of private pathology, the "precise diagnosis" of which could only be the source of contentious debate.

As limited as probation officers' ability to conceive the problems of delinquency is in this way, their ability to design and implement treatment plans according to those conceptions is more limited still. Forced to construe delinquency causation in terms of family or personal pathology, probation officers do not even have the authority to ensure parental cooperation in their attempts to address family problems. For the most part, then, they are constrained to focus their treatment efforts on the personal pathologies they find in delinquents.

In "easy" cases, probation officers can use their public offices to strengthen the private orders of households, by coaching receptive parents in more effective parenting techniques, and by persuading ambivalent delinquents to be more obedient as children. Most parents and delinquents, however, are not receptive to such influence, because of either stubbornness or reasons beyond their control. (Recall that Jerome's probation officer was unable to arrange the participation of Jerome's guardian in intensive community-based parenting training—because it turned out the guardian [Jerome's sister] had herself taken refuge in a shelter for battered women.)

In most cases then, probation officers and parents engage in reciprocal maneuvering to claim authority over casework decisions while disclaiming responsibility for children's problems, further blurring the public-private boundary. Parents can refuse to participate in family counseling with impunity. Indeed, parents can virtually choose to ignore court proceedings entirely. Consider how Harold's mother eluded the jurisdiction of local social service workers simply by moving back and forth across the county line, and how difficult it was locate her (or Henry's mother, for that matter) for court hearings. Or consider how the judge refused to hold Rose's mother in contempt for failing to provide clothing or supplies for her daughter's wilderness school.

Parents can thwart the court's treatment plans for their children by enlisting the support of religious leaders. Despite the seriousness of the arson charge against Joseph, his probation officer had to subject his own personal religious beliefs to the examination of the fundamentalist family pastor in a series of prayer sessions before Joseph's parents would even consent to speak with him. A psychologist working for a Christian counseling center was successfully able to contravene the shared recommendation of other experts to remove Joseph from his home.

Joseph's mother persisted in sexually abusing him. It was strongly suspected—but never proven—that Joseph's father had physically abused him as a child, to the extent of causing brain damage. Indeed all the children described in part 1 of this book experienced parental abuse or neglect. Neither the court nor other related public agencies were effectively able to control this perversion of family life.

Despite the court's formal authority, even left to their own devices parents are largely able get their way concerning their children. They can obstruct the court's treatment plans by withholding necessary cooperation themselves, or sabotage them by merely encouraging their children's recalcitrance. Thus Rose's mother encouraged her daughter to quit the wilderness program prematurely, even though the mother felt no obligation to keep her at home. On the other hand, parents (such as Henry's) seeking to abandon their children to the state can usually manipulate the court to that end, by advocating court-ordered institutionalization. As the statistical cohort analysis presented in chapter 10 indicates, family situation exerts a greater influence than recidivism risk over the court's decision to remove a child from home.

Privatizing Institutionalization

Not only does the court privatize public issues by reducing problems of social ecology to ones of private pathology, it also privatizes delinquency treatment. Constrained by the absence of effective techniques for reforming recalcitrant parents and youth, and confronting the evasions of related public agencies, probation officers can in effect only broker contract services provided in large part by private, sectarian, and—increasingly—for-profit organizations. Public correctional facilities provide a treatment option of "last resort," although their capacities are severely strained and their quality of care is, if at all possible, to be avoided. Residential placement in private institutions thus becomes the normal remedy for children's untenable community and family situations.

A burgeoning industry of such institutions has arisen, subject only to ceremonial public oversight, even though dependent for its revenues on tax dollars. These institutions mix delinquents and nondelinquents from a variety of public and private referral sources. As Paul Lerman (1982) has documented, this privatization of treatment long antedates the policy initiatives of the Reagan administration, having received its most dramatic impetus from the Social Security amendments of the sixties. Abdicating responsibility for the actual treatment of delinquents to the private sector is a trend consistent with the more general development of corporatism in the modern state noted by Roberto Unger:

> The spearhead of corporatism is the effacement both in organization and in consciousness of the boundary between state and society, and therefore between the public and the private realm. As the state reaches into society, society itself generates institutions that rival the state in their power and take on many attributes formerly associated with public bodies. (1976: 200–201)

Despite a misnamed policy of "de-institutionalization," Lerman documents a consistent, long-range growth of institutional youth admissions, increasingly in private rather than public facilities, though for diminishing lengths of stay.

Not only does the court cede responsibility for treating delinquents after their placement to private institutions, but in effect the court often cedes the very placement decisions themselves. Since they are private, these institutions are often in a position to accept only whom they please. Thus placement decisions depend as much on the needs of those institutions and the breadth of probation officers' brokerage networks as on the court's judgment of children's needs.

None of the approved residential institutions within the state, for example, would accept either Larry, Michael, or Joseph. Larry's probation officer, as well as the director of the court's diagnostic team, wasted six solid weeks of daily efforts to place Larry before devising the inspired plan of persuading Boys' Town to accept him. Despite finally gaining the cooperation of the schools and the Department of Social Services (DSS), it took Joseph's probation officer over seven months to find a private institution outside the state willing to accept him; so desperate was this collaborative search, it was even expanded to include nonaccredited institutions. Although the search to find residential placement for Michael was no less collaborative, it failed altogether. Over a hundred inquiries during a five-month period proved fruitless, since no institution was willing to take on the challenge posed by Michael's particular combination of problems. By contrast however, despite Rose's disruptive nature, her probation officer was able to place her in a wilderness school on a moment's notice—and without even the means to pay the first week's tuition—because that school sought to attract referrals from the court and happened to need one other resident to start a new group.

At the same time, then, as the court publicizes certain household matters better left private, it privatizes the pervasive public problems that form the ecological basis of delinquency, reducing those problems to the dimensions of individual or family pathology, and abdicating to the private sector not only their treatment but even the very decisions about treatment. This double-edged blurring of the distinction between the public and private spheres is related to another aspect of the no-fault society, the laxity of the rule of law.

Laxity of the Rule of Law

Authoritative law at once requires and sustains a clear distinction between the public and the private. In the Greek *polis,* as Arendt reminds us, the law (*nomos*) was literally a wall that provided a clear demarcation between the separate spaces that physically constituted those realms. By contrast, the confused blurring of the realms undermines the rule of law in modern society. For Unger, "the rule of law is defined by the interrelated notions of neutrality, uniformity, and predictability. Governmental power must be exercised within the constraints of rules that apply to simple categories of persons and acts, and these rules, whatever they may be, must be uniformly applied" (1976: 176–77). Yet under conditions of the corporatist and welfare state—in its complexity and instability, responsiveness to the proliferation of organized interests, and concern with distributive justice—law embraces "open-ended standards and general clauses" (194), turning away from formalistic reasoning. In respect to this decline of law, Unger's analysis of "postliberal" society converges with Theodore Lowi's (1969) analysis of the "end of liberalism."

273

Manipulating Obedience

It is not surprising that the juvenile court sometimes shields children from the punitive rigors of legal formalism, since that is a crucial part of the court's distinctive mission. Thus, because the boy was only sixteen, a judge refused to sentence Larry to the adult jail on new charges including grand larceny and auto theft, even though he had already completed a term in a Nebraska training school as an accomplice to armed robbery, abduction, and attempted rape. Similarly, the court did no more than return Mary to a different mental hospital than the one from which she had escaped, despite a forty-five-day spree of over 120 larcenies. Whatever harm these decisions ultimately caused the public and the children themselves, they appeared reasonable at the time.

However other abridgements of the rule of law do not befit the court's mission. Under the pressure of mass dockets, judges conduct hearings in such haste that children and their parents cannot always comprehend what is transpiring. Even probation officers find it challenging to express themselves fully and accurately in court. The presence of lawyers in juvenile court—whether for the prosecution or the defense—is sporadic. Lawyers in attendance are often unfamiliar with the court's special nature, and hence are ineffective.

Because they cannot rely on the force of law, probation officers rely on manipulation to exact obedience from their clients. Although they are the ones dealing most directly with court-involved children and their parents, probation officers themselves have limited knowledge of the legal Code. They are frustrated by the inconsistency among judges in sanctioning probation violations and new offenses, just as judges are frustrated by the inconsistency among probation officers in bringing those violations to their attention. Probation officers use juvenile detention as an informal sanction, in technical violation of legal criteria. They also resort to such legal technicalities as "relabeling" status offenders to gain a manipulative edge.

The rhetoric of the casework narrative serves these strategies of manipulation. The tragic narrative expresses the probation officer's sense of empathy and presumes to chart a behavioral course in the child's best interest. Compliance with the scripted role promises to shield the child from the force of law. This however may not turn out to the child's advantage. Tragic narratives create new orders of prohibitions, as probation officers enforce their narratives rather than the law. Remember, for instance, how Rose's probation officer charged her with making "threatening phone calls" many months after the fact, to make her eligible for commitment to a state training school after she insisted on leaving the wilderness school "prematurely." Probation officers punish children for deviation from their cast roles, even in the absence of serious new legal offenses.

The laxity of the rule of law and the ineffectiveness of attempting to manipulate delinquents into obedience are measured by the statistical findings of chapter 10: despite their greater exposure to removal-from-home, children assigned directly to probation supervision upon completion of their social investigations are no less likely to recidivate than those not so assigned.

Manipulating Entitlement

Just as probation officers must attempt to manipulate delinquents into obedience, they must similarly attempt to manipulate other public officials into providing basic services to delinquents. Recall how one probation officer had to obtain a mental petition against Mary in order to arrange medical treatment for her hepatitis and heroin withdrawal. Or how another probation officer had to prolong Jerome's term of probation in order to ensure continuation of his special education services. Or how the court director criticized a parole officer and judge for attempting to invoke the force of law to protect Henry from harassment in a state correctional institution, rather than attempting to work behind the scenes at the Department of Corrections.

How could DSS and the community mental health centers get away with their evasions of service to the children described in part 1? Why did probation officers have to go to such lengths of adversarial maneuvering to establish special education eligibility for Rose, Harold, Joseph, and Henry? The erosion of legal formalism in juvenile justice impedes the exercise not only of authority over delinquents, but also of delinquents' rights to basic social and educational services.

The result of the process Lowi describes as "interest group liberalism" produces laws that establish only frameworks for ad hoc bargaining rather than authoritative guides to conduct. This is the nature of the child welfare legislation which sets the terms on which probation officers must seek special education and foster care services for their clients (Jacobs 1986). The Title XX Amendments (P.L. 93–647) and the Education for All Handicapped Act (P.L. 94–142) were the most expansive child welfare laws of the seventies, promising to extend rights to those on the periphery formerly excluded from them, and widening the role of government to encompass new areas of programmatic activity. Yet upon closer examination these laws represent vague expressions of general sentiment rather than clear and coherent statements of public policy. Reflecting the play of organized special interests, they base eligibility for service on categorical rather than universal criteria of need. Nor do they provide unambiguous definitions of eligibility categories or services, but rather only "open-ended clauses and general standards" which, as Unger notes, "force courts and administrative agencies to engage in ad hoc balancings of interests that resist reduction to general rules" (1976: 197).

Even though the Education for All Handicapped Act, for example, promises a "free appropriate public education" to all students, and offers special education services to "emotionally disturbed" youth among others, it specifically excludes "socially maladjusted" youth from special education eligibility. Eligibility committees of local school boards must therefore decide whether particular students are "emotionally disturbed" or "socially maladjusted." Not surprisingly, they are inclined to fit delinquents into the latter category. Neither federal nor state legislation, nor case law, nor administrative regulations, nor clinical practice provide any meaningful definition of the distinction between categories of applicants.

Consequently probation officers must resort to artifice and special pleading in seeking special education eligibility for their clients. Since diagnostic nuances are critical to such eligibility decisions, probation officers attempt to influence diagnoses by manipulating the situations of their production. Thus, for example, Rose's probation officer managed to exclude from the schools' administrative review hearing the court psychologist whose report undermined Rose's eligibility claim, while commissioning a neurological evaluation that countered the unfavorable report. In similar fashion, Harold's probation officer exploited a lapse in the schools' own testing cycle to have required evaluations commissioned by the court's diagnostic team rather than the schools' eligibility committee. Even the school psychologist reported to the diagnostic team that Harold required residential treatment. Psychologists naturally tailor evaluations to particular audiences; as in Henry's case, for example, the same psychologist may report slightly—but significantly—different findings to different judicial and administrative bodies.

Probation officers also pursue services for their clients by trading personal favors with line workers in other agencies with whom they are linked by networks of informal exchange. By exchanging client information and information about agency procedures as well as mutual services, line workers can circumvent the formal obstacles to interagency cooperation by which the various agencies defend their organizational boundaries. It is largely through membership in such informal networks that probation officers learn at once to make "appropriate" interagency referrals and to persuade others of their appropriateness.

Probation officers' tragic casework narratives provide the medium of this persuasion. While the jargon of clinical evaluations provides the official rhetoric of eligibility decisions, the ultimate decision criteria are related to character: is a particular child "deserving" or not? In the absence of clear-cut clinical grounds for distinguishing "emotional disturbance" from "social maladjustment," special education officials confer eligibility on students whose problems seem to be the result of remediable handicaps rather than willful character disorders. Tragic casework narratives emphasize precisely those elements of children's characters and situations which most effectively evoke feelings of personal sympathy for them. The rhetorical effect of these narratives is to justify special pleading by indicating the redemptive potential of conferring service eligibility.

Contradictory Legal Statutes

Probation officers must resort to strategies of artifice and special pleading to obtain services for their clients because the law is not only vague and ambiguous but also in significant respects contradictory. Most of the funding for the court's placement of children in residential institutions is jointly governed by a pair of federal statutes, enacted within a year of each other, which embody diametrically opposing attitudes toward the practice of institutionalization. The Title XX Amendments to the Social Security Act encourage institutionalization as one of their stated purposes. By contrast, the Education for All Handicapped Act insists on the principle that educationally handicapped students receive an education in the "least restrictive environment" or most normal setting. The former act specifically prohibits using Title XX funds to pay special education costs for children placed in residential institutions, so that in effect the tuition costs associated with residential placement must be funded under the terms of the latter act. Yet that latter act, whose stated purpose is to ensure the universal availability of special education, only provides funds for children placed residentially on *educational* grounds. Even though enacted after the Title XX legislation, the Education for All Handicapped Act simply fails to contemplate placing children in residential institutions for noneducational reasons.

Thus the combined effect of these two critical statutes is to create an administrative catch-22. In the particular jurisdiction under study, the director of special education studies decreed a policy of refusing to collaborate with either DSS or the juvenile court in arranging residential placement: if a child was found to require institutional placement for educational reasons, the schools would pay all costs, educational and related; if not, they would pay nothing at all. This policy made it impossible for DSS to arrange residential placements altogether, even though the state superintendents of education and welfare had expressly negotiated a set of procedures for overcoming the contradiction in federal law, by prescribing the schools' participation in the private placement of educationally handicapped students even for noneducational reasons. The local school official, exploiting the local school board's legal autonomy from the state, simply chose to disregard the state superintendents' directive, instead requesting the state to provide the following "clarification":

> My question is this: If a social service agency places a handicapped child in a treatment or residential setting for non-educational reasons, is the local school division required to pay the educational costs for that child even though the local school division believes that the handicapped child should be educated in a less restrictive environment?

This stubborn decision by the local director of special education studies helped create the context for the flurry of interagency litigation involving Rose, Harold, Henry, and Joseph, among others. The contradictions in federal law help explain why such litigation could produce only ad hoc interagency accommodations rather than agreements in principle, even though the special education services at issue were defined by federal statute to be basic rights of citizenship. The head of the schools' special education eligibility committee was eventually embarrassed to confess that the director of special education studies had flatly ordered him to find against Joseph, for example, even before the case was ever heard.

Although the unclear enforceability of formal claims to legal entitlement compels caseworkers' recourse to strategies of informal manipulation, that recourse is costly. Contesting the evasive practices of related public agencies through the informal exchange of personal favors entails sacrificing the benefits of rational authority classically enumerated by Max Weber (1968, chaps. 3, 11): reliability, efficiency, impartiality, and due process. It is only possible to work out an exchange of informal favors if workers in other agencies prove receptive and trustworthy. (It is especially difficult to get cooperation from workers in remote jurisdictions, beyond the reach of local exchange networks. Think how difficult it was merely to get Larry's records from the adjoining state.) At best, the artifice required to circumvent formal procedures is inordinately time-consuming, requiring court workers to invade the domains of other agencies' specialized competencies. Responses to special pleading are by definition particularistic rather than universalistic. The informal exchange of casework favors abridges client confidentiality and does not provide for appeal.

Laxity of law imposes yet another cost on public officials. Without a firm legal foundation for their actions, public officials face a special double burden of accountability. The rule of law not only protects citizens from the arbitrary exercise of state power, but also legitimates the actions of public officials. (In a formulation that usefully complements Roberto Unger's, Friedrich Hayek defines the rule of law to mean that "government in all its actions is bound by rules fixed and announced beforehand—rules which make it possible to foresee with fair certainty how the authority will use its coercive powers in given circumstances" [1944: 72].) Good law facilitates acceptance of bureaucratic decision-making by cloaking official roles with a set of clearly limited responsibilities and powers in relation to recognizable problems. Law that merely designates vague and contradictory remedies for amorphous problem areas exposes public officials to challenge by fraying that cloak of legitimacy. Laxity of law, then, intensifies the demands on public officials to submit their decisions to explicit account, even as it undermines the credibility of those accounts by eliminating their authoritative basis.

Eroding the Bases of Accountability

The very laxity of law that poses this dilemma of accountability for public officials also offers them a way out of it, by allowing them to manipulate the standards of their own evaluation. As with other public agencies, the administrative oversight exercised over the juvenile court is largely ceremonial. In the state where this particular study was conducted, juvenile courts receive formal certification upon triennial review of a few dozen case files, identified in advance so that court staff can put them in order for the officials of other juvenile courts who serve as the reviewers. Agencies have wide discretion in operationalizing categorical definitions of service eligibility and in keeping decision criteria to themselves. The schools for example managed to withhold from juvenile court judges, among others, the memorandum from the state superintendent of education requiring payment of special education funds for the tuition costs of educationally handicapped students placed in private institutions for noneducational reasons. Thus in Henry's court case the schools' lawyers were able to misrepresent, without challenge, the contents of that memorandum. Although formal procedures exist for the appeal of casework decisions, in practice the inordinate time and expense entailed by those procedures preclude effective appeal in most cases. In any event, agencies control those procedures until the advanced

279

stages of appeal. By illustration, the Department of Corrections simply invoked the reform school's own internal investigation to deny Henry's allegations of harassment.

The narrowly specialized way in which public agencies define their own domains, constrained only vaguely by the ambiguous terms of federal statute, also enables them to escape accountability for evading their responsibilities. The very activity of contesting particular eligibility decisions on ad hoc categorical grounds helps ratify this more general evasion, by acceding to its basic terms. Yet there is no better alternative for imposing accountability. Reliance on the informal exchange of personal favors shields casework decisions from exposure to public accounting altogether. Even the enforced formal collaboration of different agencies in particular cases may obscure accountability, as when a DSS counselor and juvenile probation officer each attribute primary casework responsibility to the other.

The blurred delineation of public and private spheres of action similarly contributes to the deniability of individual and institutional accountability characteristic of the no-fault society. Where does responsibility inhere for delinquency causation, treatment decisions, or treatment outcomes? As Harold's probation officer successfully argued before the schools' special hearing examiner, how was it possible to determine whether the family or the school was primarily responsible for Harold's problems of school adjustment? If probation officers are successful in "laying the seed" of approval to remove children from home, are probation officers or parents then accountable for those decisions? How can case outcomes be evaluated, when the juvenile court loses track of children placed in private residential institutions—institutions themselves unevaluated? There is not even a straightforward accounting of the numbers of children placed in those institutions, to say nothing of the public costs involved. Indeed due to the multiplicity of funding sources, the arcane nature and lax enforcement of reporting requirements, and the fragmentation of record-keeping responsibilities, the federal government had to hire the private accounting firm of Arthur D. Little, Inc., to sort out expenditures for the "de-institutionalization" of status offenders alone (Lerman 1984).

If the eroding basis of governmental accountability is one side of the no-fault society, the eroding basis of civic accountability is another. Although probation officers attribute many of delinquents' problems to the parents, probation officers have no way of enforcing accountability for the civic obligations of parenthood. Nor is the juvenile court effective in enforcing even minimal standards of civility among delinquents themselves. In its ambiguity and allowance for special pleading, juvenile court law contains the seeds of its own neutralization, as David Matza (1964) observes. Probation officers formulate case plans according to the pathos of delinquents' situations rather than the severity of their offenses. Most basically, through the ideological confusion that Matza describes, the assumption that delinquents suffer patterns of community and family disorganization reflecting societal injustice and inequality may inhibit the juvenile court from holding delinquents openly accountable to law for their delicts.

Probation officers' tragic casework narratives, which function perhaps most significantly as the medium of accounting for decisions taken without the clear authoritative guidance of law, at once express and foster this mutually exculpatory spirit of the no-fault society. Unger notes that "the willingness, in criminal as well as private law, to admit a growing list of exculpatory conditions" (1976: 199) is one aspect of the decline in legal formalism. As a more forgiving variant of Goffman's "sad tale," the tragic casework narrative reconstructs creditable moral identities for both delinquents and probation officers, exculpating the crimes of the former and the failures of the latter by attributing to each a paradoxical mixture of heroism and disability in their complementary struggles against handicapping societal conditions. Exculpation for both appeals to a vague sentiment Lionel Trilling calls "the inculpation of society" (1971: 161), which may be conceived as the displacement of accountability onto an unidentifiably diffuse and generalized "other."

It is important to emphasize that the no-fault society is not at all a society without punishment. The exculpatory attitude is fundamentally ambivalent, so that the provisional tolerance it breeds can upon revocation turn to vengeance all the more severe for having been deferred. Recall from the last chapter how angrily a probation officer reacted to a boy's plans for a holiday weekend away, after having arranged a lenient disposition of a new assault charge against him. Because probation officers must employ casework narratives for manipulative purposes, those narratives confuse the nature of their actions rather than clarify them. Tragic narratives conflate treatment and punishment, advocacy and deception. They inspire probation officers to heroic efforts on behalf of particular children, but they also rationalize the failure of those efforts.

In constructing accounts, public officials profess to hold themselves up to standards of evaluation. But casework narratives corrode the bases of such evaluation by confounding the very criteria of success and failure. Their spirit of tragedy is specifically *modern* in embodying the assumption of moral unintelligibility. Indeed, in their hedged, ambiguous, and shifting nature as accounts, tragic narratives promote and serve precisely the manipulability of evaluative standards which corrodes the no-fault society at its shadowy core.

Larry's Case Revisited

The themes of mutual exculpation and immunity from evaluation pervade the narratives related by court workers at various stages in Larry's case, starting with the judge's eloquent referral note to the diagnostic team cited in the opening passage of chapter 1. This note embodies a poetics of tragedy. It assumes that although there is hope for redemption, both Larry and the probation staff will need to summon heroic efforts of will to alter the troubled course of his destiny. ("The young man I am sending you today is in great need of help. . . . His educational and emotional needs are enormous. Shortly, his hurt will turn to bitterness, his confusion to violence and we will have a very dangerous adult felon in our community.") It exculpates Larry by attributing the cause of his delinquency to abuse and neglect suffered first at the hands of his own family, then at the hands of public officials from a neighboring state. ("The conduct of the authorities in this case has been incredibly inept.") In consideration of these circumstances, the narrative commits the court to Larry's assistance and grants him immediate relief from further punishment. ("I will not send Larry to the Department of Corrections. . . . I dare you to do your best.") However this commitment and relief are conditioned on the good faith of Larry's struggle for self-reform. Larry will have to learn to recognize his character flaws and adhere to a treatment regimen designed to help him overcome them. Thus the ultimate responsibility is Larry's; the tragic nature of these circumstances exonerate the court in advance from probable failure. ("There is perhaps no way that we at this point can reverse the failures of the past. . . . In short, I am asking you to do the impossible.") Nevertheless, it is the court which stands to gain the credit in the unlikely case of success. ("I am confident that if over the next five years we can turn Larry into a functioning adult we all will have done a service for the community of inestimable value.")

This explains the triumphant pride with which Larry's probation officer, the director of the diagnostic team, and the judge celebrated the most promising imaginable disposition of Larry's case, placement at Boys' Town. ("We really did it—we made the system do something it heretofore had never done—we really screwed the system and made it work, for one impossible kid.") It also explains the mood of fatalism with which Larry's probation officer reflected upon the ultimate devolution of the case into a series of increasingly violent new offenses:

> I started out thinking the system ruined this kid. That's not true; this kid was destroyed by age eight. We could not have saved him, if save is the word. There is probably no institutional program that could have helped him. . . . My impression now is that it's always been hopeless, that we were fooling ourselves, that we acted—consciously—not with the facts in front of us, but from our hearts. Still, what the judge did then was noble.

While acknowledging "fooling ourselves," this narrative denies accountability for misjudging the severity of Larry's case or for shifting liability to a private institution. While the court freely blamed Larry's troubles on the authorities from whom they had inherited the case, this narrative denies the reciprocal verdict brought against them by the probation officer in Nebraska who inherited the case in turn: "You dumped on us, and didn't even bother to notify us."

Confronting the contentious evasions of delinquents on the one hand and related public officials on the other, court workers too must seek to obscure the bases of their accountability; in the no-fault society, evasions of mutual obligation feed each other. Continually thrown back on their own personal resources in managing systemic casework dilemmas, probation officers resort to manipulative strategies of artifice and special pleading in attempting to enforce civic obligations and entitlements. As the statistical findings of chapter 10 indicate, the resulting interventions into the lives of children are neither effective nor fair. Those findings also indicate that the court's environment exercises greater influence on the court than the court exercises back on its environment. Despite the unmistakably resourceful dedication of probation officers to helping children—efforts that belie stereotypes of probation officers as "street-level bureaucrats"—the juvenile court is severely constrained by the more general weakness of social control in which it operates.

Juvenile delinquency can only be treated effectively by families, schools, communities, and workplaces supporting each other in authoritatively coordinated ways to integrate growing children into the emergent social order. Constrictive individualism, the blurred delineation of public and private responsibilities, and laxity in the rule of law impede such interinstitutional cooperation in the no-fault society. Synchronizing community institutions will require a formidable program of political reform, community organization, and institution building, at once impelling and impelled by an associated set of cultural changes: expanding civic consciousness, clarifying the increasingly complex division of public and private responsibilities, and strengthening the rule of law. It is unclear how such a reform program could ever develop in the no-fault society, but there is no alternative path to effective delinquency treatment. However inspired, the manipulations of isolated individuals cannot compensate for the absence of authoritative institutional means for achieving valued collective goals. Like vain struggles for a foothold in a steeply banked sand dune, attempts to out-manipulate the no-fault society produce only a deeper rut. In the no-fault society, as Larry's court workers sorrowfully learned, merely screwing the system cannot make it work.

References

Allen, Francis A. 1964. *The Borderland of Criminal Justice*. Chicago: University of Chicago Press.

———. 1981. *The Decline of the Rehabilitative Ideal*. New Haven: Yale University Press.

Arendt, Hannah. 1958. *The Human Condition*. Chicago: University of Chicago Press.

Aristotle. 1958. *Poetics*. In *Aristotle on Poetry and Style*. Trans. George Grube. New York: Bobbs-Merrill.

Austin, John. 1962. *How to Do Things with Words*. Cambridge: Harvard University Press.

Becker, Howard S. 1963. *Outsiders*. New York: Free Press.

Bell, Daniel. 1976. *The Cultural Contradictions of Capitalism*. New York: Basic Books.

Bellah, Robert. 1975. *The Broken Covenant*. New York: Seabury.

Bennett, James. 1981. *Oral History and Delinquency*. Chicago: University of Chicago Press.

Blos, Peter. 1962. *On Adolescence: A Psychoanalytic Interpretation*. New York: Free Press.

———. 1979. *The Adolescent Passage*. New York: Free Press.

Breuer, Mark. 1979. "The Intellectual Development in Parole Prediction." M.A. thesis, Department of Sociology, University of Chicago.

Burke, Kenneth. [1935] 1984. *Permanence and Change*. Reprint. Berkeley: University of California Press.

———. [1945] 1969. *A Grammar of Motives*. Reprint. Berkeley: University of California Press.

———. [1952] 1968. *Counter-statement*. Reprint. Berkeley: University of California Press.

———. [1961] 1970. *The Rhetoric of Religion*. Reprint. Berkeley: University of California Press.

———. [1962] 1969. *A Rhetoric of Motives*. Reprint. Berkeley: University of California Press.

Burke, Kenneth. 1966. *Language as Symbolic Action*. Berkeley: University of California Press.

――――. [1937] 1984. *Attitudes towards History*. 3d ed. Berkeley: University of California Press.

Cicourel, Aaron. 1968. *The Social Organization of Juvenile Justice*. New York: Wiley.

Davis, Kenneth. 1969. *Discretionary Justice*. Urbana: University of Illinois Press.

Dewey, John. [1934] 1980. *Art as Experience*. Reprint. New York: Perigree.

Eliot, T. S. 1951. *Poetry and Drama*. Cambridge: Harvard University Press.

Emerson, Robert. 1969. *Judging Delinquents*. Chicago: Aldine.

――――. 1981. "On Last Resorts." *American Journal of Sociology* 89 : 1–22.

Emerson, Robert, and Sheldon Messinger. 1977. "The Micro-politics of Trouble." *Social Problems* 25 : 121–34.

Erikson, Erik. 1968. *Identity: Youth and Crisis*. New York: Norton.

Erikson, Kai. 1966. *Wayward Puritans*. New York: Wiley.

Farrington, David P., and Roger Tarling. 1985. "Criminological Prediction: The Way Forward." In David P. Farrington and Roger Tarling, eds., *Prediction in Criminology*. Albany: State University of New York Press.

Freud, Sigmund. 1957. "On Narcissism." In *The Standard Edition of the Complete Psychological Works of Sigmund Freud*, vol. 14. London: Hogarth.

Frye, Northrop. [1957] 1968. *Anatomy of Criticism*. Reprint. New York: Atheneum.

Garfinkel, Harold. 1967. *Studies in Ethnomethodology*. Englewood Cliffs, N.J.: Prentice-Hall.

Geertz, Clifford. 1983. *Local Knowledge*. New York: Basic Books.

Glaser, Daniel. 1964. *The Effectiveness of a Prison and Parole System*. Indianapolis: Bobbs-Merrill.

Goffman, Erving. 1961. *Asylums*. Garden City, N.J.: Anchor.

Greenberg, David. 1979. *Mathematical Criminology*. New Brunswick, N.J.: Rutgers University Press.

Hayek, Friedrich. 1944. *The Road to Serfdom*. Chicago: University of Chicago Press.

Heinz, John, and Edward Laumann. 1982. *Chicago Lawyers*. New York: Russell Sage Foundation.

Hindelang, Michael, Travis Hirschi, and J. G. Weis. 1981. *Measuring Delinquency*. Beverly Hills, Calif.: Sage.

Jacobs, Mark D. 1978. "Delay and the Subcultures of Probation Units in a Juvenile Court." M.A. thesis, Department of Sociology, University of Chicago.

――――. 1986. "The End of Liberalism in the Administration of Social Casework." *Administration and Society* 18 : 7–27.

Janowitz, Morris. 1978. *The Last Half-Century: Societal Change and Politics in America*. Chicago: University of Chicago Press.

Katz, Jack. 1975. "Essences as Moral Identities." *American Journal of Sociology* 80 : 1369–90.

Klapp, Orrin. 1962. *Heroes, Villains, and Fools.* Englewood Cliffs, N.J.: Prentice-Hall.

Kornhauser, Ruth. 1978. *Social Sources of Delinquency.* Chicago: University of Chicago Press.

Krieger, Murray. [1960] 1966. *The Tragic Vision.* Reprint. Chicago: University of Chicago Press.

Langer, Suzanne. 1953. *Feeling and Form.* New York: Scribners.

Lerman, Paul. 1982. *Deinstitutionalization and the Welfare State.* New Brunswick, N.J.: Rutgers University Press.

———. 1984. "Child Welfare, the Private Sector, and Community-based Corrections." *Crime and Delinquency* 30:5–38.

Lipsky, Michael. 1980. *Street-level Bureaucracy.* New York: Russell Sage.

Lowi, Theodore. 1969. *The End of Liberalism.* New York: W. W. Norton.

Lubove, Roy. 1969. *The Professional Altruist.* Cambridge: Harvard University Press.

Lyman, Sanford, and Marvin Scott. 1968. "Accounts." *American Sociological Review* 33:46–62.

MacIntyre, Alasdair. 1981. *After Virtue.* Notre Dame, Ind.: University of Notre Dame Press.

Mahoney, Anne Rankin. 1987. *Juvenile Justice in Context.* Boston: Northeastern University Press.

Maltz, Michael. 1984. *Recidivism.* Orlando, Fla.: Academic Press.

Mannheim, Hermann, and Leslie Wilkins. 1955. *Prediction Methods in Relation to Borstal Training.* London: Her Majesty's Stationery Office.

Marshall, T. H. 1964. *Class, Citizenship, and Social Development.* New York: Doubleday.

Martinson, Robert. 1974. "What Works? Questions and Answers about Prison Reform." *Public Interest* 35:22–54.

Matza, David. 1964. *Delinquency and Drift.* New York: Wiley.

Merton, Robert. 1968. "Social Structure and Anomie." In *Social Theory and Social Structure.* New York: Free Press.

Murray, Gilbert. 1951. *The Five Stages of Greek Religion.* New York: Doubleday.

Nietzsche, Friedrich. 1956. *The Birth of Tragedy.* Trans. Francis Golffing. New York: Doubleday.

Parsons, Talcott. 1951. *The Social System.* New York: Free Press.

Piaget, Jean. 1965. *The Moral Judgment of the Child.* Trans. Marjorie Gabain. New York: Free Press.

Reiss, Albert. 1951. "Delinquency as a Failure of Personal and Social Controls." *American Sociological Review* 16:196–208.

Rosenberg, Harold. 1960. "Character Change and the Drama." In Lionel Abel, ed., *Moderns on Tragedy.* Greenwich, Conn.: Fawcett.

Rosenheim, Margaret. 1976. "Notes on Helping Juvenile Nuisances." In Margaret Rosenheim, ed., *Pursuing Justice for the Child.* Chicago: University of Chicago Press.

References

Rothman, David. 1980. *Conscience and Convenience*. Boston: Little, Brown.
Rueckert, William. 1982. *Kenneth Burke and the Drama of Human Relations*. Berkeley: University of California Press.
Sahlins, Marshall. 1976. *Culture and Practical Reason*. Chicago: University of Chicago Press.
Scheff, Thomas. 1979. *Catharsis in Healing, Ritual, and Drama*. Berkeley: University of California Press.
Schlossman, Steven. 1977. *Love and the American Delinquent*. Chicago: University of Chicago Press.
Schmidt, Peter, and Ann Witte. 1984. *An Economic Analysis of Crime and Justice*. Orlando, Fla.: Academic Press.
Selznick, Philip. 1957. *Leadership in Administration*. New York: Harper and Row.
Sewall, Richard. 1980. *The Vision of Tragedy*. New Haven: Yale University Press.
Shaw, Clifford, and Henry McKay. [1942] 1969. *Juvenile Delinquency and Urban Areas*. Reprint. Chicago: University of Chicago Press.
Shils, Edward. [1961] 1975. "Center and Periphery." Reprinted in *Center and Periphery: Essays in Macrosociology*. Chicago: University of Chicago Press.
Stapleton, Vaughn, David Aday, and Jeanne Ito. 1982. "An Empirical Typology of American Metropolitan Juvenile Courts." *American Journal of Sociology* 88:549–564.
Sullivan, William. 1986. *Reconstructing Public Philosophy*. Berkeley: University of California Press.
Trilling, Lionel. 1971. *Sincerity and Authenticity*. Cambridge: Harvard University Press.
Unger, Roberto Mangabeira. 1976. *Law in Modern Society*. New York: Free Press.
Weber, Max. 1968. *Economy and Society*. 3 vols. Ed. Guenther Roth and Claus Wittich. New York: Bedminster Press.
West, D. J., and David Farrington. 1973. *Who Becomes Delinquent?* London: Heinemann.
Williams, Raymond. 1966. *Modern Tragedy*. Palo Alto, Calif.: Stanford University Press.

288

Index

Accountability: civic, 280; by delinquents, 103, 245, 281; individual, 5, 247, 262, 265, 280, 283, 235–36, 254–56; institutional, 5, 129, 135, 184, 247, 254, 256, 262, 265, 280, 283; by parole officers, 60; by probation officers, 5, 281; by public officials, 279–81

Accounts, theory of, 232

Adolescence, social psychology of, 1, 19–21, 226–27, 266, 268

Adult jail, 36, 189

Allen, Francis, 23, 231

Ambiguity: of behavior, 166; of case outcomes, 97, 114–15, 280; of casework prospects, 247, 256; of character, 251–52, 262, 267; of children's problems, 22, 27–29, 39, 44, 64, 76, 101, 266, 270, 279; of clinical diagnoses, 44, 64, 76, 270; of goals and objectives, 1, 19, 23, 102, 130; of mission, 232; of modern tragedy, 241–42, 244, 262; of the probation role, 113, 126; of tragic casework narratives, 256 (*see also* Tragic casework narratives: moral ambiguity and incoherence of)

Ambivalence: of moral essences, 252; of the no-fault society, 281; of parents, 154–55; of personal attitudes towards adolescents, 1; of the probation role, 113, 115, 268; of public purpose, 130, 254–56; of tragic narratives, 5, 254–57

Appeals of special education eligibility denials: to the circuit court, 43, 76, 84–87; at a due process hearing, 43, 72, 75, 79–80, 83; to the juvenile court, 43, 75,

81, 83–84, 148; to the schools' administrative review committee, 43, 72, 75, 78–79, 276

Arendt, Hannah, 273

Aristotle, 238, 256–57

Austin, John, 244

Becker, Howard, 243

Bellah, Robert, 234

"Benefit of the doubt" in treatment, by age, 200–204, 229

Bennett, James, 255–56

Booth, Wayne, 255

Boys Town, 12–15, 269, 272, 282

Breuer, Mark, 229

Burgess, Ernest, 229, 255

Burke, Kenneth, 234, 239–40, 255, 257–58

Career stages: of delinquents, 63, 188, 204, 221–28; of a "moral career," 245–47; of probation officers, 122–24, 172, 176

Case files, 108–9, 129, 162, 191–92, 279

Case plans, 108, 126, 128

Caseload pressures, 25, 34, 54, 106–7, 126, 132, 187, 233

Caseload standards, 129

Casework dilemmas, 3–4, 31–34, 283

Casework "fires," 73, 106, 109–11, 116–17, 124

Ceremonial oversight: of the juvenile court, 129, 185, 279; of private residential institutions, 183–84, 272; of selection for residential institutions, 183; of state training schools, 89–90